Mometrix
TEST PREPARATION

# Virginia SOL Grade 4 Secrets Study Guide

# DEAR FUTURE EXAM SUCCESS STORY

First of all, **THANK YOU** for purchasing Mometrix study materials!

Second, congratulations! You are one of the few determined test-takers who are committed to doing whatever it takes to excel on your exam. **You have come to the right place.** We developed these study materials with one goal in mind: to deliver you the information you need in a format that's concise and easy to use.

In addition to optimizing your guide for the content of the test, we've outlined our recommended steps for breaking down the preparation process into small, attainable goals so you can make sure you stay on track.

We've also analyzed the entire test-taking process, identifying the most common pitfalls and showing how you can overcome them and be ready for any curveball the test throws you.

Standardized testing is one of the biggest obstacles on your road to success, which only increases the importance of doing well in the high-pressure, high-stakes environment of test day. Your results on this test could have a significant impact on your future, and this guide provides the information and practical advice to help you achieve your full potential on test day.

**Your success is our success**

**We would love to hear from you!** If you would like to share the story of your exam success or if you have any questions or comments in regard to our products, please contact us at **800-673-8175** or **support@mometrix.com**.

Thanks again for your business and we wish you continued success!

Sincerely,
The Mometrix Test Preparation Team

**Need more help? Check out our flashcards at:**
**http://MometrixFlashcards.com/SOL**


Written and edited by the Mometrix Exam Secrets Test Prep Team
Printed in the United States of America

# TABLE OF CONTENTS

# Introduction

**Thank you for purchasing this resource!** You have made the choice to prepare yourself for a test that could have a huge impact on your future, and this guide is designed to help you be fully ready for test day. Obviously, it's important to have a solid understanding of the test material, but you also need to be prepared for the unique environment and stressors of the test, so that you can perform to the best of your abilities.

For this purpose, the first section that appears in this guide is the **Secret Keys**. We've devoted countless hours to meticulously researching what works and what doesn't, and we've boiled down our findings to the five most impactful steps you can take to improve your performance on the test. We start at the beginning with study planning and move through the preparation process, all the way to the testing strategies that will help you get the most out of what you know when you're finally sitting in front of the test.

We recommend that you start preparing for your test as far in advance as possible. However, if you've bought this guide as a last-minute study resource and only have a few days before your test, we recommend that you skip over the first two Secret Keys since they address a long-term study plan.

If you struggle with **test anxiety**, we strongly encourage you to check out our recommendations for how you can overcome it. Test anxiety is a formidable foe, but it can be beaten, and we want to make sure you have the tools you need to defeat it.

# Secret Key #1 – Plan Big, Study Small

There's a lot riding on your performance. If you want to ace this test, you're going to need to keep your skills sharp and the material fresh in your mind. You need a plan that lets you review everything you need to know while still fitting in your schedule. We'll break this strategy down into three categories.

## Information Organization

Start with the information you already have: the official test outline. From this, you can make a complete list of all the concepts you need to cover before the test. Organize these concepts into groups that can be studied together, and create a list of any related vocabulary you need to learn so you can brush up on any difficult terms. You'll want to keep this vocabulary list handy once you actually start studying since you may need to add to it along the way.

## Time Management

Once you have your set of study concepts, decide how to spread them out over the time you have left before the test. Break your study plan into small, clear goals so you have a manageable task for each day and know exactly what you're doing. Then just focus on one small step at a time. When you manage your time this way, you don't need to spend hours at a time studying. Studying a small block of content for a short period each day helps you retain information better and avoid stressing over how much you have left to do. You can relax knowing that you have a plan to cover everything in time. In order for this strategy to be effective though, you have to start studying early and stick to your schedule. Avoid the exhaustion and futility that comes from last-minute cramming!

## Study Environment

The environment you study in has a big impact on your learning. Studying in a coffee shop, while probably more enjoyable, is not likely to be as fruitful as studying in a quiet room. It's important to keep distractions to a minimum. You're only planning to study for a short block of time, so make the most of it. Don't pause to check your phone or get up to find a snack. It's also important to **avoid multitasking**. Research has consistently shown that multitasking will make your studying dramatically less effective. Your study area should also be comfortable and well-lit so you don't have the distraction of straining your eyes or sitting on an uncomfortable chair.

The time of day you study is also important. You want to be rested and alert. Don't wait until just before bedtime. Study when you'll be most likely to comprehend and remember. Even better, if you know what time of day your test will be, set that time aside for study. That way your brain will be used to working on that subject at that specific time and you'll have a better chance of recalling information.

Finally, it can be helpful to team up with others who are studying for the same test. Your actual studying should be done in as isolated an environment as possible, but the work of organizing the information and setting up the study plan can be divided up. In between study sessions, you can discuss with your teammates the concepts that you're all studying and quiz each other on the details. Just be sure that your teammates are as serious about the test as you are. If you find that your study time is being replaced with social time, you might need to find a new team.

# Secret Key #2 – Make Your Studying Count

You're devoting a lot of time and effort to preparing for this test, so you want to be absolutely certain it will pay off. This means doing more than just reading the content and hoping you can remember it on test day. It's important to make every minute of study count. There are two main areas you can focus on to make your studying count.

## Retention

It doesn't matter how much time you study if you can't remember the material. You need to make sure you are retaining the concepts. To check your retention of the information you're learning, try recalling it at later times with minimal prompting. Try carrying around flashcards and glance at one or two from time to time or ask a friend who's also studying for the test to quiz you.

To enhance your retention, look for ways to put the information into practice so that you can apply it rather than simply recalling it. If you're using the information in practical ways, it will be much easier to remember. Similarly, it helps to solidify a concept in your mind if you're not only reading it to yourself but also explaining it to someone else. Ask a friend to let you teach them about a concept you're a little shaky on (or speak aloud to an imaginary audience if necessary). As you try to summarize, define, give examples, and answer your friend's questions, you'll understand the concepts better and they will stay with you longer. Finally, step back for a big picture view and ask yourself how each piece of information fits with the whole subject. When you link the different concepts together and see them working together as a whole, it's easier to remember the individual components.

Finally, practice showing your work on any multi-step problems, even if you're just studying. Writing out each step you take to solve a problem will help solidify the process in your mind, and you'll be more likely to remember it during the test.

## Modality

*Modality* simply refers to the means or method by which you study. Choosing a study modality that fits your own individual learning style is crucial. No two people learn best in exactly the same way, so it's important to know your strengths and use them to your advantage.

For example, if you learn best by visualization, focus on visualizing a concept in your mind and draw an image or a diagram. Try color-coding your notes, illustrating them, or creating symbols that will trigger your mind to recall a learned concept. If you learn best by hearing or discussing information, find a study partner who learns the same way or read aloud to yourself. Think about how to put the information in your own words. Imagine that you are giving a lecture on the topic and record yourself so you can listen to it later.

For any learning style, flashcards can be helpful. Organize the information so you can take advantage of spare moments to review. Underline key words or phrases. Use different colors for different categories. Mnemonic devices (such as creating a short list in which every item starts with the same letter) can also help with retention. Find what works best for you and use it to store the information in your mind most effectively and easily.

# Secret Key #3 – Practice the Right Way

Your success on test day depends not only on how many hours you put into preparing, but also on whether you prepared the right way. It's good to check along the way to see if your studying is paying off. One of the most effective ways to do this is by taking practice tests to evaluate your progress. Practice tests are useful because they show exactly where you need to improve. Every time you take a practice test, pay special attention to these three groups of questions:

- The questions you got wrong
- The questions you had to guess on, even if you guessed right
- The questions you found difficult or slow to work through

This will show you exactly what your weak areas are, and where you need to devote more study time. Ask yourself why each of these questions gave you trouble. Was it because you didn't understand the material? Was it because you didn't remember the vocabulary? Do you need more repetitions on this type of question to build speed and confidence? Dig into those questions and figure out how you can strengthen your weak areas as you go back to review the material.

Additionally, many practice tests have a section explaining the answer choices. It can be tempting to read the explanation and think that you now have a good understanding of the concept. However, an explanation likely only covers part of the question's broader context. Even if the explanation makes perfect sense, **go back and investigate** every concept related to the question until you're positive you have a thorough understanding.

As you go along, keep in mind that the practice test is just that: practice. Memorizing these questions and answers will not be very helpful on the actual test because it is unlikely to have any of the same exact questions. If you only know the right answers to the sample questions, you won't be prepared for the real thing. **Study the concepts** until you understand them fully, and then you'll be able to answer any question that shows up on the test.

It's important to wait on the practice tests until you're ready. If you take a test on your first day of study, you may be overwhelmed by the amount of material covered and how much you need to learn. Work up to it gradually.

On test day, you'll need to be prepared for answering questions, managing your time, and using the test-taking strategies you've learned. It's a lot to balance, like a mental marathon that will have a big impact on your future. Like training for a marathon, you'll need to start slowly and work your way up. When test day arrives, you'll be ready.

Start with the strategies you've read in the first two Secret Keys—plan your course and study in the way that works best for you. If you have time, consider using multiple study resources to get different approaches to the same concepts. It can be helpful to see difficult concepts from more than one angle. Then find a good source for practice tests. Many times, the test website will suggest potential study resources or provide sample tests.

# Practice Test Strategy

If you're able to find at least three practice tests, we recommend this strategy:

### Untimed and Open-Book Practice

Take the first test with no time constraints and with your notes and study guide handy. Take your time and focus on applying the strategies you've learned.

### Timed and Open-Book Practice

Take the second practice test open-book as well, but set a timer and practice pacing yourself to finish in time.

### Timed and Closed-Book Practice

Take any other practice tests as if it were test day. Set a timer and put away your study materials. Sit at a table or desk in a quiet room, imagine yourself at the testing center, and answer questions as quickly and accurately as possible.

Keep repeating timed and closed-book tests on a regular basis until you run out of practice tests or it's time for the actual test. Your mind will be ready for the schedule and stress of test day, and you'll be able to focus on recalling the material you've learned.

# Secret Key #4 – Pace Yourself

Once you're fully prepared for the material on the test, your biggest challenge on test day will be managing your time. Just knowing that the clock is ticking can make you panic even if you have plenty of time left. Work on pacing yourself so you can build confidence against the time constraints of the exam. Pacing is a difficult skill to master, especially in a high-pressure environment, so **practice is vital**.

Set time expectations for your pace based on how much time is available. For example, if a section has 60 questions and the time limit is 30 minutes, you know you have to average 30 seconds or less per question in order to answer them all. Although 30 seconds is the hard limit, set 25 seconds per question as your goal, so you reserve extra time to spend on harder questions. When you budget extra time for the harder questions, you no longer have any reason to stress when those questions take longer to answer.

Don't let this time expectation distract you from working through the test at a calm, steady pace, but keep it in mind so you don't spend too much time on any one question. Recognize that taking extra time on one question you don't understand may keep you from answering two that you do understand later in the test. If your time limit for a question is up and you're still not sure of the answer, mark it and move on, and come back to it later if the time and the test format allow. If the testing format doesn't allow you to return to earlier questions, just make an educated guess; then put it out of your mind and move on.

On the easier questions, be careful not to rush. It may seem wise to hurry through them so you have more time for the challenging ones, but it's not worth missing one if you know the concept and just didn't take the time to read the question fully. Work efficiently but make sure you understand the question and have looked at all of the answer choices, since more than one may seem right at first.

Even if you're paying attention to the time, you may find yourself a little behind at some point. You should speed up to get back on track, but do so wisely. Don't panic; just take a few seconds less on each question until you're caught up. Don't guess without thinking, but do look through the answer choices and eliminate any you know are wrong. If you can get down to two choices, it is often worthwhile to guess from those. Once you've chosen an answer, move on and don't dwell on any that you skipped or had to hurry through. If a question was taking too long, chances are it was one of the harder ones, so you weren't as likely to get it right anyway.

On the other hand, if you find yourself getting ahead of schedule, it may be beneficial to slow down a little. The more quickly you work, the more likely you are to make a careless mistake that will affect your score. You've budgeted time for each question, so don't be afraid to spend that time. Practice an efficient but careful pace to get the most out of the time you have.

# Secret Key #5 – Have a Plan for Guessing

When you're taking the test, you may find yourself stuck on a question. Some of the answer choices seem better than others, but you don't see the one answer choice that is obviously correct. What do you do?

The scenario described above is very common, yet most test takers have not effectively prepared for it. Developing and practicing a plan for guessing may be one of the single most effective uses of your time as you get ready for the exam.

In developing your plan for guessing, there are three questions to address:

- When should you start the guessing process?
- How should you narrow down the choices?
- Which answer should you choose?

## When to Start the Guessing Process

Unless your plan for guessing is to select C every time (which, despite its merits, is not what we recommend), you need to leave yourself enough time to apply your answer elimination strategies. Since you have a limited amount of time for each question, that means that if you're going to give yourself the best shot at guessing correctly, you have to decide quickly whether or not you will guess.

Of course, the best-case scenario is that you don't have to guess at all, so first, see if you can answer the question based on your knowledge of the subject and basic reasoning skills. Focus on the key words in the question and try to jog your memory of related topics. Give yourself a chance to bring the knowledge to mind, but once you realize that you don't have (or you can't access) the knowledge you need to answer the question, it's time to start the guessing process.

It's almost always better to start the guessing process too early than too late. It only takes a few seconds to remember something and answer the question from knowledge. Carefully eliminating wrong answer choices takes longer. Plus, going through the process of eliminating answer choices can actually help jog your memory.

**Summary**: Start the guessing process as soon as you decide that you can't answer the question based on your knowledge.

## How to Narrow Down the Choices

The next chapter in this book (**Test-Taking Strategies**) includes a wide range of strategies for how to approach questions and how to look for answer choices to eliminate. You will definitely want to read those carefully, practice them, and figure out which ones work best for you. Here though, we're going to address a mindset rather than a particular strategy.

Your odds of guessing an answer correctly depend on how many options you are choosing from.

| **Number of options left** | 5 | 4 | 3 | 2 | 1 |
|---|---|---|---|---|---|
| **Odds of guessing correctly** | 20% | 25% | 33% | 50% | 100% |

You can see from this chart just how valuable it is to be able to eliminate incorrect answers and make an educated guess, but there are two things that many test takers do that cause them to miss out on the benefits of guessing:

- Accidentally eliminating the correct answer
- Selecting an answer based on an impression

We'll look at the first one here, and the second one in the next section.

To avoid accidentally eliminating the correct answer, we recommend a thought exercise called **the $5 challenge**. In this challenge, you only eliminate an answer choice from contention if you are willing to bet $5 on it being wrong. Why $5? Five dollars is a small but not insignificant amount of money. It's an amount you could afford to lose but wouldn't want to throw away. And while losing $5 once might not hurt too much, doing it twenty times will set you back $100. In the same way, each small decision you make—eliminating a choice here, guessing on a question there—won't by itself impact your score very much, but when you put them all together, they can make a big difference. By holding each answer choice elimination decision to a higher standard, you can reduce the risk of accidentally eliminating the correct answer.

The $5 challenge can also be applied in a positive sense: If you are willing to bet $5 that an answer choice *is* correct, go ahead and mark it as correct.

**Summary**: Only eliminate an answer choice if you are willing to bet $5 that it is wrong.

# Which Answer to Choose

You're taking the test. You've run into a hard question and decided you'll have to guess. You've eliminated all the answer choices you're willing to bet $5 on. Now you have to pick an answer. Why do we even need to talk about this? Why can't you just pick whichever one you feel like when the time comes?

The answer to these questions is that if you don't come into the test with a plan, you'll rely on your impression to select an answer choice, and if you do that, you risk falling into a trap. The test writers know that everyone who takes their test will be guessing on some of the questions, so they intentionally write wrong answer choices to seem plausible. You still have to pick an answer though, and if the wrong answer choices are designed to look right, how can you ever be sure that you're not falling for their trap? The best solution we've found to this dilemma is to take the decision out of your hands entirely. Here is the process we recommend:

**Once you've eliminated any choices that you are confident (willing to bet $5) are wrong, select the first remaining choice as your answer.**

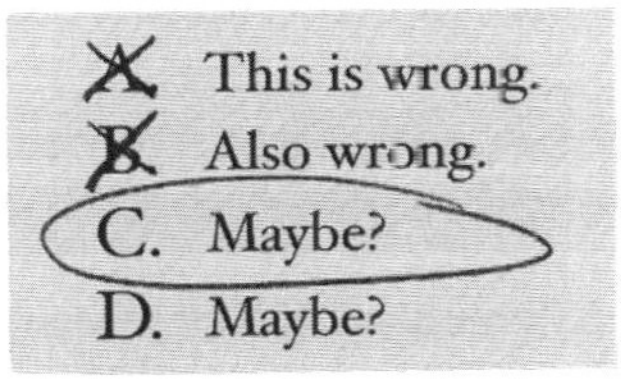


Whether you choose to select the first remaining choice, the second, or the last, the important thing is that you use some preselected standard. Using this approach guarantees that you will not be enticed into selecting an answer choice that looks right, because you are not basing your decision on how the answer choices look.

This is not meant to make you question your knowledge. Instead, it is to help you recognize the difference between your knowledge and your impressions. There's a huge difference between thinking an answer is right because of what you know, and thinking an answer is right because it looks or sounds like it should be right.

**Summary**: To ensure that your selection is appropriately random, make a predetermined selection from among all answer choices you have not eliminated.

# Test-Taking Strategies

This section contains a list of test-taking strategies that you may find helpful as you work through the test. By taking what you know and applying logical thought, you can maximize your chances of answering any question correctly!

It is very important to realize that every question is different and every person is different: no single strategy will work on every question, and no single strategy will work for every person. That's why we've included all of them here, so you can try them out and determine which ones work best for different types of questions and which ones work best for you.

## Question Strategies

### ✓ READ CAREFULLY

Read the question and the answer choices carefully. Don't miss the question because you misread the terms. You have plenty of time to read each question thoroughly and make sure you understand what is being asked. Yet a happy medium must be attained, so don't waste too much time. You must read carefully and efficiently.

### ✓ CONTEXTUAL CLUES

Look for contextual clues. If the question includes a word you are not familiar with, look at the immediate context for some indication of what the word might mean. Contextual clues can often give you all the information you need to decipher the meaning of an unfamiliar word. Even if you can't determine the meaning, you may be able to narrow down the possibilities enough to make a solid guess at the answer to the question.

### ✓ PREFIXES

If you're having trouble with a word in the question or answer choices, try dissecting it. Take advantage of every clue that the word might include. Prefixes can be a huge help. Usually, they allow you to determine a basic meaning. *Pre-* means before, *post-* means after, *pro-* is positive, *de-* is negative. From prefixes, you can get an idea of the general meaning of the word and try to put it into context.

### ✓ HEDGE WORDS

Watch out for critical hedge words, such as *likely, may, can, often, almost, mostly, usually, generally, rarely,* and *sometimes*. Question writers insert these hedge phrases to cover every possibility. Often an answer choice will be wrong simply because it leaves no room for exception. Be on guard for answer choices that have definitive words such as *exactly* and *always*.

### ✓ SWITCHBACK WORDS

Stay alert for *switchbacks*. These are the words and phrases frequently used to alert you to shifts in thought. The most common switchback words are *but, although,* and *however*. Others include *nevertheless, on the other hand, even though, while, in spite of, despite,* and *regardless of*. Switchback words are important to catch because they can change the direction of the question or an answer choice.

### ☑ Face Value

When in doubt, use common sense. Accept the situation in the problem at face value. Don't read too much into it. These problems will not require you to make wild assumptions. If you have to go beyond creativity and warp time or space in order to have an answer choice fit the question, then you should move on and consider the other answer choices. These are normal problems rooted in reality. The applicable relationship or explanation may not be readily apparent, but it is there for you to figure out. Use your common sense to interpret anything that isn't clear.

## Answer Choice Strategies

### ☑ Answer Selection

The most thorough way to pick an answer choice is to identify and eliminate wrong answers until only one is left, then confirm it is the correct answer. Sometimes an answer choice may immediately seem right, but be careful. The test writers will usually put more than one reasonable answer choice on each question, so take a second to read all of them and make sure that the other choices are not equally obvious. As long as you have time left, it is better to read every answer choice than to pick the first one that looks right without checking the others.

### ☑ Answer Choice Families

An answer choice family consists of two (in rare cases, three) answer choices that are very similar in construction and cannot all be true at the same time. If you see two answer choices that are direct opposites or parallels, one of them is usually the correct answer. For instance, if one answer choice says that quantity *x* increases and another either says that quantity *x* decreases (opposite) or says that quantity *y* increases (parallel), then those answer choices would fall into the same family. An answer choice that doesn't match the construction of the answer choice family is more likely to be incorrect. Most questions will not have answer choice families, but when they do appear, you should be prepared to recognize them.

### ☑ Eliminate Answers

Eliminate answer choices as soon as you realize they are wrong, but make sure you consider all possibilities. If you are eliminating answer choices and realize that the last one you are left with is also wrong, don't panic. Start over and consider each choice again. There may be something you missed the first time that you will realize on the second pass.

### ☑ Avoid Fact Traps

Don't be distracted by an answer choice that is factually true but doesn't answer the question. You are looking for the choice that answers the question. Stay focused on what the question is asking for so you don't accidentally pick an answer that is true but incorrect. Always go back to the question and make sure the answer choice you've selected actually answers the question and is not merely a true statement.

### ☑ Extreme Statements

In general, you should avoid answers that put forth extreme actions as standard practice or proclaim controversial ideas as established fact. An answer choice that states the "process should be used in certain situations, if..." is much more likely to be correct than one that states the "process should be discontinued completely." The first is a calm rational statement and doesn't even make a definitive, uncompromising stance, using a hedge word *if* to provide wiggle room, whereas the second choice is far more extreme.

### ⊘ BENCHMARK

As you read through the answer choices and you come across one that seems to answer the question well, mentally select that answer choice. This is not your final answer, but it's the one that will help you evaluate the other answer choices. The one that you selected is your benchmark or standard for judging each of the other answer choices. Every other answer choice must be compared to your benchmark. That choice is correct until proven otherwise by another answer choice beating it. If you find a better answer, then that one becomes your new benchmark. Once you've decided that no other choice answers the question as well as your benchmark, you have your final answer.

### ⊘ PREDICT THE ANSWER

Before you even start looking at the answer choices, it is often best to try to predict the answer. When you come up with the answer on your own, it is easier to avoid distractions and traps because you will know exactly what to look for. The right answer choice is unlikely to be word-for-word what you came up with, but it should be a close match. Even if you are confident that you have the right answer, you should still take the time to read each option before moving on.

## General Strategies

### ⊘ TOUGH QUESTIONS

If you are stumped on a problem or it appears too hard or too difficult, don't waste time. Move on! Remember though, if you can quickly check for obviously incorrect answer choices, your chances of guessing correctly are greatly improved. Before you completely give up, at least try to knock out a couple of possible answers. Eliminate what you can and then guess at the remaining answer choices before moving on.

### ⊘ CHECK YOUR WORK

Since you will probably not know every term listed and the answer to every question, it is important that you get credit for the ones that you do know. Don't miss any questions through careless mistakes. If at all possible, try to take a second to look back over your answer selection and make sure you've selected the correct answer choice and haven't made a costly careless mistake (such as marking an answer choice that you didn't mean to mark). This quick double check should more than pay for itself in caught mistakes for the time it costs.

### ⊘ PACE YOURSELF

It's easy to be overwhelmed when you're looking at a page full of questions; your mind is confused and full of random thoughts, and the clock is ticking down faster than you would like. Calm down and maintain the pace that you have set for yourself. Especially as you get down to the last few minutes of the test, don't let the small numbers on the clock make you panic. As long as you are on track by monitoring your pace, you are guaranteed to have time for each question.

### ⊘ DON'T RUSH

It is very easy to make errors when you are in a hurry. Maintaining a fast pace in answering questions is pointless if it makes you miss questions that you would have gotten right otherwise. Test writers like to include distracting information and wrong answers that seem right. Taking a little extra time to avoid careless mistakes can make all the difference in your test score. Find a pace that allows you to be confident in the answers that you select.

### ✓ KEEP MOVING

Panicking will not help you pass the test, so do your best to stay calm and keep moving. Taking deep breaths and going through the answer elimination steps you practiced can help to break through a stress barrier and keep your pace.

## Final Notes

The combination of a solid foundation of content knowledge and the confidence that comes from practicing your plan for applying that knowledge is the key to maximizing your performance on test day. As your foundation of content knowledge is built up and strengthened, you'll find that the strategies included in this chapter become more and more effective in helping you quickly sift through the distractions and traps of the test to isolate the correct answer.

Now that you're preparing to move forward into the test content chapters of this book, be sure to keep your goal in mind. As you read, think about how you will be able to apply this information on the test. If you've already seen sample questions for the test and you have an idea of the question format and style, try to come up with questions of your own that you can answer based on what you're reading. This will give you valuable practice applying your knowledge in the same ways you can expect to on test day.

**Good luck and good studying!**

# Reading

## Word Analysis and Vocabulary

### Using Context to Determine the Meaning of Words

Readers of all levels will encounter words that they have either never seen or that they have seen before but still don't know what it means. The best way to define a word in **context** is to look for nearby words that can assist in learning the meaning of the word.

#### *Context Clues*

Context clues are hints about the meaning of a word. They are the words or phrases in the sentence or sentences before and after a new or unfamiliar word. Context clues give the reader an idea about what a word means. A context clue may also contain words that help define the new word or an example of what the new word means. sing context clues to figure out meaning can be helpful when learning a new set of vocabulary words or reading a difficult text. The dictionary definition of a word can always be looked up to double-check intended meaning.

##### Example

Read the following sentences and determine the meaning of the word *absorbed* based on context clues:

> Kamal was so *absorbed* by his video game that he didn't hear his grandmother calling him for dinner.

The dictionary definition of the word *absorbed* is "having one's attention fully engaged; greatly interested." In this sentence, the words "didn't hear" show that Kamal is not paying attention to anything other than what he's doing. The explanation that he's playing a video game tells us that he's most likely doing something he enjoys. The clues present in the sentence help the reader figure out that the word *absorbed* most likely means very interested. This word can also mean "liquid taken in or soaked up," but because Kamal is a person and not a liquid substance, the reader can determine that is not the correct meaning in this sentence.

#### *Substitution to Find Meaning*

One way to find out if you have figured out the correct meaning of a new word is to **substitute** the meaning for the word. Using the example for *absorbed*, if the reader substituted in "very interested," the sentence would read

> Kamal was so "very interested" by his video game that he didn't hear his grandmother calling him for dinner.

This is a way for the reader to confirm that they have used the context clues in the sentence correctly.

#### *Synonyms and Antonyms*

When you understand how words relate to each other, you will discover more in a passage. This is explained by understanding **synonyms**, which are words that mean the same thing, and **antonyms**, which are words that mean the opposite of one another. As an example, *dry* and *arid* are synonyms, and *dry* and *wet* are antonyms.

### EXAMPLE

Read the following sentences and determine the meaning of the word *reluctant* based on context clues:

> Sam was *reluctant* to be in the play, so he told the director that he was too busy to rehearse and didn't go to tryouts. He felt too shy to get up on a stage.

In this example sentence, the words "too busy" show that Sam made an excuse about why he couldn't be in the school play. The sentence also says that he "didn't go to tryouts." The second example sentence has other clues. It says, "He felt too shy to get up on stage." These clues give the reader hints about what the word *reluctant* means. It means "not willing."

## ROOT WORDS, PREFIXES, AND SUFFIXES

The root, prefix, and suffix are parts of a word. The **root** is the main part of a word. It is what a **prefix** or **suffix** is attached to. A prefix goes on the front of a root word to make a new word. A suffix goes on the end of a root word to make a new word. Some words have both a prefix and a suffix. Many words have one or the other. The root, prefix, and suffix all have different meanings. By studying the parts of a word, the reader can figure out the meaning of a word.

Here are some common Greek Root words:

| Root | Meaning | Example |
|---|---|---|
| auto | self | automobile (a self-propelled vehicle) |
| graph | writing | graphic (are, especially involving drawing or lettering) |
| meter | measure | thermometer (an instrument for measuring temperature) |

Here are some common prefixes:

| Prefix | Meaning | Example |
|---|---|---|
| mis- | wrongly | misspell (to spell wrongly) |
| sub- | under | submerge (to sink below the surface) |
| dis- | not | disagree (not agree) |
| pre- | before | preview (to view before) |

Here are some common suffixes:

| Suffix | Meaning | Example |
|---|---|---|
| -it/ity | state of | activity (state of being active) |
| -ful | full of | wonderful (full of wonder) |
| -er | a person connected with | teacher (a person connected with teaching) |
| -able | can be done | likeable (can be liked) |
| -ment | result of | payment (the result of being paid) |

### EXAMPLE

Using current knowledge of prefixes and suffixes, determine the meaning of the word *misjudged* in the following sentence:

> After seeing him stop to help someone who had tripped, Tiffany realized she may have *misjudged* the new student.

A reader may know that *judge* means to make a decision. The prefix *mis-* means wrongly. Putting the entire word together, the reader can see that *misjudged* means to make a decision that is wrong. This makes sense in the context of the sentence. When people make quick decision about another person without knowing them long, they are more likely to judge them incorrectly. By paying close attention to the meaning of a root word plus any prefixes and suffixes, the reader can figure out what the author is trying to say.

### EXAMPLE

Figure out the meaning of *harmful* from its word parts.

*Harmful* is made up of a root and a suffix. The root is *harm.* The word *harm* means "to hurt." The suffix is *-ful.* This suffix means "full of." A reader can figure out that the meaning of *harmful* is "full of hurt or harm."

## SYNONYMS, ANTONYMS, HOMOPHONES, HOMOGRAPHS, AND IDIOMS

### SYNONYMS AND ANTONYMS

**Synonyms** are words that have similar or the same meaning. For example, *happy* and *glad* mean the same thing, so they are synonyms. A word may have many synonyms. Other synonyms for *happy* are *content* and *pleased.*

**Antonyms** are words that have opposite meanings. For example, *big* is an antonym for *small.* A word may have many antonyms. Other antonyms for *little* are *large* and *huge.*

Here are some common words with possible synonyms and antonyms:

| Word | Synonym | Antonym |
|---|---|---|
| Fast | Quick | Slow |
| Loud | Noisy | Soft |
| Pretty | Beautiful | Ugly |
| Rich | Wealthy | Poor |
| Sick | Unwell | Healthy |
| Start | Begin | End |
| Tired | Sleepy | Energetic |

**Review Video: Synonyms and Antonyms**
Visit mometrix.com/academy and enter code: 105612

#### Example

Determine if there is a synonym or an antonym for the word *silly* in the following sentence:

> Danny was so silly that his teacher had to keep reminding him to be serious and stop fooling around.

To figure out if there is a synonym for *silly*, the reader needs to look at the context of the sentence. A synonym means the same as another word. Danny's teacher reminds him to "stop fooling around." The sentence also says that Danny "was so silly." The term *fooling around* means almost the same as *silly*. The reader can tell this from the context clues because context clues are hints. An antonym means the opposite of another word. The teacher tells Danny "to be serious." The reader can figure out that *serious* means the opposite of *silly*. The reader can tell that *serious* is an antonym of *silly* because the context gives clues about the meaning of *serious* and *silly*.

### Homographs and Homophones

There are several types of words that sound alike but that have different meanings. **Homographs** are words that are spelled the same way, but have different meanings and that aren't always pronounced the same way. **Homophones** are words that sound alike, but are spelled differently and have different meanings.

Because some words have many meanings, the reader has to decide which meaning of the word is being used. To figure out which meaning is being used, the reader needs to look for context clues to find hints about the meaning of the word. For example, the word *spot* is a homograph. It can mean "a place" or "a stain or blot." In the sentence "After my lunch, I saw a spot on my shirt," the word *spot* means "a stain or blot." Context clues help the reader figure this out. The hints include "lunch" and "on my shirt."

### Homographs

| Homographs | |
|---|---|
| Quarter | |
| It's a quarter past noon. | I put a quarter in the vending machine. |
| Bat | |
| I love to watch bats fly through the sky. | I had practice today, but I forgot my bat. |
| Left | |
| Look both right and left before you cross the road. | The plane left for New York at three o'clock. |

### Homophones

| Homophones | |
|---|---|
| Bare | Bear |
| The trees already look bare. | These parks are full of bears. |
| Blue | Blew |
| My favorite color is blue. | My coffee was too hot, so I blew on it. |
| Reign | Rain |
| The kingdom wished the new queen a long and prosperous reign. | My garden will keep drying up is we do not get some rain soon. |

### *Idioms*

Idioms create comparisons, and often look like similes or metaphors. An **idiom** is a phrase that has a meaning that is different from the literal meaning of its individual words. For example, "break a leg" is a common idiom that is used to wish someone luck or tell them to perform well. Literally, the phrase "break a leg" means to injure a person's leg, but the phrase takes on a different meaning when used as an idiom. Another example is "call it a day," which means to temporarily stop working on a task. The phrase does not mean to literally refer to something as "a day."

## Dictionary

A print or digital dictionary can be used to find out many things about a word. A dictionary will show the correct pronunciation of a word, provide its meaning, and identify what part of speech the word is. It will also tell how the word was derived—that is, what words it came from originally. A dictionary will have a **pronunciation guide** for each word that shows how to sound it out and where its syllables start and end. It will use symbols to indicate sounds, and will also use sample sounds (the "a" in "bad," for instance). A dictionary lists all of the meanings of a word and the parts of speech the word can be used as.

> **example** \ ig-'zam-pəl\ noun
> 1. something that shows what a group of things is like
> 2. a model that should be either copied or avoided
> 3. a punishment meant to serve as a warning to others

### *Example:*

Julia used her dictionary to check the various meanings of the word *clear*. She found this entry:

> **clear** (klîr) adjective
> 1. obvious.
> 2. easily seen through
> 3. free from flaw or blemish
> 4. free from guilt; untroubled
> 5. out of the way
> 6. to tidy *v*
> 7. to free *v*
> 8. to earn *v*

Identify which definition of *clear* is used in the following sentence:

Janet stood *clear* of the crowd pushing to get through the door.

The correct answer is meaning 5: "out of the way." If you substitute that definition for the word, the sentence makes sense. Meanings 1, 2, 3, and 4 do not fit with the context of the sentence. Meanings 6, 7, and 8 are verbs and "clear" as it is used in the sample is an adjective. When considering which meaning is being used, always check for context clues in the sentence or in the sentences before or after the sentence in which the word is used.

## Thesaurus

A thesaurus is a reference book that gives **synonyms** of words. It is different from a dictionary because a thesaurus does not give definitions. A thesaurus can be helpful in finding the meaning of an unfamiliar word when reading. If the meaning of a synonym is known, then the meaning of the unfamiliar word will be known. Another time in which a thesaurus can be helpful is when writing. Using a thesaurus helps authors to vary their word choice.

## Glossary

A glossary is a **list of terms and their definitions** that can be found **at the back** of certain types of books, such as textbooks or reference books. A glossary does not have the definitions of all words, like a dictionary, but instead gives the definitions of the important terms within that particular book which are either uncommon or newly introduced. One may use a glossary when reading a book about economics or a chapter in a science textbook, for example, to define some of the technical terms within the text.

## Multiple-Meaning Words

A multiple-meaning word has different **definitions** in the dictionary. Many words have multiple meanings, so the reader has to pay attention to how a word is used in a sentence to figure out which meaning is intended. A multiple-meaning word is spelled the same, no matter how it is used. So, to find the meaning of a multiple-meaning word, the reader needs to look at the information presented in the rest of the sentence. For example, look at the word *leaves* in the following two sentences:

- Michelle *leaves* the building at 5 o'clock every day.
- The *leaves* fell off the oak tree in September.

In the first sentence, *leaves* means exits. In the second sentence, *leaves* refers to parts of a tree. By looking at the rest of each sentence, the reader can understand which definition of the multiple-meaning word the author is referring to.

### *Example*

Figure out the meaning of the multi-meaning word *part* from the context of the following sentence:

> Anita wanted to have a *part* in figuring out when the school trip would take place.

Possible meanings of the word *part* include "piece," "quantity," and "role." The example sentence says that Anita wanted to have a *part* in figuring out when the school trip would take place." If the reader substitutes each meaning of the word *part* for the word itself, the reader can figure out that the correct meaning is "role." It is the only word that makes sense in this example sentence. Anita wanted to have a role in figuring out when the school trip would take place. "Role" is the correct meaning of *part* as used here.

### *Example*

Read the following sentence from *Charlie and the Chocolate Factory* by Roald Dahl and determine the meaning of the word *spellbound* based on context clues:

> "Little Charlie Bucket was staring at her absolutely *spellbound*, watching her huge rubbery lips as they pressed and unpressed with the chewing, and Grandpa Joe stood beside him, gaping at the girl."

In the context of the sentence, *spellbound* refers to not being able to turn away. The character Little Charlie Bucket is staring at a girl as she chews, which means that he is looking at her without moving. The character Grandpa Joe is looking at the girl as well, while standing right next to Charlie. The reader can decide, based on the sentence, that the two characters are viewing something unusual and do not want to look away. Even if the reader does not know the meaning of an unfamiliar word, looking at the surrounding sentence or sentences can help the reader to figure out the meaning.

# Elements of Story

## Setting

The setting is where a story **takes place**. The setting of a story may stay the same for the entire story, or change as events in the story unfold. For example, an entire story may take place in one room, or on the other end, a story could cross continents as the reader follows the characters along on a trail of events. Every story has to take place somewhere. The setting of story is described by the author in terms of what it looks like, how the character feels, and anything that is happening at that location at the time. For example, a character may be caught on a doorstep on a cold, rainy day. The character may feel frustrated as he shivers in the doorway, waiting for the heavy rain to let up a bit.

### *Example*

When listing ways that a story set in the city has a different backdrop from a story set in the countryside, answers will vary based on current knowledge of common characteristics for each setting. A story set in a city may be different from a story set in the countryside based on the following factors:

- Number of passersby: many people on a sidewalk vs. no other people around
- Background noise: car horns vs. bird calls
- Types of surroundings: tall buildings vs. fields of corn
- Types of transportation: subways and taxis vs. horses and farm trucks
- Daily activities being carried out: sitting at a desk in a skyscraper vs. plowing fields for planting
- Type of attire: a business suit vs. dirty jeans and boots

### *Shaping a Character with Setting or Plot*

The setting of a story shapes character because it helps to define the situation that a character finds herself in. A character is limited to the setting of a story. For example, if a story takes place in a cold environment filled with snow and ice, this is certain to impact what actions a character can and will take. Frequently, the setting changes the way characters behave based on time. For example, the character of a woman who is a single mother in 1920 would be seen and behave very differently than a single mother in 2020.

#### Example

Read the excerpt and determine how the setting influences the character in this excerpt.

> She had swum too far out. The waves were higher than she thought. She was struggling hard to get to shore. She wondered if she would make it. She thought of her childhood. Had she been right to run away from home, she wondered? Just then, a lifeguard grabbed her and helped her to shore.

The setting of the ocean and the high waves creates a conflict in the character. She is worried. She thinks about her childhood and her parents. She doesn't know if she will make it to shore. This is how the setting affects the character in this excerpt. Without the high waves and the struggle, she would not become so worried and start to think about her past. She probably would not have questioned herself. This is an example of how a setting influences a character. If the waves had not been high, there probably would not have been a struggle or any self-searching of the swimmer's past.

### *HISTORICAL AND CULTURAL SETTING*

Historical context influences literature in a number of ways. The style of the author's writing can be impacted by the historical period during which it was written (e.g., Dickens wrote at a time when authors were paid by the word; this is why his novels are so long). Obviously, the setting of the book includes its historical context. In addition, dialect may be a function of the historical period of the book. When a reader understands the historical context of a particular book, he or she can have a deeper understanding of the novel. Knowing about the time period during which the author wrote, as well as the time period discussed in the novel, helps the reader understand some of the author's choices, including character motivations.

### STYLE AND VOICE

Style and voice play an important role in the development of a story. The reader's impression of a story can vary based on the style and voice used by the author. **Style** refers to the way an author uses words, phrases, and sentence structure. The style of the text can change depending on whether the author uses short, choppy sentences, long, elaborate sentences, formal language, or informal language. **Voice** refers to the characteristics of a text that show the author's personality and distinguish the author from other writers. An author's voice may be recognized through the way they use words or the way they organize and present their thoughts. Voice is specific to each writer, and it can be as specific and unique as personality.

### PLOT

The term **plot** refers to the series of events that take place in a story. The events in a story may take place in one location or many, in a short amount of time or over many years. A story always has to start somewhere, and the first event in a story signals the beginning of the plot. Stories may vary in length from half a page to novel-length, but they all follow a progression of events that the author winds together to form the plot. The characters and events in the story determine what the plot will be. Readers may find a **plot line** useful as they try to put the events in the text in order and determine the relationships between events.

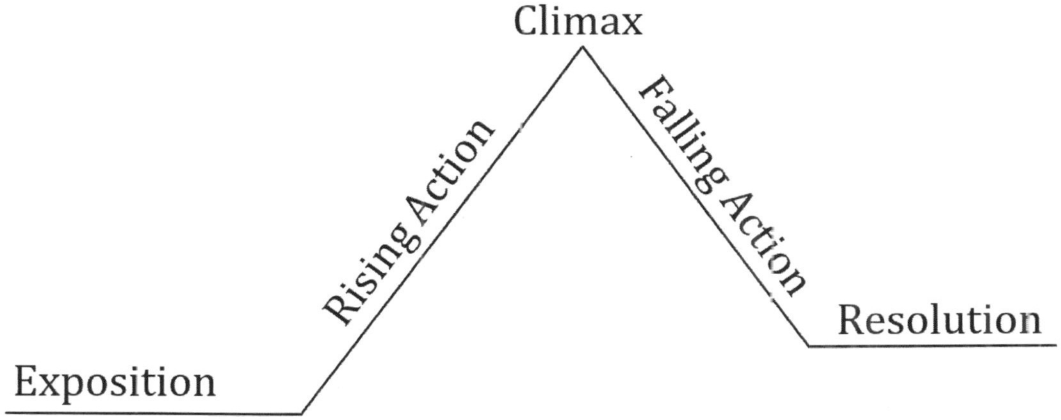


**Review Video: Plot Line**
Visit mometrix.com/academy and enter code: 944011

Every plot will begin with **exposition**, which introduces the characters and the setting of the story. The plot will continue to develop as new ideas and events centered on the main conflict in the story are revealed, which is called the **rising action**. The action in the story will rise until a **climax** is reached within the conflict. The climax can also be referred to as the turning point in the story, since the climax is where each character makes an important decision. After the climax, the action starts to wind down during the **falling action**. At this point, the characters begin to follow the paths they chose in during climax. The events of the story reach **resolution** in some way by the end of the story. Some conflicts are left open-ended, so that the reader is left to decide what really happened at the end of the story. Keep in mind that not all resolutions are happy or peaceful.

### *Example*

Read the following plot and determine what the missing event is in the plot sequence:

> Sarita went to the store to buy eggs for her mother. She bought the eggs and got back on her bicycle to bring the eggs home. Her mother was angry that the eggs were all broken.

The reader has to guess based on the plot sequence what happened between events. The reader knows that Sarita got on her bicycle to go home. The reader also knows that the eggs were broken when she arrived at the house. Based on the context, the reader can assume that Sarita fell off her bicycle or dropped the eggs on the way home, causing them to all be broken when she arrived. The reader can assume that Sarita would have noticed if the eggs were already broken in the store. Plot often follows a logical sequence of events, but sometimes it is difficult to decide what actually happened between two events. In the example, the reader can logically assume that the eggs were broken on the way home.

### *Conflict*

Conflict creates the basis for the plot of a story. A conflict may be between characters, a character and their own mind, or an outside influence. The main point of a conflict is that there is a problem that needs to be resolved. The problem may be a disagreement or an obstacle that has arisen and needs to be overcome.

An important part of analyzing the plot of a passage is identifying the **main conflict**. There will likely be many smaller conflicts in the story, but there will be one main problem that influences the characters and events. To identify the main conflict, first look at who the main character is. Now ask yourself what they want. They may want to something to happen or not happen, another character to do or not do something, or to confront or avoid a problem, among other things. Once you know what they want, now ask yourself what is standing in the character's way. It may be a person, an event, or something less tangible like the passing of time. Combining what the main character wants and why they do not currently have leaves the reader with a summary of the main conflict.

#### Example

Read the following sentence and explain the main conflict between the two characters:

> Joe stared angrily at Jamie's retreating back as Jamie raced away down the field with Joe's soccer ball.

The main conflict in the sentence is that Jamie has Joe's soccer ball. There may be additional conflicts between the two characters, but none are evident from the evidence shown in the sentence. In any story, a conflict may be minor and only affect part of the story, or be the main focus, taking an entire story to solve a conflict between characters. In the context of the sentence, it is not clear whether or not the entire story will revolve around Jamie taking Joe's soccer ball.

### *Resolution*

The term **resolution** usually indicates the result of a conflict in a story. Conflict between characters, within a character, or against an external element is necessary in order to have a plot for a story. Without conflict, no events would occur to form the story. A conflict will come to a climax, and then conclude in some way. The resolution of a problem may be open-ended, end tragically, or end in a way that is good for everyone involved. The problem resolution typically occurs near the end of a story, after the climax has happened. A problem may be resolved by the characters involved within the conflict or by an external event; an upcoming resolution may be foreshadowed in the text, or may be completely unexpected by the reader. If the resolution is completely unexpected, it is considered to be a **twist** in the story.

### *Effect of Plot on a Story's Characters*

The plot of a story unfolds as each event follows another, shaping the characters as they react to the various events that occur. Some characters are able to resolve their problems by the end of the story, while some characters fail to overcome their predicaments. As characters respond to the events around them, they reveal more and more about their personalities. Some grow and some do not. The reader can use the events of the plot to interpret the meaning of the story and understand its characters.

#### Example

Read the excerpt and explain how finding the chest affects Marta.

> The map said this was the spot. Marta held her breath. Her fists were clenched into two tight balls. She lifted the shovel and scooped more sand out of the hole. There it was; she had found the chest with the diamonds. She opened the top. She would never need to work again She smiled. It was really happening.

The event affects Marta by making her happy. The reader gets several clues that she is anxiously waiting ("Marta held her breath" and "her fists were clenched"), and that she is happy with what she found ("She smiled"). Events can cause characters to have all kinds of feelings. Here, something wonderful happened. However, events in stories are not always quite so happy. For instance, if a robber had suddenly seen Marta and the chest, he might have stolen the chest. That event would have had a very different effect on her. Readers need to pay attention to how characters are reacting to events, whether they are simply hinted at or stated in the story. In this way a reader will learn what characters are like.

## Characters

### *Character Trait*

The traits of a character may include how they act and physical characteristics; a character trait is a behavior or physical characteristic that is unique to a specific character. For example, a character may be outgoing, which means he or she likes to talk a lot, or they may have bright red hair. These are both character traits.

An author uses character traits to describe a character in a story and help the reader to learn more about how the character acts and what they look like. By comparing the character traits in a story, the reader can see similarities and differences between characters. The author includes character traits to help the reader understand why a character may act a certain way in the story. For example, a character who is shy may not want to talk with a lot of people in a new classroom, but a character who is outgoing may want to talk with many people.

An author typically provides many details about a character so that the reader can learn more about the character's traits, motivations, relationships, and any conflicts they may have in the story. The traits of a character may include how they act and how they look. Characters are often motivated by things that have already happened in their life or how they feel about a topic. The author will often give the reader enough information about the character so that the reader can figure out why the character responds to a situation in a certain way. The author will also often give details about the relationships between characters and points they may conflict on. For example, a character may be good friends with another character; however, the two characters may disagree on where to play outside if one character likes being near the water and the other character does not.

#### EXAMPLE

Read the following description of a character and decide, logically, whether the character is likely to go hiking outdoors:

> Jeremy lived in a high-rise in Chicago. He was studious, and not very athletic. Jeremy preferred to stay indoors and read a book, rather than enjoy outdoor weather.

Based on the description of the character's traits, preferences, and personality, he is not likely to go hiking outdoors. The description indicates that the character prefers reading, rather than enjoying outdoor weather. In addition, the character lives in a tall building in the middle of a large city, in order for him to enjoy the outdoors, he would have to travel away from where he lives. The character is not likely to change his preferences. A situation may lead the character to go hiking, but he is not likely to initiate the action on his own. A description of a character that is likely to go hiking outdoors may include a preference for outdoor activity and living near trails.

### *CHARACTER RELATIONSHIPS*

A relationship is the way one character acts with another character in a story. The characters are often called **major characters** if they have a main part in the story and **minor characters** if they have a smaller part. There are many different kinds of relationships. For example, two children in a story may be friends, but they could be angry with each other, competing with each other, or helping each other. An author may tell the reader what kind of relationship the characters have. An author might give hints about a relationship. For example, the author may show one child making fun of the other child, which would suggest that the two children do not have a friendly relationship. The author might show one child teaching the other child how to read, which would suggest that the two children have a friendly relationship.

#### EXAMPLE

Read the following sentences and describe the relationship Jill and Anna have:

> Jill came over to Anna and asked if she wanted an apple. "Sure, I'd love one. Thanks," Anna answered. Anna took a bite of the apple and started to chew it. Her chewing was so loud that they both started to laugh.

The author does not tell what the relationship between Jill and Anna is. The reader must figure it out from their actions. These actions are the clues the author gives. Jill asks Anna if she wants an apple. Anna says yes and starts to eat it. Her chewing is very loud. Both Jill and Anna start to laugh. They seem to like each other. Jill seems generous to Anna because she gives Anna an apple. They laugh together, and friends often laugh together. The reader can use personal experience to decide that it seems as though Jill and Anna are friends.

### *Characters' Feelings*

An author can show how a character feels in many ways. For example, the character may laugh a lot, which shows that the character is happy. The character could cry, which shows that the character is sad. There are other ways an author shows a character's feelings. A character may say something that shows he or she is sad. For example, a character may say that she misses her old school. This statement would show that the character is sad. A character may say something about enjoying her new school. This statement would show that the character is happy. An author knows that a character's feelings are important in a story. Sometimes the author says how a character is feeling; other times the author gives hints or clues about what a character feels.

#### Example

Read the following sentences and describe how Lorna feels:

> Lorna walked forward very slowly. The strange scratching noise was growing louder. She thought about calling out for help, but she knew no one would hear her. She decided to keep going anyway.

The author does not tell the reader directly how Lorna feels, but there are many clues about how Lorna feels from her actions. The sentences say that Lorna walks forward slowly and that there is a strange scratching noise. The sentence also says that she thinks about calling for help. These clues all suggest that Lorna is frightened. She doesn't know what is making the scratching noise. She wants to call for help, but she cannot. She is scared. The sentences also suggest another feeling. Lorna doesn't run away. She decides to keep going. This is another clue. It shows that Lorna is also feeling brave.

### *Character Changes*

Characters can change in a multitude of ways throughout a story; however, there are main aspects of a character that change. A character's identifying characteristics, such as personality or behavior traits, may change as the result of a prominent event in the story, current motivations, and conflicts. As conflicts change or are resolved, a character may no longer be motivated by striving toward a goal that was previously important to them. As the plot of a story moves along, characters can constantly change in relation to events that occur. Relationships between characters and the points of view of characters may change throughout a story as well.

Each story will have many different types of characters and each of these characters will have a different relationship with other characters. Stories usually have a protagonist, antagonist, and a variety of other characters including round, flat and stock characters.

#### Protagonist

The main character in a drama, movie, novel, or other fictional text. The author portrays the protagonist in a way that the audience is most like to identify with themselves. The protagonist is generally undertaking some type of personal challenge throughout the story. The author writes the story so that the reader becomes aware of the protagonist's emotions and is generally able to empathize with the personal challenge.

#### Antagonist

The character that actively opposes the protagonist by trying to prevent them from succeeding. The antagonist is usually presented in such a way as to make the audience dislike them, and want them to fail at stopping the protagonist. The protagonist and antagonist oppose each other, so their relationship is almost always one of dislike.

#### Flat Characters

Does not have any substantial changes throughout the story. They stay the same despite the conflict, and do not learn any lessons. They are usually minor characters that might interact with the main character in some way.

#### Round Characters

Major characters in the story that will be more fully developed than other minor characters. They will usually encounter some type of conflict that they must overcome, and usually learn a lesson about life or themselves along the way.

#### Stock Characters

Often get their characteristics and mannerisms from stereotypes of people that are widely recognized. These types of characters are often repeated and well-known. Readers should be aware that stereotypes are rarely accurate in reality, and are generally intended to be humorous or dramatic. Some examples are evil stepmothers, unintelligent blondes, rude athletes, and loyal servants.

## Main Idea and Theme

### Key Ideas and Supporting Details

Identifying **key ideas** helps the reader see what a text or story is mostly about. They are the **most important ideas** in a text, and everything else in the text builds around and supports them. Every piece of writing has key ideas. The **supporting details** in a story, such as the characters, events, and settings, will work together to reveal the key ideas. The details are not key ideas, themselves. They make the key ideas clear and show the reader the author's purpose for writing the text.

### Theme

The **theme** of a story, essay, or poem is the lesson that it teaches, or the message the author wants to get across. The theme is linked to the characters, the setting, and the events in a story. Some themes are fairly common. These themes are called **universal themes** and they suggest things about life, society, and human nature.

The theme of a story is not the same as the topic of a story. The topic is what the story is about, but the theme is what a reader is meant to learn. Themes are very rarely stated in the text. Instead, the reader has to **infer** the theme by reading closely and thinking carefully about what the author is saying.

Themes are an important part of literature because they serve the purpose of teaching the reader or listener a truth about life. The theme is developed by how a character or characters respond to their situations and challenges.

#### *Example*

Read the following and consider the theme of the excerpt.

> Jeanie arrived at the bake sale early. She bought the biggest cake at the sale. Sally had to work late. When she finally got to the sale, no cakes were left. She got only two cookies. She was lucky to get anything.

The saying "the early bird gets the worm" is one way to explain the theme of the story. In the story we read that Jeanie arrived early at the bake sale and got the biggest cake. But when Sally arrived, all that was left were two cookies. The point of the story is that the early bird gets the worm—the worm in this case is a large cake. In this story, the topic is a bake sale, but the theme is not "bake sale" because the words "bake sale" do not teach the reader anything.

## Point of View

Authors choose which character tells the story they are writing. This is called **point of view**. The point of view affects the story in many ways. There are three general types of point of view:

### *First Person*

- Tells a story through the eyes of one character.
- Uses the pronouns 'I,' 'me,' 'we,' and 'my.'
- The reader gets only one side of the story, without any other angles on what may have happened in the text

### *Second Person*

- Tells a story using the pronoun 'you.'
- The least common point of view.

### *Third Person*

- Tells a story about a character or group of characters from an outside viewpoint.
- Uses the words 'her', 'his,' 'they,' or a name to talk about a character or characters.
- A common way to show action in a story which allows the author to easily and realistically tell a story from more than one person's viewpoint.
- Gives readers a more complete view of a story as it is told from many different perspectives.

### *Poet Versus Speaker*

The author of a poem is called a **poet**. Many poems are written in first person, which means the **stanzas** (groups of lines) include words like "I" and "me." However, the poet is not always the **speaker** of the poem. In a novel, the author can create characters with different points of view. The characters can argue or have different roles to play in telling the story. Similarly, a poet may write a poem from a different point of view or even include more than one voice. The speaker is the voice of the poem, and is not always the same person as the poet him or herself. The reader or listener should know that the person telling the story is a character, and not always a real person.

For example, this excerpt from a poem by Dr. Seuss reads:

> When you think things are bad,
> when you feel sour and blue,
> when you start to get mad...
> you should do what I do!
> Just tell yourself, Duckie,
> you're really quite lucky!
> Some people are much more...
> oh, ever so much more...
> oh, muchly much-much more
> unlucky than you!

Even though one line has the word "I" in it, the poem is not from the perspective of Dr. Seuss. He is the author of the poem, but not the speaker. The person saying "I" is a character, just like in a story.

# Imagery and Figurative Language

## Imagery

Imagery is the use of **descriptive language** to add life or feeling to a work of literature. Many authors add literary and sound devices to create vivid pictures in the minds of their readers. Most of the time, imagery is thought to be one of the best ways to help readers fully understand and remember a work.

The most common forms of imagery are those that appeal to the sense of sight and sound. Imagery that appeals to the sense of sight, or **visual imagery**, helps the reader picture an event in their mind, usually by including specific details in the text that are not strictly necessary for the purpose of the story, but allow the reader to more easily "see" the scene. Some common forms of figurative language can help create visual imagery.

**Review Video: Sensory Language**
Visit mometrix.com/academy and enter code: 177314

## Literal and Figurative Language

Many types of text use both **literal language**, which means just what it says, and **figurative language**, which means something more than the literal words being used. Figurative language is a literary device that allows the author to expand reality in a vivid way. When an author uses figurative language, she connects things in an exaggerated way in order to create a memorable image, which helps to describe a situation in a new way for the reader.

**Review Video: Figurative Language**
Visit mometrix.com/academy and enter code: 584902

### *Simile*

- Shows similarity between two ideas or objects, using the words "**like**" or "**as**"
- For example, an author might write "The princess is as beautiful as a rose" to compare the appearance of a woman to a beautiful flower.

### *Metaphor*

- Puts one idea in place of another to draw a parallel between the two ideas.
- For example, an author might write "Her room was a pigsty," to compare a person's bedroom to a dirty spot where pigs sleep.

### *Hyperbole*

- An extreme exaggeration of an idea.
- For example, a character might say "I'm starving to death!" to show that they are really hungry. Most of the time a character who says this is not literally going to die from hunger, they are just ready for a snack.

### *Irony*

- Uses sarcasm or humor (usually with an emphasis on the opposite) to show difference from literal meaning.
- For example, if a character says "Well today must be my lucky day!" after they left their homework on the kitchen table, they are being ironic. The irony used here helps show that it is definitely *not* the character's lucky day.

### PERSONIFICATION

- Gives life or human characteristics to an inanimate object
- For example, if an author writes "The trees whispered to each other across the wide blue sky," they are using personification to help the reader imagine the scene. Trees are not human beings, so they do not whisper, but the image created in the reader stands out more than a literal description would.

### SOUND DEVICES

Sound devices allow authors to add another level to their texts by tapping into the spoken part of language. Authors may use many sound devices to create meaning and help readers understand them better, including:

#### ONOMATOPOEIA

- Appeals to the reader's sense of hearing by using words that copy the noises objects or people make, like sound effects.
- For example, an author might write "The soccer ball whooshed across the field into the goalie's net, scoring the winning point!" The word "whooshed" is an **onomatopoeia** because it mimics the sound of air moving quickly. Because the writer chose to include an onomatopoeia, the reader is able to better picture the action in the sentence.

#### ALLITERATION, ASSONANCE, AND CONSONANCE

- Alliteration, assonance, and consonance all deal with using the same sound throughout a line or sentence. **Alliteration** is the use of words that begin with the **same sound** in a sentence or in a line of poetry. **Assonance** refers to alliteration with a repeated **vowel** sound, whereas **consonance** refers to alliteration with **consonant** sounds.
- For example, the following line contains two sets of alliteration: "I saw a fly fly past my eye, straight into a fresh cherry pie. I felt a flea flee away from my knee and onto the sleeping dog." The first line uses the same sound in the words *I, fly, eye,* and *pie,* which is assonance. The second line uses both assonance and consonance, using the same vowel sound in *flea, flee, knee,* and, *sleeping*. The repeated consonants show up in the words *felt, flea*, and *flee.*

**Review Video: Alliteration in Everyday Expressions**
Visit mometrix.com/academy and enter code: 462837

# Author's Purpose

## Author's Purpose

An author may write a text for many different purposes. Four of the most common purposes are to inform, to persuade or influence, to express, or to entertain readers.

| | Definition | Example |
|---|---|---|
| **Informational Texts** | Inform the reader on a topic that they previously knew nothing about, such as many non-fiction texts. | An informative paper on kangaroos would detail where kangaroos live, what they look like, what they eat, and other habits. |
| **Persuasive Texts** | Influence the reader to think a certain way about a topic, calling them to action or pointing them toward resources that would help them to learn more about the topic. | An author may try to persuade the reader that waterparks are the best place to go in the summer when it is hot outside. The author would present information about waterparks and explain *why* they are good places to visit. |
| **Expressive Texts** | Express the author or speaker's opinion or emotions about a topic. Lots of descriptive words are used to clearly show the reader how the author or speaker feels. | The author may think that a new playground in town is a good idea, and write an essay about why a playground would be great for the community. |
| **Entertaining Texts** | Entertain the reader, such as in most fictional texts. | Kate DiCamillo, the author of *Because of Winn Dixie*, entertains her readers with the story of a young girl named Opal and the stray dog who teaches Opal the meaning of friendship. |

Authors usually write to entertain, to inform, or to persuade their readers. The organization structure or pattern they use is related to what the author's purpose is. It is important to choose the pattern that best presents the information, as not all patterns will work for every piece of writing.

### *Example*

Read the following sentence. State the author's point in writing the sentence, whether it is to inform, persuade, express an opinion, or entertain:

> The rollercoaster reached a peak and paused for a second, before gliding down the other side of the hill with a roar.

The purpose of the sentence is to entertain the reader. The author does not state his or her opinion on the topic, and the sentence doesn't inform the reader about an important topic. The sentence does not persuade the reader to accept a certain point of view, and is instead meant to entertain the reader by giving them the feeling they might get from riding an exciting roller coaster.

Notice that the text describes an event, rather than an issue or conflict. The event is part of a larger tale, where a series of events occur to form an entire story. The reader may notice that the author uses descriptive words to present the setting, such as gliding and roar. The reader can better picture a story when the setting is clearly presented.

# Types of Texts

## Children's Literature

There are types of texts that are specifically meant to be read by children or younger audiences. Children's literature contains many different **genres**, which are categories that texts can be divided into. Some types of children's literature are

- **Folktales** -Songs, stories, myths, or proverbs belonging to a group of people. Often passed down from generation to generation by word of mouth.
- **Fairy tales** are stories that include fictional creatures or characters with fantastical traits and abilities. Fairy tales often end happily and depict the victory of good over evil. The plots and characters in fairy tales are often far-fetched and whimsical.
- **Fables** –Story told (often by a narrator) full of supernatural features like speaking animals. The tale demonstrates a useful truth at the end.
- **Legends** -A story featuring a national or folk hero. Often has a basis in actual fact, but also contains imaginative material.
- **Myth** -A legend or traditional narrative, often based on a historical event. The story reveals something about human behavior or the natural world, and often involves actions of gods.
- **Tall Tales** -A story full of outlandish exaggerations, often humorous and containing heroes who perform impossible acts easily.

## Poetry

### *Poet Versus Speaker*

The author of a poem is called a **poet**. Many poems are written in first person, which means the **stanzas** (groups of lines) include words like "I" and "me." However, the poet is not always the **speaker** of the poem. In a novel, the author can create characters with different points of view. The characters can argue or have different roles to play in telling the story. Similarly, a poet may write a poem from a different point of view or even include more than one voice. The speaker is the voice of the poem, and is not always the same person as the poet him or herself. The reader or listener should know that the person telling the story is a character, and not always a real person.

For example, this excerpt from a poem by Dr. Seuss reads:

> When you think things are bad,
> when you feel sour and blue,
> when you start to get mad...
> you should do what I do!
> Just tell yourself, Duckie,
> you're really quite lucky!
> Some people are much more...
> oh, ever so much more...
> oh, muchly much-much more
> unlucky than you!

Even though one line has the word "I" in it, the poem is not from the perspective of Dr. Seuss. He is the author of the poem, but not the speaker. The person saying "I" is a character, just like in a story.

### Sensory Language in Poetry

Sensory language is when the author uses descriptive words and specific details that appeal to a reader's senses (sight, touch, taste, hearing, smell, emotion). For example, the author can use scents that the reader is familiar with to help them imagine what the setting of the poem smells and feels like. This use of sensory language is also called **imagery**.

### Rhyme in Poetry

Poets use rhymes to help readers understand poems. Words **rhyme** when they sound similar to each other, especially when the similar sound is at the end of the words, like *cat* and *hat*, or *roar* and *soar*. Rhyming words usually have endings that are spelled the same way, but sometimes they are spelled differently, like *wait* and *hate* or *bear* and *snare*.

Famous poet Shel Silverstein uses rhyme in many of his poems. For example, in his poem "Listen to the Mustn'ts", the last word of the first- and second-lines rhyme with each other, and the last word of the third- and fourth-line rhyme with each other.

> Listen to Mustn'ts, child, listen to the Don'ts.
> Listen to the Shouldn'ts, the Impossibles, the Won'ts.
> Listen to the Never Haves, then listen close to me.
> Anything can happen, child, Anything can be.

The pattern of the rhymes in this poem forms a **rhyme scheme**. Sometimes poets use a rhyme scheme that makes every other line of the poem rhyme instead.

## Drama

Dramas are texts that are written to be performed by people reading the lines or acting the stories out. They can also be presented as monologues (one character speaks), dialogues (two character speak to each other), or pantomimes (body movements are used instead of spoken words). Dramatic texts are called plays or **scripts**, and they are written differently than other texts.

### Text Structure in Drama

Plays are divided into **acts** (large units) and **scenes** (small sections inside acts) instead of chapters. There are also **stage directions**, which are instructions from the playwright about where items go, where actors should move, and what the characters should be doing during the scene. Stage directions are usually in italics to set them apart from other parts of the play. When it is time for a character in a play to speak, there will be **character tag** on the left side of the page which shows the name of the character (all letters of the name are capitalized) followed by a colon.

Here is an example of how a page from a play might look:

Title of Play

Act Number

Scene Number

*The setting of the scene is being described here. The reader is being introduced to the characters and the things happening around them. Characters will enter speak to one another during the scene.*

CHARACTER 1:

I am speaking. These are words I say. *(stage directions)* I am still speaking.

CHARACTER 2 *enters and does something.*

CHARACTER 2:

Now I am speaking. This is my dialogue.

### Dialogue and Stage Directions

**Dialogue** refers to what the characters say in a play when they are talking to each other, talking to themselves, or even talking to the audience. The type of speech, word choice, and accent a character uses is specific to the role he is playing. For example, a person cast to play a cowboy would have certain words in his vocabulary that a character from a big city in the North would not have.

A playwright also uses stage directions to make the play flow smoothly. Character interaction helps the viewer to understand the mood of the scene. If two characters are confrontational, the viewer is aware that there is some type of conflict occurring. Stage directions create order when all the characters are on stage together.

## Informational Text

### Controlling Idea

The controlling idea, also called the main idea or thesis, of a passage is usually located in the first paragraph or two of text. Having the controlling idea near the beginning of the passage allows the author to grab the reader's attention and let them know what the rest of the passage will discuss.

To find the controlling idea in a passage, there are questions the reader can ask while reading: What is this passage about? What does the author want the reader to know about the topic? The supporting details will provide evidence that the controlling idea is correct and are found in the body of a passage. The supporting details often provide examples of the controlling idea.

### Supporting Details

Supporting details provide evidence and backing for the main point. All texts contain details, but they are only classified as supporting details when they serve to reinforce some larger point. Supporting details are most commonly found in informative and persuasive texts. In some cases, they will be clearly indicated with words like **for example** or **for instance**, or they will begin with words like **first**, **second**, and **last**. However, these special words are not a requirement. As a reader, it is important to consider whether the author's supporting details really back up his or her main point. Supporting details can be factual and correct but still not relevant to the author's point. Sometimes, supporting details can seem important but they might not support the main idea in the story well because they are based on opinion that cannot be proven.

### EXAMPLE

Read the following two sentences. State which sentence is a main idea and which sentence is a supporting detail. Explain the difference between the two sentences:

> She went fishing with her cousin Vinny.
>
> Jayden visited her relatives in Louisiana over the summer.

The first sentence is a supporting detail, and the second sentence is the main idea. A main idea gives the overall concept, or point, of the story. A supporting detail adds more information to the point of the story. The reader already knows that the name of the character needs to be introduced before using the pronoun she. Therefore, it makes sense that Jayden visiting her relatives in Louisiana over the summer must come before the supporting detail about her going fishing with her cousin Vinny. Once the reader knows the overall point of the text, supporting details help to explain what else happens in the story. The reader knows from the main point that the character Jayden is visiting her relatives in Louisiana, which is where she went fishing.

### *STRUCTURAL FEATURES OF INFORMATIONAL TEXT*

Texts which intend to inform the reader about a topic are often accompanied by visual aids or graphics. Some common examples are listed below.

- **Insets and sidebars** show additional information related to the text in boxes or on the sides of the page. Insets can contain pictures or text, and sometimes have different colored backgrounds or font types to make them stand out from the text.
- **Visual aids** include features like diagrams, graphs, and charts. These can help the user think about information in a different way. They do this by visually presenting the relationship between the information in the text.
- **Timelines** are a visual aid which show how events from the text happened over time, and usually contain dates, locations, or other related information.
- **Tables** are visual aids that organize information in a way that shows the relationship between the information. Tables are made using rows and columns, and the pieces in the rows and columns are called cells. Usually, the first row or column will contain a title or heading that categorizes or defines the other cells in that row or column.
- **Bullet points** list items separately, making facts and ideas easier to see and understand.
- **Numbers** can also be used to list separate items. Usually, numbers are used to show that the items are part of a sequence. For example, in a list of instructions, each instruction may be numbered to show the reader the order in which each instruction should be completed.
- **Italics** are a formatting technique that makes text appear slanted. Italics can be used to emphasize text because they cause the text to look different and lead the reader to notice it more easily. Italics are also often used in fiction to show that text is part of a character's thoughts. They are also commonly used to show that a word or section of text is written in a foreign language.
- **Boldface** is a way to format text to make it stand out. Boldface, or bold, text can be used to emphasize a word, phrase, or idea. Boldface can also be used to let the reader know that they can find more information about a term in a glossary, sidebar, or other feature of the text.

### ORGANIZATIONAL PATTERNS

Authors want to have an effective text that the reader can understand. If ideas do not follow a logical order, the reader will become confused and not know what the author is trying to say. When writing, there are a variety of ways that an author can choose to organize a written work. It is important to choose the pattern that best presents the information, as not all patterns will work for every piece of writing. An author may organize ideas according to a timeline, cause and effect, or description of an event or setting.

#### ORDER OF IMPORTANCE

The author puts the information in the text in order of what is most important. Order of importance can be either increasing or decreasing, depending on how the writer wants to structure the work.

#### CHRONOLOGICAL ORDER

The author organizes the progression of events based upon when they occurred and what was included in each step of the story. By organizing the text in this way the author presents all necessary information about the six questions readers can ask to help themselves understand the text: who, what, when, where, why, and how.

#### PROBLEM AND SOLUTION

The author presents some information as a problem and then discusses a solution or attempted solution to that problem. In problem and solution, there is generally one main problem, but that one problem may have several possible solutions.

For example, suppose Billy wants a new video game but does not have the money. There are several possible solutions to this. He might try asking his mom to buy it for him. If that does not work, he could offer to do small jobs to earn enough money to buy it. A third possibility might be to wait until his birthday and ask for it then.

#### PROPOSITION AND SUPPORT

The author states a proposition that they believe to be true, and then provides support for that proposition in the paper. The topics that use this type of structure are generally things that reader might feel uncertain about or might not already have an opinion about. The support that the author gives for the proposition should include facts, statistics, logic, and reasoning. The more hard evidence an author can give the reader, the better it will help convince them to see things from the author's point of view.

#### CAUSE AND EFFECT

The author will write about relationship between two events that occur, where the second event occurs as a result of the first.

For example, a text may discuss a school policy stating that when a student is late to school too many times, they receive a detention. Later in the text, we might see a student repeatedly arriving late to school, after which he is given a detention. In this example, the **cause** is the student being late to school, and the **effect** is the student receiving a detention.

#### COMPARE AND CONTRAST

The author will show similarities and differences between items or events.

For example, the author may write about cats and dogs. They might start by giving a brief description of the two. Then they will want to point out all of the similarities, such as; they both have tails, and both are kept as pets. Next, they will explain the differences, such as; dogs are canines, while cats are felines. They will try to provide as much detail as possible about both the similarities and the differences.

### *Identifying Organizational Patterns*

**Example**

Read the following paragraph from a story. Describe how the author organizes information in the paragraph:

> First, John stopped at the grocery store to pick up some bread. Next, he went home and checked the mail. Finally, John sat down on the couch and opened up a book to where he had stopped reading.

The author uses chronological order to present information to the reader. The points in the story follow the order in which they occurred in time. The reader can look for words that give a clue as to progression of time, such as first, next, and finally. The paragraph does not use cause and effect, because one event does not lead to the occurrence of another. Each event is separate based upon when it occurred during the day. A progression of events can be placed on a timeline, to provide a visual image of when each event occurred. This is a helpful way to organize information in a lengthy story. The information in the paragraph is not overly descriptive, nor does it show where each event occurred in relation to another.

**Example**

Read the following paragraph from a news story and describe how the author organizes information in the story:

> The parade in honor of the town's 200th anniversary began at the corner of 57th Street at 9:00 a.m. on Saturday morning. Members of the fire department led the parade, dressed in their bright red hats and heavy yellow coats. At 9:15 a.m., members of the high school band gave a performance.

The news story uses chronological order organize ideas. The reader is given information about what type of event occurred, when the event occurred, what the event was about, and who was included.

**Example**

Identify organizational pattern that is used in the following sentence from *Morte d'Arthur* by Sir Thomas Malory:

> The king had given his promise, so he was obliged to agree.

The text structure of cause and effect is used in this sentence. The cause in the sentence is that the king gave his promise, and the effect is that he had to agree.

## Argumentative Texts

### *Identifying the Claim*

In a persuasive or argumentative text, the author is writing in order to make and support a claim. A claim is similar to the key idea of an informational text. However, a claim can be argued, which means that some readers may not agree with it. The author of the text will need to use the body of the text to support the claim and show readers why they should agree with it. To identify the claim of a text, first identify the topic. Then, read the introduction text to see what the author writes about the topic.

The claim should be clearly stated in the introduction. However, if the claim is still not clear, read the body to see what kind of evidence the author uses to support the claim. The way that the author gives and applies evidence may also show what the claim of the text is.

#### CALL TO ACTION

Another strategy is to look for a call to action in the text. A call to action is a statement that instructs the reader to do something after reading the text. Often, the call to action will tell the reader to do something that shows that he or she agrees with the author's claim. For example, if an author's claim is that reading is better than watching a movie, the author may include a call to action that says "Turn off the TV and dig in to a new book today!" By including this statement, the author is telling the readers to show their agreement by choosing to read rather than watch a movie.

### *IDENTIFYING HOW THE AUTHOR SUPPORTS A CLAIM*

In a persuasive or argumentative text, the author must use information to support his or her claim. This information is called evidence. Below are common types of evidence an author may use to support a claim:

- **Facts:** Authors may use facts that show that their claim is true. For example, a claim that fish are better pets than dogs can be supported by the fact that fish cannot make a mess inside a house.
- **Examples:** Authors may give examples of events or experiences that suggest that their claim is true. For example, an author may claim that people should exercise because it will make them healthier. The author could give an example of how exercise can improve a person's health in order to support this claim.
- **Quotes:** An author can support a claim by using quotes from other people or texts. If the person or text makes a statement that shows that the author's claim is true, the author can include that quote in his or her text. When authors include quotes in their work, they must always tell the reader where the quote came from.

The author must use enough evidence to support the claim. If the evidence does not fully support the claim in the text, then the author must continue working to find evidence for the claim. The evidence used to support a claim must also be believable and come from a reliable source.

### *IDENTIFYING THE INTENDED AUDIENCE*

Authors of persuasive and argumentative texts want to convince others to agree with a claim or take a certain action. Because of this, they will often write to a specific audience. Often, the target audience will include people who disagree with the author's claim. The author's desire is to give these people information that will lead them to change their minds or actions.

#### STRATEGIES FOR IDENTIFYING THE INTENDED AUDIENCE

One way to identify the intended audience of a persuasive or argumentative text is to first identify the author's claim. Then, consider who would disagree with the author's claim. This group of people is likely the group that the author wants to persuade.

Another way to identify the audience is to look for clues in the text. Sometimes, authors will clearly state which people are included in the intended audience. For example, imagine that an author includes the statement, "Teachers should reward their students every time they make a good grade on a test." This shows that the text is written to persuade teachers who do not already reward their students for good test grades. Similarly, a call to action may show who the target audience is by instructing the members of the audience to take a certain action.

# Drawing Conclusions and Making Inferences

## Facts and Opinions

Writers and readers must always be aware of the difference between fact and opinion. A **fact** can be tested and proven to be true. An **opinion**, on the other hand, is someone's personal thoughts or feelings. Opinions are often not changed by information. If an author writes that a newborn elephant is about five times taller than a newborn giraffe, then he or she is stating a fact. If the author writes that giraffes are more interesting than elephants, then he or she is giving an opinion because this cannot be proven to be true or false. Opinions are often supported by facts. For instance, the author might use a comparison between the way that giraffes eat and the way elephants eat as evidence of how giraffes are more interesting. An opinion supported by facts tends to be more convincing. On the other hand, when authors support their opinions with other opinions, readers should seriously think about and read the argument carefully to see whether it is logical and trustworthy.

**Review Video: Distinguishing Fact and Opinion**
Visit mometrix.com/academy and enter code: 870899

## Making Inferences and Drawing Conclusions

An **inference** is a **conclusion** or generalization that the reader makes based on the information provided within a text. Certain facts are included to help a reader come to a specific conclusion.

For example, a story may open with a man trudging through the snow on a cold winter day, dragging a sled behind him. The reader can infer from the setting of the story that the man is wearing heavy winter clothes in order to stay warm. Information is implied based on the setting of a story, which is why setting is an important element of the text. If the same man in the example was trudging down a beach on a hot summer day, dragging a surf board behind him, the reader would assume that the man is not wearing heavy clothes. The reader makes inferences based on their own experiences and the information presented to them in the story.

Readers may come to their own conclusion about a topic, or the author may state a conclusion at the end of a story. When readers are in the middle of a story, they can predict what will happen at the end of it based on the events that have occurred so far and the typical characteristics that have been presented by the author up to that point. A reader needs to consider all of the information that an author has presented, including the main point and supporting points, to make logical conclusions and inferences about the story.

### *Example*

Describe what can be inferred from the following sentences:

> Sometimes after a big storm, the beaches are covered with dead fish, seaweed, broken shells, and pieces of wood. Most seaweed is brown or gold, but there are often pieces of white seaweed. If people visit the beaches, the white seaweed disappears very quickly. It makes a delicious pudding.

To make an inference a reader needs to look for clues in a text. The author does not tell an inference directly; the author hints at one. Here the text says that fish, seaweed, and shells are on the beach after a storm. It also says that some of the seaweed is white and adds that the white seaweed is used for pudding. Another clue is that the white seaweed disappears quickly if people visit the beaches. The inference that a reader can figure out is that the people take the seaweed. It disappears quickly because it can be used to make a delicious pudding.

### EXAMPLE

Draw a conclusion based on the following sentence from "The Sing-Song of Old Man Kangaroo" by Rudyard Kipling:

> "He hopped through the Flinders; he hopped through the Cinders; he hopped through the deserts in the middle of Australia."

Based on the wording in the sentence, the character appears to be a kangaroo. The fact that the character hopped through the deserts in the middle of Australia lends the reader to believe that the character is a kangaroo. The reader needs to use personal knowledge of geography, animals, and context clues to draw this conclusion. The title of the story includes the word kangaroo, as well, which gives the reader a clue that the character described in the story is that type of animal.

Using context clues, or wording in a sentence, is an important way to identify what the author is talking about in the story. An author will often leave blanks for the reader to fill in on their own using information that has been presented up to that point in the story.

# Graphic Features in Texts

## Print and Graphic Features

An author may show information in a chart, a graph, in paragraph format, or as a list. Information may also be shown in a picture or a diagram. The way an author chooses to show information is often based on the purpose of the text and the audience that the text is meant to reach.

A reader may be asked to answer questions based on the graphic by itself, how the graphic relates to the text, or how the text would best be shown in a graphic form. Some common examples of graphics are cause and effect organizers, circle graphs, bar graphs, illustrations, and diagrams.

### *Cause and Effect Graphic Organizers*

Cause-and-effect graphic organizers are often used to map the **elements of a story**. A reader might read a story about a string of events and then be asked to correctly fill in either the **cause** or **effect** of an event in the story.

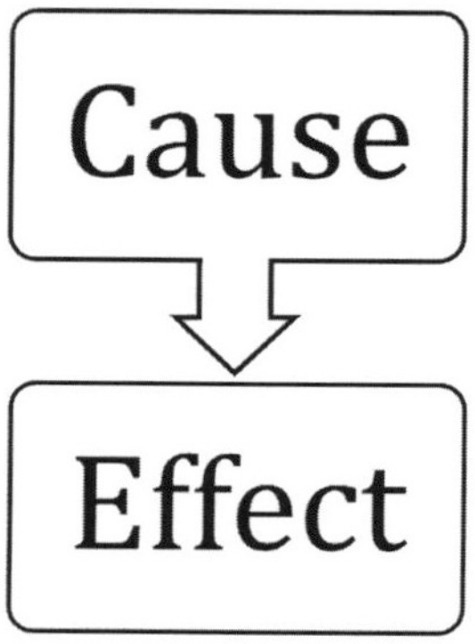


Example

Read the following excerpt from *Ramona Quimby, Age 8* by Beverly Cleary and decide what the cause of the hectic morning at the Quimby house is.

> With all four members of the family leaving at different times in different directions, mornings were flurried in the Quimby household.

A **cause and effect** graphic organizer for this excerpt might look something like this:

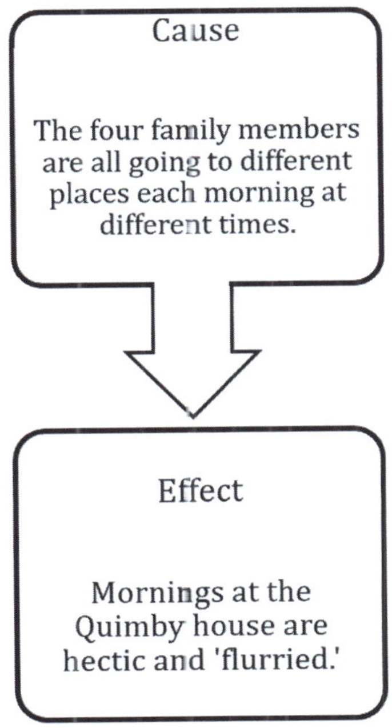


### *CIRCLE GRAPHS*

Circle graphs, also called pie charts, are often used to represent information that can be shown as **parts of a whole**. For example, this graph shows the results of people being asked about their favorite color:

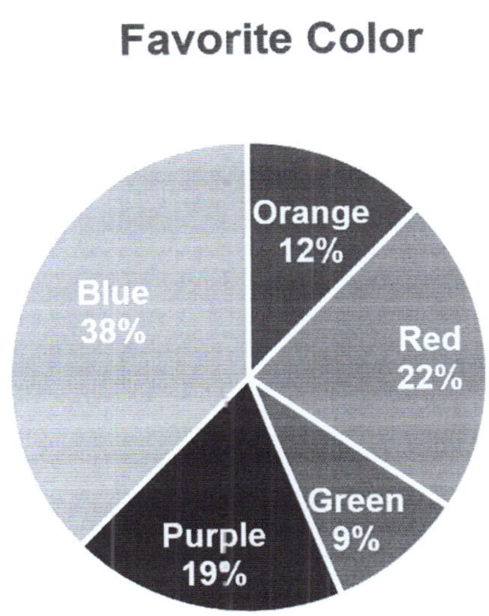

### *BAR GRAPHS*

Bar graphs are used to show information about **numbers**. For example, this graph is a different way of representing the same results as those in the circle graph.

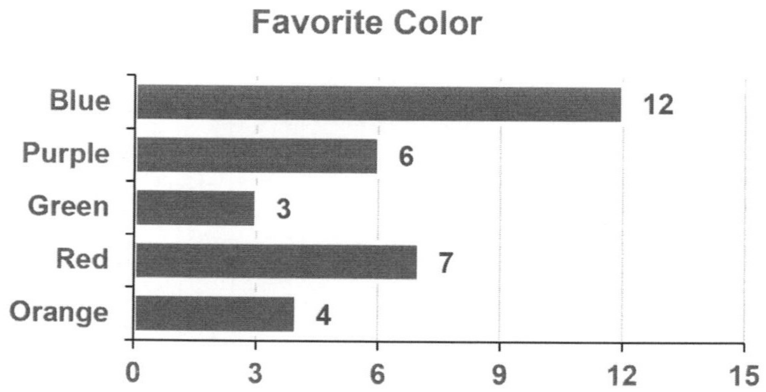


### *ILLUSTRATIONS AND PHOTOGRAPHS*

Authors may choose to include **illustrations** or **photographs** (or both) with their texts. These two image types both show something from the text or give more information about the text.

Illustrations are drawings of an object. They may be based on reality, or they may represent an artist's abstract idea. For example, this is an illustration of a 1903 automobile:

Photographs are pictures of objects. They are generally extremely realistic, and most often show an object as it actually existed at that moment in time. For example, this is a photograph of a 1917 automobile:

Both illustrations and photographs give the reader another way to relate to and understand the text. The reader may be asked how the image relates to the text, what type of caption the image should be given, or why the author chose to include the image with the text.

### DIAGRAMS

Diagrams are used to show information in a visual way. There are many different types of diagrams, including:

Diagrams that show the parts of an object, how they work together, or how they should be put together. This is an example of a diagram which shows how gears turn together

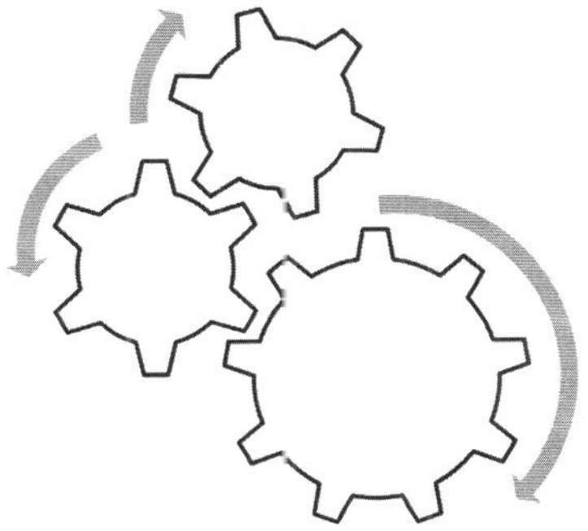

Diagrams that show how information is related are called **Venn Diagrams**. These are ways to visually see the way in which two different ideas overlap. This is an example of a Venn Diagram comparing cats and dogs:

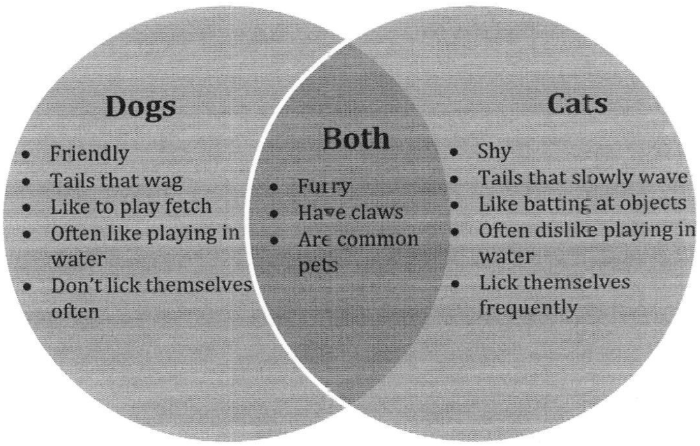

# Mathematics

## Number and Number Sense

### Base-Ten Number System

In the **base ten number system**, digits **increase** by a **factor of 10** as you move to the **left** and **decrease** by a factor of 10 as you move to the **right**. For example, 3,928,473.561 shows 3 in the millions place, 9 in the hundred thousands place, 2 in the ten thousands place, 8 in the thousands place, 4 in the hundreds place, 7 in the tens place, 3 in the ones place, 5 in the tenths place, 6 in the hundredths place, and 1 in the thousandths place. The first place to the right of the decimal point is the tenths place, the second place is the hundredths place, and so on. Notice that each place value to the right of the decimal point has the letters "ths" at the end of it to signify that is to the right of the decimal point. Digits are 10 times as large as you move to the left. As you move to the right, the digits are one-tenth the previous digit.

Moving to the left:

$\frac{5}{10}$ or 0.5 is 10 times as large as $\frac{5}{100}$ or 0.05.

5 is 10 times as large as $\frac{5}{10}$ or 0.5.

50 is 10 times as large as 5.

Moving to the right:

5 is $\frac{1}{10}$ of 50.

$\frac{5}{10}$ or 0.5 is $\frac{1}{10}$ of 5.

$\frac{5}{100}$ or 0.05 is $\frac{1}{10}$ of $\frac{5}{10}$ or 0.5.

### Place Value

Numbers can be broken apart and composed based on their **place value**. For example, the number 129,548 can be expressed in **expanded form** as 100,000 + 20,000 + 9,000 + 500 + 40 + 8. You should also be comfortable going from expanded form to standard form. For example, what number is represented by 30,000 + 400 + 80 + 2? Notice 3 groups of ten-thousands, 0 groups of thousands, 4 groups of hundreds, 8 groups of tens, and 2 groups of ones. This becomes 30,482.

## Expanded Notation

**Expanded notation** shows the value of each digit in a number. For example, 45.3 can be "expanded" into 4 tens, 5 ones, and 3 tenths. In expanded form, it is 40 + 5 + 0.3.

The following number is in **standard form**: 1,234,567,891.23

When writing numbers in expanded form, consider the place value of each number.

The first 1 represents 1,000,000,000.
The first 2 represents 200,000,000.
The first 3 represents 30,000,000.
The 4 represents 4,000,000.
The 5 represents 500,000.
The 6 represents 60,000.
The 7 represents 7,000.
The 8 represents 800.
The 9 represents 90.
The second 1 represents 1.
The second 2 represents 0.2.
The second 3 represents 0.03.

Put it all together in expanded form:

$$1,000,000,000 + 200,000,000 + 30,000,000 + 4,000,000 + 500,000 + 60,000 + 7,000 + 800 + 90 + 1 + 0.2 + 0.03$$

**Review Video: Place Value**
Visit mometrix.com/academy and enter code: 205433

### *Example*

Write the number 567.92 in expanded form.

Standard form: 567.92

Expanded form: 500 + 60 + 7 + 0.9 + 0.02

### *Example*

What is the value of the first 5 in the number 45,105,000?

The first 5 is in the millions place, so its value is 5,000,000.

## Whole Numbers

### *Comparing Whole Numbers*

When comparing whole numbers, compare each digit from left to right. For example, consider the comparison between the numbers 46,241,733 and 46,243,946. At first glance, the numbers might seem very close. To precisely compare the numbers, compare each digit, one by one, starting at the **farthest left digit**.

46 , 241 , 733

46 , 243 , 946

Both digits have 4 in the ten millions place.

Both digits have 6 in the millions place.

Both digits have 2 in the hundred thousands place.

Both digits have 4 in the ten thousands place.

The top number has 1 in the thousands place, but the bottom number has 3 in the thousands place. 3 > 1 so 46,243,946 > 46,241,733.

#### Symbols for Comparing Numbers

Remember that the symbol > means "is **greater** than." When using this symbol, the larger number must appear first, or to the left of the symbol. The symbol < means "is **less** than." So when using this symbol, the smaller number must appear first, or to the left of the symbol. When using the symbol =, the equal sign, the numbers on both sides of the symbol should have the **same** value.

### *Rounding Whole Numbers*

When rounding whole numbers, look at the number to the **right** of the digit you are **rounding**. If the number to the right is **5 or more**, the digit you are rounding rounds **up**. If the number to the right is **less than 5**, the digit you are rounding stays the **same**. All the digits to the right of the one you are rounding become **zeros**.

Round to the nearest ten: 2,392,537

Find the digit in the tens place (3). Look to the right. 7 is "5 or more", so the digit 3 will round up to 4. All digits to the right of 4 become 0.

2,392,537 becomes 2,392,540.

Round to the nearest hundred: 2,392,537.

Find the digit in the hundreds place (5). Look to the right. 3 is "less than 5", so the digit 5 will stay the same. All digits to the right of 5 become 0.

2,392,537 becomes 2,392,500.

Round to the nearest thousand: 2,392,537.

Find the digit in the thousands place (2). Look to the right. 5 is "5 or more", so the digit 2 will round up to 3. All digits to the right of the rounded 3 become 0.

2,392,537 becomes 2,393,000.

Round to the nearest ten thousand: 2,392,537.

Find the digit in the ten thousands place (9). Look to the right. 2 is "less than 5", so the digit 9 will stay the same. All digits to the right of 9 become 0.

2,392,537 becomes 2,390,000.

Round to the nearest hundred thousand: 2,392,537.

Find the digit in the hundred thousands place (2). Look to the right. 9 is "5 or more", so the digit 3 will round up to 4. All digits to the right of the rounded 4 become 0.

2,392,537 becomes 2,400,000.

## FRACTIONS

### *UNIT FRACTIONS*

A **unit fraction** is any fraction with a numerator of 1. For example, $\frac{1}{2}, \frac{1}{3}, \frac{1}{4}$, and $\frac{1}{5}$ are considered unit fractions. When a unit fraction is added to itself multiple times, the result is a larger fraction. For example, $\frac{1}{8} + \frac{1}{8} + \frac{1}{8} = \frac{3}{8}$.

The opposite of this is **decomposing** a fraction into the sum of its unit fractions.

$\frac{5}{6}$ is the result of combining $\frac{1}{6}$ five times.

$$\frac{5}{6} = \frac{1}{6} + \frac{1}{6} + \frac{1}{6} + \frac{1}{6} + \frac{1}{6}$$

This is true for **mixed numbers** and **improper** fractions as well. Mixed numbers are values that are written using a whole number and a fraction. For example, $2\frac{1}{3}$ is a mixed number that consists of 7 groups of $\frac{1}{3}$.

$$2\frac{1}{3} = \frac{1}{3} + \frac{1}{3} + \frac{1}{3} + \frac{1}{3} + \frac{1}{3} + \frac{1}{3} + \frac{1}{3}$$

Improper fractions are fractions that have a numerator that is greater than the denominator. $\frac{4}{3}$ is an improper fraction that consists of 4 groups of $\frac{1}{3}$.

$$\frac{4}{3} = \frac{1}{3} + \frac{1}{3} + \frac{1}{3} + \frac{1}{3}$$

### *Decomposing Fractions*

When a fraction is decomposed, it is **split up** into **smaller** fractions. The sum of these smaller fractions is the original fraction. For example, $\frac{7}{8}$ can be split up into the sum of $\frac{1}{8}+\frac{1}{8}+\frac{1}{8}+\frac{1}{8}+\frac{1}{8}+\frac{1}{8}+\frac{1}{8}$. However, this is not the only way to decompose $\frac{7}{8}$.

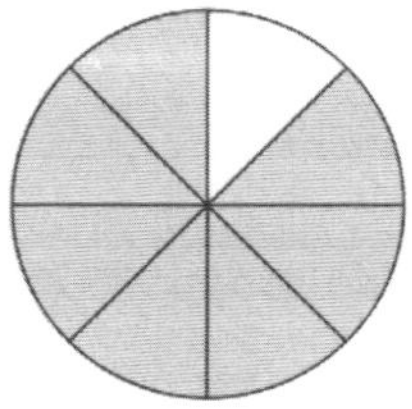

For example, the model below shows 7 shaded shares out of 8, or the fraction $\frac{7}{8}$. The fraction $\frac{7}{8}$ can be created in many ways. For example, $\frac{2}{8}+\frac{4}{8}+\frac{1}{8}$ has a sum of $\frac{7}{8}$.

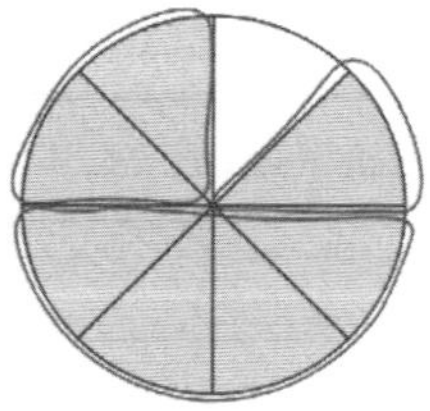

### *Equivalent Fractions*

Fractions are considered **equivalent** if they represent the same amount. There are a few ways to determine if fractions are equivalent.

#### Models

Fractions can be compared by drawing a quick sketch. For example, consider the fractions $\frac{6}{8}$ and $\frac{3}{4}$. Create two circles that are the same size. Divide one circle into 8 equal shares, and the other circle into 4 equal shares. Notice how 6 out of 8 is the same size as 3 out of 4. Since $\frac{6}{8}$ and $\frac{3}{4}$ cover the same amount of each circle, they are considered equivalent. Creating a sketch or a model is a great way to compare fractions with denominators that are small. However, when denominators are larger, like $\frac{1}{40}$ or $\frac{39}{100}$, a sketch is unreasonable.

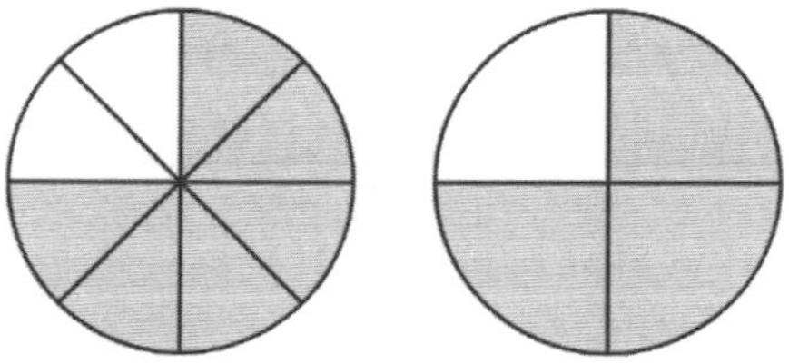

### Common Denominators

For larger denominators, consider using a common denominator to determine if fractions are equivalent. For example, consider the fractions $\frac{46}{100}$ and $\frac{70}{150}$. The fractions cannot be compared until they have the same denominator. The lowest common multiple of 100 and 150 is 300. Set up each fraction with 300 as the denominator.

$\frac{46}{100}$ becomes $\frac{x}{300}$.

$\frac{70}{150}$ becomes $\frac{y}{300}$.

Now adjust the numerators.

$\frac{46}{100}$: The denominator is multiplied by 3 to get 300, so multiply the numerator by 3 as well: $\frac{46\times3}{100\times3} = \frac{138}{300}$.

$\frac{70}{150}$: The denominator is multiplied by 2 to get 300, so multiply the numerator by 2 as well: $\frac{70\times2}{150\times2} = \frac{140}{300}$.

Now that the two fractions have the same denominator, they can be compared. $\frac{138}{300}$ is not equivalent to $\frac{140}{300}$ because the numerators are different while the denominators are the same.

### Comparing Fractions

It can be difficult to compare fractions when the numerators and denominators are different. For example, consider the fractions $\frac{7}{9}$ and $\frac{8}{11}$. It is difficult to know which fraction is larger because one fraction is out of 9, and one fraction is out of 11. To compare these fractions, create a common denominator.

One denominator is 9, and the other is 11. A common denominator can be calculated by determining the least common multiple (LCM). The LCM of 9 and 11 is 99. Set up each fraction with 99 as the new denominator.

$\frac{7}{9}$ becomes $\frac{x}{99}$.

$\frac{8}{11}$ becomes $\frac{x}{99}$.

Now adjust the numerators.

The denominator in $\frac{7}{9}$ was multiplied by 11 to reach $\frac{x}{99}$. Multiply the numerator by 11 as well: $\frac{7\times11}{9\times11} = \frac{77}{99}$.

The denominator in $\frac{8}{11}$ was multiplied by 9 to reach $\frac{x}{99}$. Multiply the numerator by 9 as well: $\frac{8\times9}{11\times9} = \frac{72}{99}$.

Now the two new fractions can be compared. $\frac{77}{99}$ is greater than $\frac{72}{99}$, or $\frac{77}{99} > \frac{72}{99}$.

**EXAMPLE**

Fill in the blank to make the statement true. $\frac{3}{5}$ __ $\frac{2}{7}$

Use one of the following symbols: >, <, or =.

$\frac{3}{5}$ and $\frac{2}{7}$ have different denominators. To compare the fractions, rewrite each fraction with a common denominator. The lowest multiple that both 5 and 7 have in common is 35. Rewrite the fractions with 35 as the denominator.

$\frac{3}{5}$ becomes $\frac{?}{35}$

$\frac{2}{7}$ becomes $\frac{?}{35}$

Now adjust the numerators.

$\frac{3}{5}$: The denominator was 5 and now it is 35. 5 was multiplied by 7, so multiply the numerator by 7 as well. $\frac{3}{5}$ becomes $\frac{21}{35}$.

$\frac{2}{7}$: The denominator was 7 and now it is 35. 7 was multiplied by 5, so multiply the numerator by 5 as well. $\frac{2}{7}$ becomes $\frac{10}{35}$.

$\frac{21}{35} > \frac{10}{35}$, therefore $\frac{3}{5} > \frac{2}{7}$.

**EXAMPLE**

Compare the two fractions using the symbol >,<, or =: $\frac{5}{6}$ __ $\frac{7}{8}$.

The fractions $\frac{5}{6}$ and $\frac{7}{8}$ can be compared once they have a common denominator. Look at the denominators: 6 and 8. The lowest common multiple of 6 and 8 is 24. Make 24 the new denominator for both fractions.

$\frac{5}{6}$ becomes $\frac{?}{24}$

$\frac{7}{8}$ becomes $\frac{?}{24}$

Now adjust the numerators. What was the original denominator multiplied by? Multiply the numerator by this same amount.

$\frac{5}{6}$: The denominator was multiplied by 4 to create $\frac{?}{24}$. Multiply the numerator by 4. $\frac{5}{6}$ becomes $\frac{20}{24}$.

$\frac{7}{8}$: The denominator was multiplied by 3 to create $\frac{?}{24}$. Multiply the numerator by 3. $\frac{7}{8}$ becomes $\frac{21}{24}$.

$\frac{20}{24} < \frac{21}{24}$, therefore $\frac{5}{6} < \frac{7}{8}$.

### *DIVISION STATEMENTS EXPRESSED AS FRACTIONS*

Division statements can be expressed or written as a fraction. For example, $50 \div 2$ can be expressed as $\frac{50}{2}$. While this can be read as fifty halves, it can also be read as fifty divided by two. This is also the same concept as multiplying 50 by $\frac{1}{2}$. The model below demonstrates 50 squares cut evenly in to two equal groups. Thus, it got cut in half because the amount shaded is one-half of the original amount.

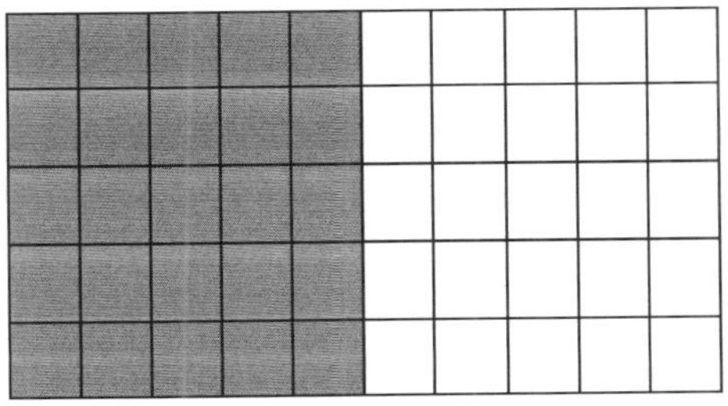

The same is true for fractions that have a smaller value in the numerator than the denominator. For example, the fraction $\frac{3}{4}$ can be written as $3 \div 4$. It is important to remember that the numerator will always be the dividend, and the denominator will always be the divisor. The dividend is the number that is being divided into or broken apart. The divisor is how many times or groups the dividend is being broken apart equally.

## DECIMALS

### *REPRESENTING DECIMALS WITH MODELS*

It can be helpful to **visualize** fractions and decimals as a **model**. For example, when one whole is divided into 10 equal shares, each share represents 1 out of 10. As a fraction this is $\frac{1}{10}$, and as a decimal this is 0.1.

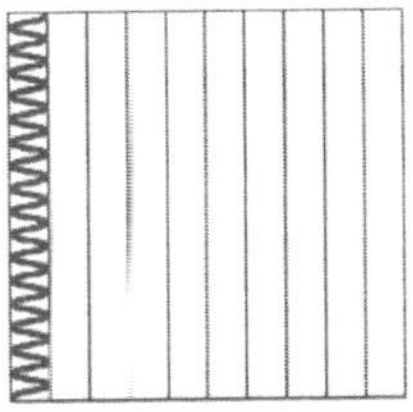

When one whole is divided into 100 equal shares, each share represents 1 out of 100. As a fraction this is $\frac{1}{100}$, and as a decimal this is 0.01.

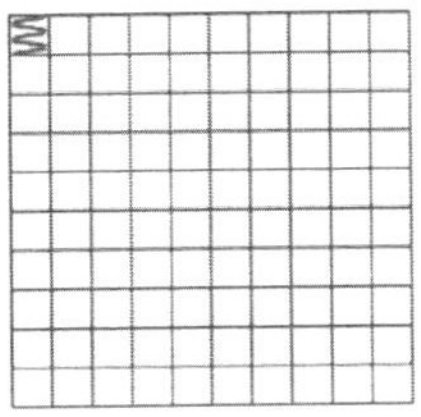

When one whole is divided into 1,000 equal shares, each share represents 1 out of 1,000. As a fraction this is $\frac{1}{1000}$, and as a decimal this is 0.001.

Notice how 1 out of 10 is the same amount as 10 out of 100. So, $\frac{1}{10}$ and $\frac{10}{100}$ are considered equivalent fractions. This means 0.1 and 0.10 are considered equivalent decimals.

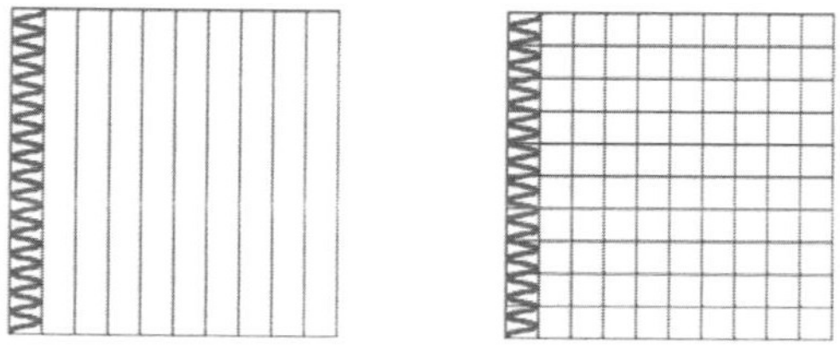

### *Representing Decimals with Money*

Money is expressed in **dollars** and **cents**. Cents are represented as **tenths** and **hundredths**. For example, $4.92 represents 4 whole dollars, 9 tenths of a dollar, and 2 hundredths of a dollar.

Express the coins as a decimal dollar amount:

4 quarters, 4 nickels, 2 pennies.

4 quarters: $\$0.25 + \$0.25 + \$0.25 + \$0.25 = \$1.00$

4 nickels: $\$0.05 + \$0.05 + \$0.05 + \$0.05 = \$0.20$

2 pennies: $\$0.01 + \$0.01 = \$0.02$

Remember, line up the decimal points when adding decimals.

$$\begin{array}{r} 1.\ 00 \\ 0.\ 20 \\ +0.\ 02 \\ \hline \$1.\ 22 \end{array}$$

#### Example

Consider the model below. What fraction would this represent? What decimal? What dollar amount?

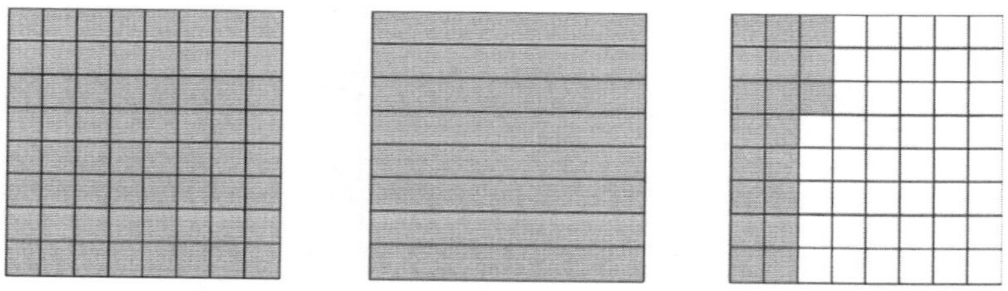

The model shows $\frac{100}{100} + \frac{10}{10} + \frac{23}{100}$.

This represents 2 wholes and 23 hundredths.

As a decimal, this is 2.23.

As a dollar amount, this represents $2.23.

### Comparing and Ordering Decimals

Decimals can be compared and ordered by **comparing each digit** from left to right. For example, 13.84 and 13.54 have the same digit in the tens place (1), the same digit in the ones place (3), but they have a different digit in the tenths place. Comparing these values, we see $8 > 5$, which means 13.84 is greater than 13.54.

This can also be seen using a visual model. For example, when comparing decimals in a model, the larger decimal value will cover a larger portion of the whole. The model on the left shows 6 out of 10, or 0.6. The model on the right shows 13 out of 100, or 0.13. Notice how 0.6 has a larger shaded region. This means 0.6 is greater than 0.13.

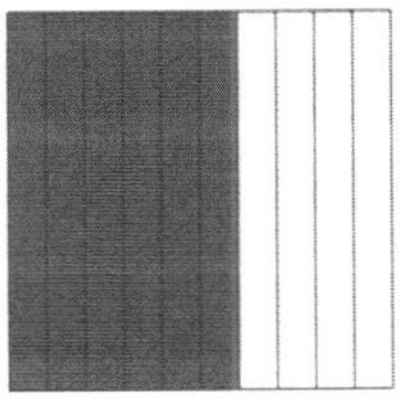
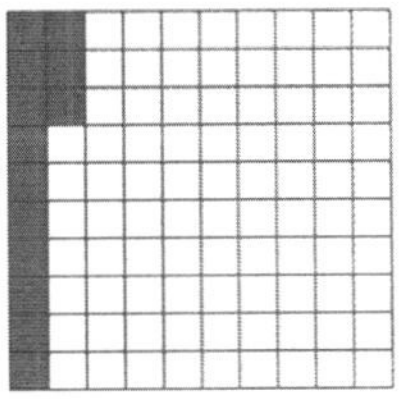

It is important to be aware of the **place value** when comparing decimal values. For example, consider the place value when comparing 0.3 and 0.03. Both values contain a 3, but one represents 3 tenths and the other represents 3 hundredths. Notice how $\frac{3}{10}$ covers more of the model than $\frac{3}{100}$.

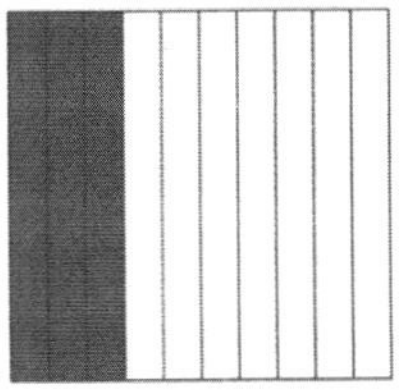
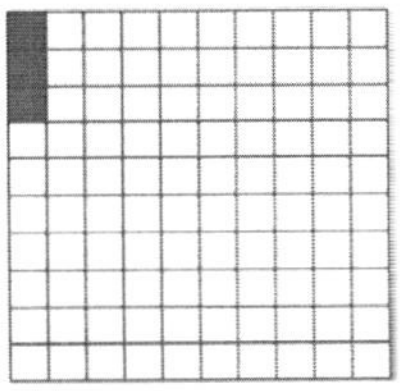

### Relating Decimals to Fractions

#### Converting Decimals to Fractions

Decimals and fractions can be used to represent values less than one whole. Remember, one decimal place value to the right of the decimal point represents tenths, and two decimal places to the right of the decimal point represents hundredths. For example, 0.4 represents 4 tenths, or as a fraction $\frac{4}{10}$. The number 0.04 represents 4 hundredths, or as a fraction $\frac{4}{100}$.

When a decimal extends to the tenths place, the fraction has a denominator of 10.

$$0.1 = \frac{1}{10}$$

$$0.2 = \frac{2}{10}$$

$$0.3 = \frac{3}{10}$$

$$0.4 = \frac{4}{10}$$

When a decimal extends to the hundredths place, the fraction has a denominator of 100.

$$0.45 = \frac{45}{100}$$

$$0.35 = \frac{35}{100}$$

$$0.25 = \frac{25}{100}$$

$$0.15 = \frac{15}{100}$$

### EQUIVALENT DECIMALS AND FRACTIONS

Notice how $\frac{40}{100}$ and $\frac{4}{10}$ cover the **same amount** of the model. This means that $\frac{40}{100}$ and $\frac{4}{10}$ are **equivalent** fractions. Since $\frac{40}{100}$ and $\frac{4}{10}$ are equivalent fractions, 0.40 and 0.4 are equivalent decimals.

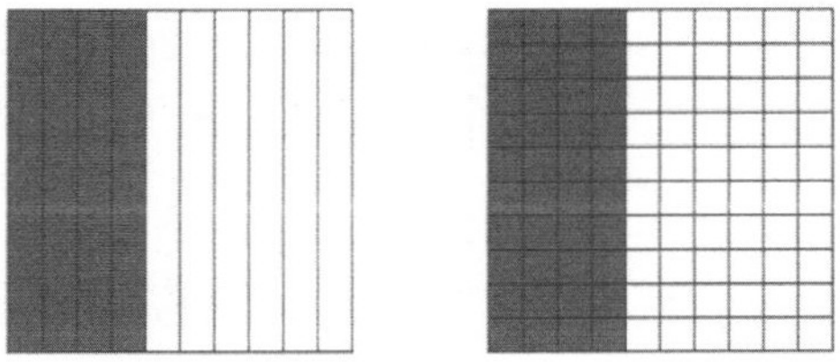

Here are some other examples of equivalent fractions and decimals:

$$\frac{1}{10} = 0.1 = 0.10 = \frac{10}{100}$$

$$\frac{2}{10} = 0.2 = 0.20 = \frac{20}{100}$$

$$\frac{3}{10} = 0.3 = 0.30 = \frac{30}{100}$$

### EXAMPLE

Express "45 hundredths" as a decimal and a fraction in simplest form.

45 hundredths represents 45 out of 100, which as a fraction is $\frac{45}{100}$. This fraction can be simplified. 45 and 100 have a factor in common. Divide both the numerator and denominator by the common factor of 5. $\frac{45}{100}$ becomes $\frac{9}{20}$.

$\frac{45}{100}$ can be expressed as a decimal. $\frac{45}{100}$ can be thought of as 4 tenths plus 5 hundredths. $\frac{4}{10}$ and $\frac{5}{100}$ is expressed as 0.45 in decimal form: $\frac{45}{100} = 0.45$.

45 hundredths as a decimal and a fraction: 0.45 and $\frac{9}{20}$.

#### EXAMPLE

Draw lines to connect the fraction and decimal values that are equivalent.

| | |
|---|---|
| 0.7 | $\frac{6}{100}$ |
| $\frac{2}{100}$ | 0.8 |
| 0.06 | 0.99 |
| $\frac{99}{100}$ | $\frac{7}{10}$ |
| $\frac{4}{5}$ | 0.02 |

0.7 represents 7 tenths. As a fraction 0.7 is $\frac{7}{10}$.

$\frac{2}{100}$ represents 2 hundredths. As a decimal $\frac{2}{100}$ is 0.02.

0.06 represents 6 hundredths. As a fraction 0.06 is $\frac{6}{100}$.

$\frac{99}{100}$ represents 99 hundredths. As a decimal $\frac{99}{100}$ is 0.99.

$\frac{4}{5}$ represents 4 fifths, or 8 tenths. As a decimal $\frac{4}{5}$ is 0.8.

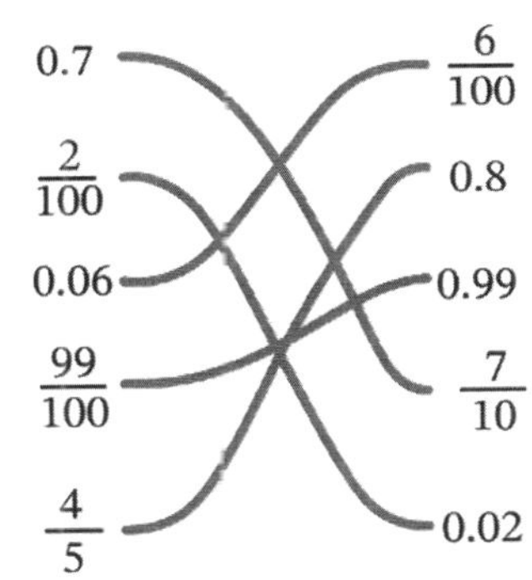

### *Decimals on a Number Line*

A number line is a great way to visualize decimals to the tenths or the hundredths places. On a number line, tenths show 10 equal segments from 0 to 1. Notice how the hash marks increase by 0.1 from left to right. The left dot is on the third hash mark, so it represents 0.3 or $\frac{3}{10}$. The right dot is on the ninth hash mark, so it represents 0.9 or $\frac{9}{10}$.

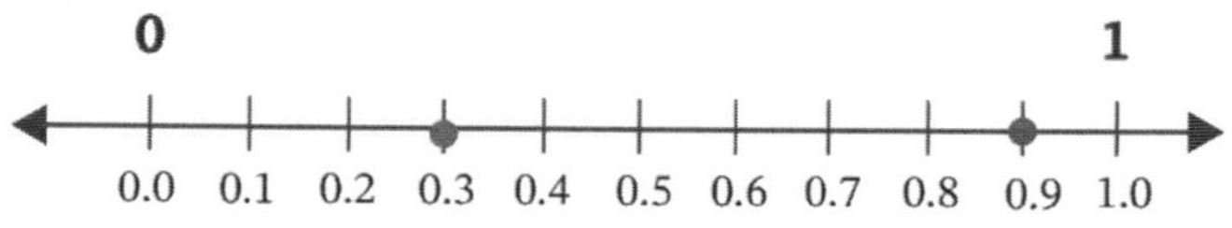


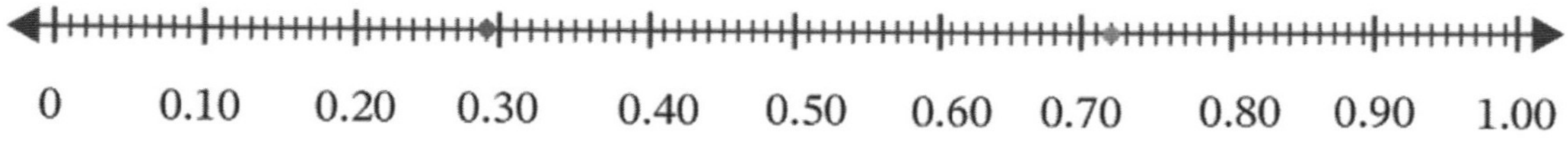


Hundredths show 100 equal segments from 0 to 100.

The left dot is on the 29th hash mark, so it represents $\frac{29}{100}$. The fraction $\frac{29}{100}$ as a decimal is 0.29. The orange dot is on the 72nd hash mark, so it represents $\frac{72}{100}$. The fraction $\frac{72}{100}$ as a decimal is 0.72.

### *Rounding Decimals*

When rounding a decimal number to the nearest whole number, always look at the tenths place. If the number in the tenths place is **5 or more**, the digit in the ones place rounds **up**. If the number in the tenths place is **less than 5**, the digit in the ones place stays the **same**. All the digits to the right of the ones place become **zeros**. Since the digits that become zeros are all to the right of the decimal place, it is not necessary to include them in the final answer. For example, 4.698 when rounded to the nearest whole number is 5.000, but it can just be written as 5.

### Decimals and Fractions on a Number Line

Fractions with a denominator of 10 can be represented as a decimal value to the tenths place. For example, $\frac{9}{10}$ written as a decimal is 0.9.

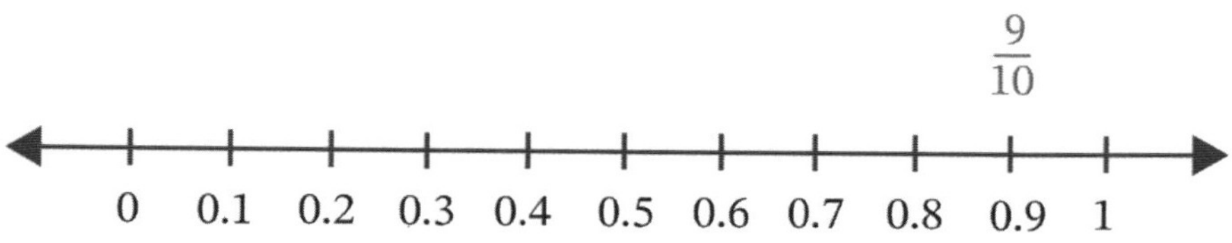

Similarly, fractions with a denominator of 100 can be represented as a decimal value to the hundredth place. For example, $\frac{9}{100}$ is 0.09 as a decimal.

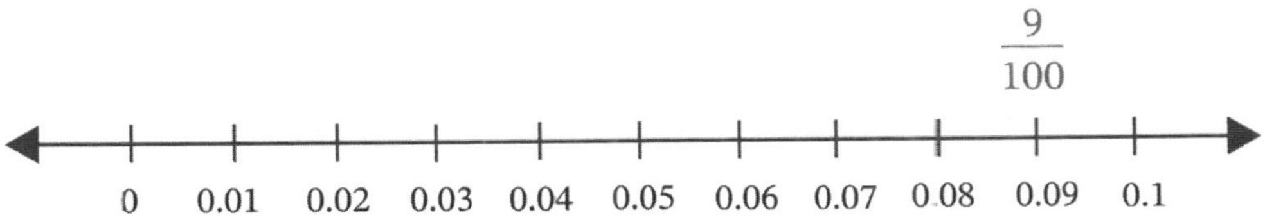


Decimals and fractions can be thought of as distances from zero on a number line. In general, the number line will extend from 0 to 1, where 1 represents 1 whole. Decimal and fraction values often represent values that are greater than 0 but less than 1 whole.

When a number line is not labeled, look for the number of equal segments. The number line below has 10 equal segments, which means each hash mark represents $\frac{1}{10}$. The dot is located on the eighth hash mark, so it represents $\frac{8}{10}$. The fraction $\frac{8}{10}$ represents the decimal 0.8 or 0.80. These values, $\frac{8}{10}$, 0.8, and 0.80, all represent the distance from zero.

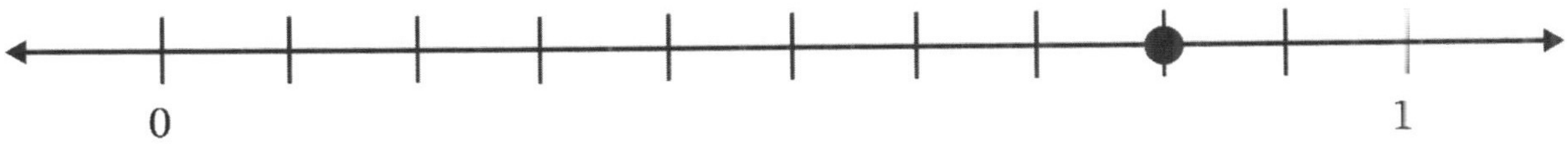


## Computation and Estimation

### Two-Step Addition and Subtraction Problems

Consider the scenario: A shopper starts with $456 in their wallet and then spends $128 on shoes. Later that day, the shopper finds a 20-dollar bill in their pocket. Altogether, how much money does the shopper have left after shoe shopping?

The scenario can be solved in two steps. The shopper starts with $456 and then spends $128. This means that $128 have been subtracted from $456. $456 consists of 4 hundreds, 5 tens, and 6 ones. $128 consists of 1 hundred, 2 tens, and 8 ones. 8 ones cannot be subtracted from 6 ones, which means **regrouping** needs to occur.

4 hundreds, 5 tens, and 6 ones becomes 4 hundreds, 4 tens, and 16 ones. Now subtraction can continue: $456 - 128 = 328$.

$$\begin{array}{r} 4\ 5\ 6 \\ -\ 1\ 2\ 8 \\ \hline \end{array} \quad \rightarrow \quad \begin{array}{r} {\scriptstyle 4\ 16} \\ 4\ \not{5}\ \not{6} \\ -\ 1\ 2\ 8 \\ \hline 3\ 2\ 8 \end{array}$$

The shopper then finds $20 in their pocket. This indicates adding 20: $328 + 20 = 348$.

The shopper has $348 after shoe shopping.

### Example

Find the value of the expression below:

$$(648 + 250) - 30$$

648 consists of 6 hundreds, 4 tens, and 8 ones. 250 consists of 2 hundreds, 5 tens, and 0 ones. Combine each place value to find the sum.

$$600 + 200 + 40 + 50 + 8 + 0 = 898$$

Now, subtract 30, which consists of 3 tens, from 898. 898 consists of 9 tens. Subtract 3 tens from this: $898 - 30 = 868$.

$$(648 + 250) - 30 = 868$$

The answer is 868.

### Example

Find the value of the expression below:

$$640 - 180$$

Think about 640 and 180 in terms of place value.

$$640 = 6 \text{ hundreds} + 4 \text{ tens} + 0 \text{ ones}$$

$$180 = 1 \text{ hundred} + 8 \text{ tens} + 0 \text{ ones}$$

640 has 4 tens, which is not enough to subtract 8 tens from.

Regrouping is necessary. 1 of the hundreds becomes 10 tens. So, 6 hundreds + 4 tens + 0 ones becomes 5 hundreds + 14 tens + 0 ones.

Now subtraction can begin.

(5 hundreds + 14 tens + 0 ones) − (1 hundred + 8 tens + 0 ones) becomes

4 hundreds + 6 tens + 0 ones. In standard form, this is 460.

$$640 - 180 = 460$$

The answer is 460.

## Recalling Multiplication Facts

Multiplication is the process of counting equally sized groups. It is a great accomplishment to memorize the multiplication and division facts from 0 to 10. This is a goal that can take some time, so keep practicing!

Some strategies that can help:

1. **Skip count by the larger number.** For example, for the problem $8 \times 3$ skip count by 8s not 3s. This can save some time. $8 + 8 + 8$ is quicker than $3 + 3 + 3 + 3 + 3 + 3 + 3 + 3$.
2. **Use facts that you do know to help you.** For example, if you are stuck on $7 \times 4$ but you know $5 \times 7$ is 35, use logic to help you. 5 groups of 7 is 7 more than 4 groups of 7, so subtract 7 from 35 to solve $4 \times 7$.
3. **Use multiplication to help with division.** Multiplication and division are inverse operations. This means they undo each other. For example, $9 \times 4 = 36$ and $4 \times 9 = 36$ represent the inverse of $36 \div 4 = 9$ and $36 \div 9 = 4$. Your multiplication facts and division facts go hand-in-hand! Remember, multiplication and division fact families use the same three numbers. For example, $8 \times 7 = 56$, $7 \times 8 = 56$, $56 \div 7 = 8$, and $56 \div 8 = 7$ all use the same three numbers.

## Strategies for Multiplication

Strategies such as mental math, skip counting, and drawing a model are great for single digit multiplication problems. However, for larger numbers, these strategies are less ideal. For example, solving $7 \times 82$ by skip counting would take quite a long time. 7, 14, 21, 28... all the way up to 574! Luckily, there are faster strategies for multiplying by two-digit numbers.

## Factors and Multiples

### *Factors and Greatest Common Factor*

Factors are numbers that are multiplied together to obtain a **product**. For example, in the equation $2 \times 3 = 6$, the numbers 2 and 3 are factors. A **prime number** has only two factors (1 and itself), but other numbers can have many factors.

A **common factor** is a number that divides exactly into two or more other numbers. For example, the factors of 12 are 1, 2, 3, 4, 6, and 12, while the factors of 15 are 1, 3, 5, and 15. The common factors of 12 and 15 are 1 and 3.

A **prime factor** is also a prime number. Therefore, the prime factors of 12 are 2 and 3. For 15, the prime factors are 3 and 5.

The **greatest common factor** (GCF) is the largest number that is a factor of two or more numbers. For example, the factors of 15 are 1, 3, 5, and 15; the factors of 35 are 1, 5, 7, and 35. Therefore, the greatest common factor of 15 and 35 is 5.

**Review Video: Factors**
Visit mometrix.com/academy and enter code: 920086

**Review Video: Prime Numbers and Factorization**
Visit mometrix.com/academy and enter code: 760669

**Review Video: Greatest Common Factor and Least Common Multiple**
Visit mometrix.com/academy and enter code: 838699

### *MULTIPLES AND LEAST COMMON MULTIPLE*

Often listed out in multiplication tables, **multiples** are integer increments of a given factor. In other words, dividing a multiple by the factor will result in an integer. For example, the multiples of 7 include: $1 \times 7 = 7, 2 \times 7 = 14, 3 \times 7 = 21, 4 \times 7 = 28, 5 \times 7 = 35$. Dividing 7, 14, 21, 28, or 35 by 7 will result in the integers 1, 2, 3, 4, and 5, respectively.

The least common multiple (**LCM**) is the smallest number that is a multiple of two or more numbers. For example, the multiples of 3 include 3, 6, 9, 12, 15, etc.; the multiples of 5 include 5, 10, 15, 20, etc. Therefore, the least common multiple of 3 and 5 is 15.

**Review Video: Multiples**
Visit mometrix.com/academy and enter code: 626738

## MULTIPLICATION WITH MULTIPLE-DIGIT NUMBERS

### *AREA MODELS*

There are a variety of strategies to choose from when multiplying multi-digit numbers. Area models and arrays can be used to show multiplication in a visual way, as opposed to the standard algorithm. For example, consider the problem $8 \times 11$. This can be represented as an **array** with 8 columns and 11 rows. There are 8 groups of 11 stars, or 11 groups of 8 stars. The total number of stars is 88, so $8 \times 11 = 88$. This strategy is great for smaller numbers. However, when multiplying two-digit numbers an area model is often preferred.

An **area model** is a visual representation of the distributive property. For example, when multiplying 27 by 35, the distributive property would be expressed as $7 \times 5 + 7 \times 30 + 20 \times 5 + 20 \times 30$. An area model shows this process using boxes. Set up each two-digit number as shown. Break apart 27 into 20 and 7. Break apart 35 into 30 and 5. Fill in each box by multiplying the outside numbers. $30 \times 20 = 600$, $30 \times 7 = 210$, $5 \times 20 = 100$, $5 \times 7 = 35$, and the sum of all the products is $600 + 100 + 210 + 35 = 945$. Therefore, $27 \times 35 = 945$.

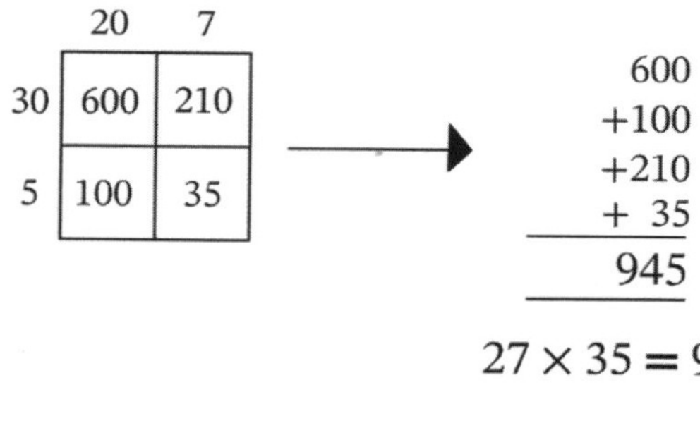


$27 \times 35 = 945$

### STANDARD ALGORITHM

Area models and arrays are great strategies for one and two-digit multiplication. However, the **standard algorithm** is a commonly preferred strategy for numbers that are more than three digits. The standard algorithm, or "vertical multiplication" is less visual but more time effective. For example, consider the product 7,482 × 8. Write the longer number on the top and the shorter number on the bottom. Push all numbers to the right so that the place value is lined up (ones lined up with ones, tens lined up with tens, etc.).

$$\begin{array}{r} {}^{3}\ \ {}^{6}{}^{1}\ \ \\ 7{,}482 \\ \times \qquad 8 \\ \hline 59{,}856 \end{array}$$

Distribute, or multiply, the 8 by each digit in the number 7,482. Work from right to left. 8 × 2, then 8 × 8, then 8 × 4, then 8 × 7. If a product has more than one digit, write the ones digit in the answer and carry the tens digit above the next number you are multiplying. For example, 2 × 8 = 16, so write 6 in the answer and 1 above 8 (the next number you will multiply by). Then, add the carried number to the next product. 8 × 8 = 64, then add 1 to get 65, and continue the multiplication process for the rest of the number. The product of 7,482 and 8 is 59,856.

### PARTIAL PRODUCTS

Using partial products is another option when multiplying multi-digit numbers. For example, consider the problem 48 × 26.

Using **partial products** is one way to express the distributive property. In the problem 48 × 26, each digit needs to be multiplied by every other digit, according to its place value. Using partial products breaks this down into pieces.

$$6 \times 8 = 48$$
$$6 \times 40 = 240$$
$$20 \times 8 = 160$$
$$20 \times 40 = 800$$

$$\begin{array}{r} 48 \\ \underline{\times 26} \\ 48 \\ 240 \\ 160 \\ \underline{+\,800} \\ 1{,}248 \end{array}$$

The sum of these "partial products" is 1,248.

## Division with Multiple-Digit Numbers

### *Area Models*

Long division is not the only way to divide multi-digit numbers. You can also use an **area model**. 620 ÷ 5 can be solved by drawing a rectangle with 5 as one side length. Now think in terms of multiplication. 5 × 100 is close to 620. Start with this. Write 100 above the rectangle. 5 × 100 = 500. So, write 500 in the first box.

620 − 500 = 120, so now think about multiplying 5 by a number to get close to 120. 5 × 20 is 100, so start there. Write 20 above the rectangle. Since 5 × 20 = 100, write 100 in the next box.

120 − 100 = 20, so now think about multiplying 5 by a number to get close to 20. 5 × 4 is 20, so write 4 above the rectangle. Write 20 in the last box.

$$620 \div 5$$

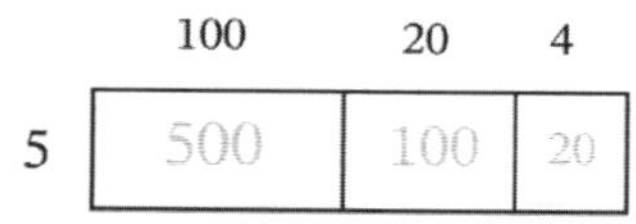


Now add up the numbers above the rectangle. 100 + 20 + 4 = 124, therefore 620 ÷ 5 = 124.

$$620 \div 5$$

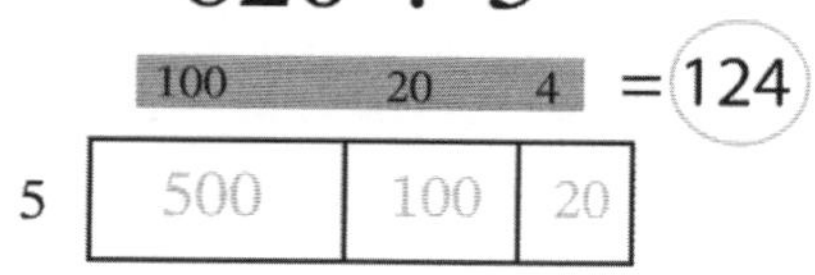


### *Long Division*

The **standard algorithm** for division, also known as **long division**, is a great option for division problems involving large numbers. The long division process involves 4 steps that repeat in a cycle.

The divisor goes to the left of the division sign, and the dividend goes under the division sign. For example, in the problem 6,488 ÷ 2, the divisor is 2 and the dividend is 6,488.

$$2\overline{)\,6,488}$$

The four steps of long division:

1. "How many times?"
2. Multiply
3. Subtract
4. Bring down

### Example

1. 2 fits into 6, 3 times. Write 3.
2. $3 \times 2 = 6$. Write 6.
3. Subtract. $6 - 6 = 0$.
4. Bring down the next digit, which is 4.

$$\begin{array}{r l} & 3 \\ 2 & \overline{)\,6,488} \\ & -6\downarrow \\ \hline & 0\,4 \end{array}$$

Repeat this 4-step process until there are no more digits to "bring down". The result is $6{,}488 \div 2 = 3{,}244$.

$$\begin{array}{r l} & 3,244 \\ 2 & \overline{)\,6,488} \\ & -6 \\ & 0\,4 \\ & -\,4 \\ & \quad 08 \\ & \quad -8 \\ & \qquad 08 \\ & \qquad -8 \\ & \qquad\;\; 0 \end{array}$$

## Estimating Solutions

Problems involving addition, subtraction, multiplication, and division can be estimated before solving. Estimating before solving allows you to check an answer for **reasonableness**. For example, consider the problem $4{,}532 \div 8$. This can be estimated using compatible numbers. 4,532 is close to 4,500, and 8 is close to 9. These are considered **compatible numbers** because 4,500 can be quickly divided by 9.

$45 \div 9$ is 5.

$450 \div 9$ is 50.

$4{,}500 \div 9$ is 500.

This can be done using mental math, and this estimate can be compared to the "actual" answer. If the actual answer is close to 500, then the answer is likely correct.

4,532 ÷ 8 can be solved using long division:

```
      5 6 6   R 4
8 )  4, 5 3 2
  -  4 0
       5 3
     - 4 8
         5 2
       - 4 8
           4
```

566 R4 is close to 500, so the answer is reasonable.

The reasonableness of an answer can be determined using estimation. For example, the product of 6,128 times 197 can be estimated quickly by rounding 6,128 to the nearest thousand, and rounding 197 to the nearest hundred.

6,128 becomes 6,000.

197 becomes 200.

$$6{,}000 \times 200 = 1{,}200{,}000$$

Remember, when rounding, first find the digit you are rounding, and then look to the digit to the right. If the digit to the right is 5 or more, the number rounds up. If the digit to the right is less than 5, the number stays the same.

For example, when rounding 6,284 to the nearest hundred, locate the digit in the hundreds place. 2 is in the hundreds place.

Now look to the right. The digit to the right of 2 is 8. 8 is 5 or more, so 2 will round up. 6,284 becomes 6,300. Notice how all digits to the right of the hundreds place become 0.

## SOLVING PROBLEMS

You and 7 friends are washing cars to earn money. The car wash costs \$5, and so far, 20 cars have been washed. If the earnings are split equally, how much money has each person earned so far?

Recall multiplication facts. Each car pays \$5, and 20 cars have been washed. $5 \times 2 = 10$, so $5 \times 20 = 100$. \$100 has been earned so far.

There are 8 friends in the group altogether. $100 \div 8$ can be solved using long division.

$$\begin{array}{r} 12\ \text{R}4 \\ 8\overline{)100} \\ \underline{-8}\phantom{0} \\ 20 \\ \underline{-16} \\ 4 \end{array}$$

There is a remainder of 4. To express R4 in terms of money, start by writing the remainder as a fraction. R4 means $\frac{4}{8}$.

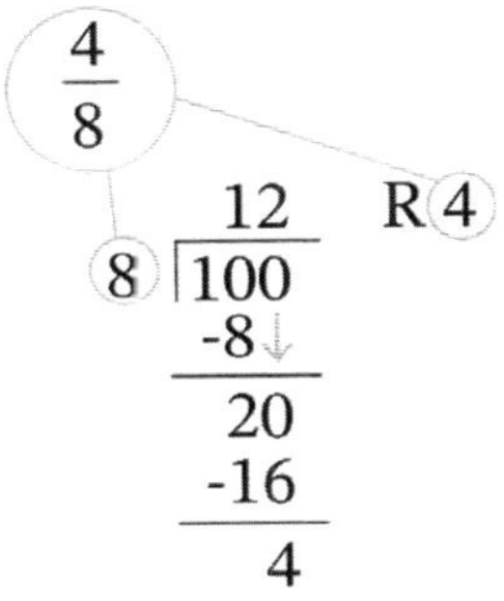


$\frac{4}{8}$ simplifies to $\frac{1}{2}$, which is the decimal 0.50. In terms of money, 0.50 is 50 cents. So, R4 represents 50 cents. Each person has earned \$12.50 so far.

### *EXAMPLE*

An artist sold 8 paintings at a craft fair. Each painting sold for \$16. The artist divided the earnings into 5 equal groups. How much money is in each group?

The scenario can be converted from word from to numeral form:

$$(16 \times 8) \div 5$$

Perform the operation in the parentheses first.

$$16 \times 8 = 128$$

Now divide 128 into 5 equal groups.

$$128 \div 5 = 25 \text{ r } 3$$

$$\begin{array}{r} 25\text{r}\,3 \\ 5\overline{)\,128} \\ -10\phantom{8} \\ \hline 28 \\ -25 \\ \hline 3 \end{array}$$

So,

$$128 \div 5 = 25 \text{ r } 3$$

In this case, remainder 3 means $\frac{3}{5}$ because the artist is dividing the money into 5 groups. $\frac{3}{5}$ is equivalent to $\frac{6}{10}$ or 0.6.

This means $128 \div 5 = 25.6$. The amount of money in each group is \$25.60.

### *EXAMPLE*

Mark has 3 boxes of cupcake mix. Each box makes 20 cupcakes. When Mark bakes the cupcakes, he can fit 10 cupcakes in each pan. If Mark uses the pan to make one batch of cupcakes at a time, how many times will he use the pan?

3 boxes that make 20 cupcakes each means 60 cupcakes: $3 \times 20 = 60$.

60 cupcakes are baked using 1 pan. Each pan holds 10 cupcakes, so divide 60 by 10: $60 \div 10 = 6$. This means the pan needs to be used 6 times.

## ADDING AND SUBTRACTING FRACTIONS

**Fractions** represent part of a whole. Fractions with the same denominator can be combined by adding the parts (the numerators, or top numbers). This can be represented using a model. For example, the model below shows 3 parts out of 6, and 1 part out of 6. In other words, the whole model shows $\frac{3}{6} + \frac{1}{6}$.

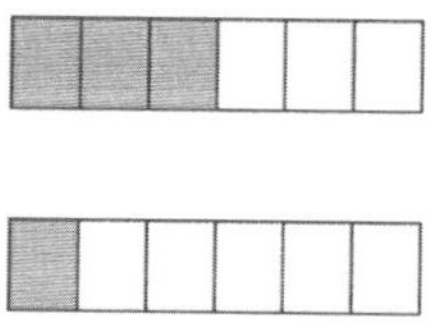

Both fractions consist of sixths, so the parts can be combined. 3 parts combined with 1 part equals 4 parts. 4 parts out of 6 parts represents the fraction $\frac{4}{6}$.

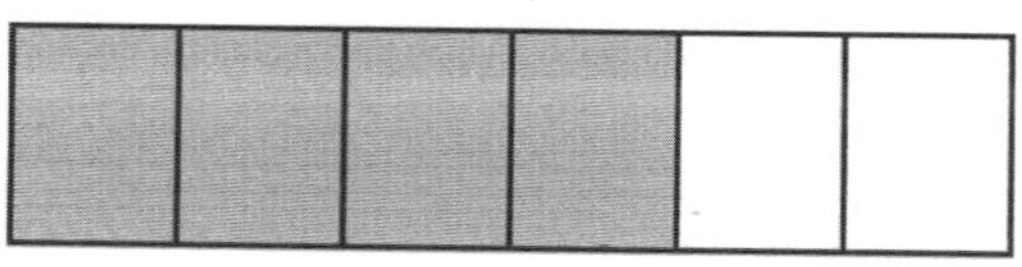

Try another example. Consider the diagram below. Each whole is divided into 8 equal shares. The circle on the left shows 2 out of 8, or $\frac{2}{8}$. The circle on the right shows 6 out of 8, or $\frac{6}{8}$.

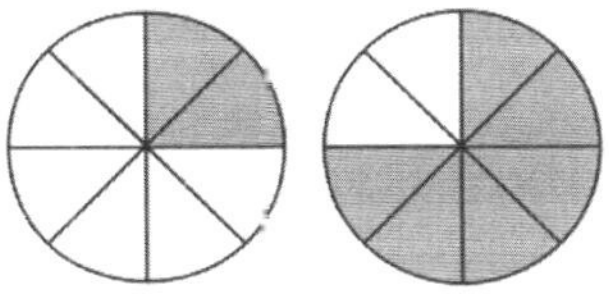

Both fractions have the same denominators so their numerators can be combined. $\frac{2}{8}+\frac{6}{8}$ combines to $\frac{8}{8}$. Another way to express $\frac{8}{8}$ is 1 whole.

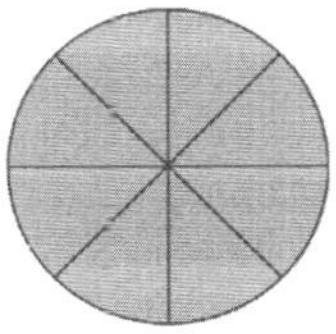

A picture or model is a great way to represent addition and subtraction of fractions. However, there is a shortcut! When denominators are the same, simply add or subtract the numerators.

$$\frac{2}{7}+\frac{4}{7}=\frac{6}{7}$$

Notice how the denominator, 7, stays the same and the numerators are added.

$$\frac{8}{9}-\frac{3}{9}=\frac{5}{9}$$

Notice how the denominator, 9, stays the same and the numerators are subtracted.

**EXAMPLE**

Write and solve an addition equation that represents adding the top fraction to the bottom fraction illustrated below.

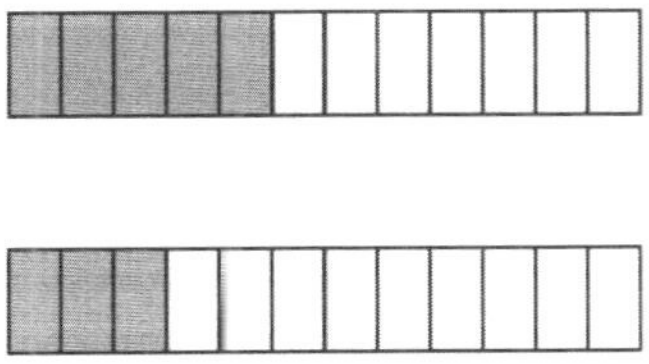

Top fraction: $\frac{5}{12}$

Bottom fraction: $\frac{3}{12}$

Both fractions have the same denominator, so they can be combined.

$$\frac{5}{12}+\frac{3}{12}=\frac{8}{12}$$

$\frac{8}{12}$ can be simplified by dividing the numerator and denominator by 4. $\frac{8}{12}$ becomes $\frac{2}{3}$.

$$\frac{5}{12} + \frac{3}{12} = \frac{8}{12} = \frac{2}{3}$$

**EXAMPLE**

Model the subtraction equation on the number line, then solve: $\frac{6}{10} - \frac{2}{10} = ?$

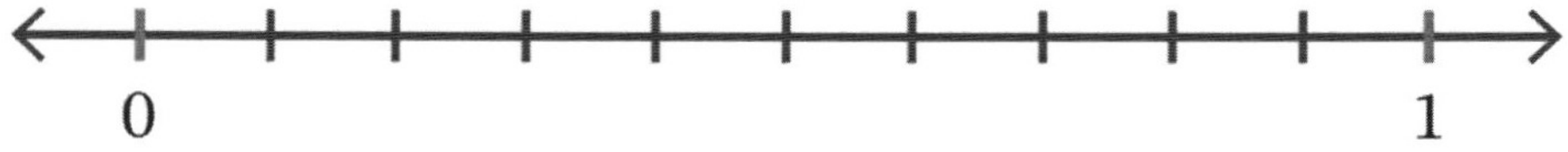


The number line is divided into 10 equal shares. Each hash mark represents $\frac{1}{10}$.

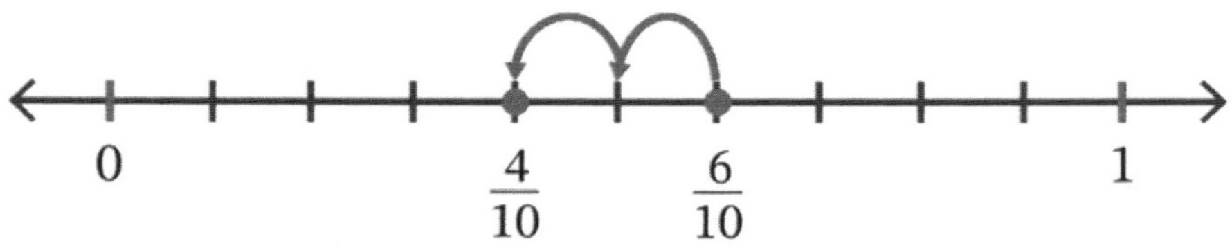


The red dot starts at $\frac{6}{10}$. The arrows show 2 jumps back, which represents subtraction of $\frac{2}{10}$: $\frac{6}{10} - \frac{2}{10} = \frac{4}{10}$.

### *REASONABLE SUMS AND DIFFERENCES OF FRACTIONS*

One way to check whether or not the sums and differences of fractions are reasonable is to use benchmark fractions. **Benchmarks fractions** are common, easy to visualize fractions such as 0, $\frac{1}{4}$, $\frac{1}{2}$, $\frac{3}{4}$, and 1.

For example, consider the following addition equation:

$$\frac{1}{12} + \frac{7}{12} = \frac{8}{12}$$

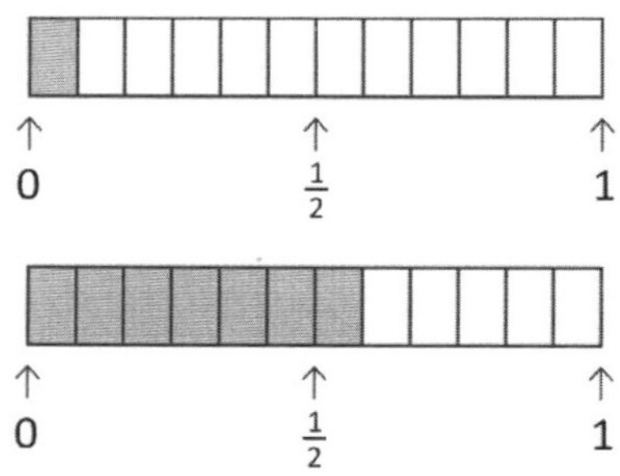


Notice how $\frac{1}{12}$ is close to the benchmark fraction 0, and $\frac{7}{12}$ is close to the benchmark fraction $\frac{1}{2}$. Since $0 + \frac{1}{2} = \frac{1}{2}$, the sum of $\frac{1}{12}$ and $\frac{7}{12}$ should be close to $\frac{1}{2}$.

$\frac{1}{12} + \frac{7}{12} = \frac{8}{12}$, and $\frac{8}{12}$ is close to $\frac{1}{2}$ since it's only one more shaded square from our picture earlier, so the sum is reasonable.

The same concept works for fractions with unequal denominators. For example, $\frac{7}{10} - \frac{2}{8} = \frac{9}{20}$. The reasonableness of the answer can be determined without solving the problem. From our picture, we can see that $\frac{7}{10}$ is close to $\frac{3}{4}$, and $\frac{2}{8}$ is the same as $\frac{1}{4}$. Therefore, the difference should be close to $\frac{3}{4} - \frac{1}{4}$ which is $\frac{2}{4}$, or $\frac{1}{2}$.

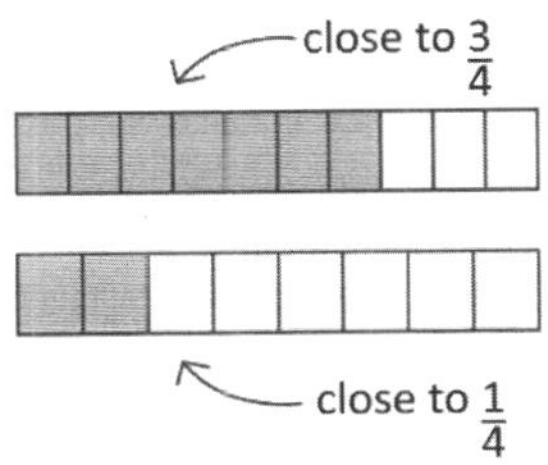


The equation shows $\frac{7}{10} - \frac{2}{8} = \frac{9}{20}$, and $\frac{9}{20}$ is very close to $\frac{2}{4}$ or $\frac{1}{2}$, so the answer seems to be reasonable.

## Adding and Subtracting Decimals and Whole Numbers

The important thing to remember when adding and subtracting decimal numbers is to **line up** the **decimal points**. Lining up the decimal points ensures that similar place values are being combined. For example, ones combine with ones, tens combine with tens.

Consider the following: A pizza costs \$27.50 and a drink costs \$4.65. The total cost of the meal can be calculated by finding the sum. Stack the numbers vertically and line up the decimal points. With addition, it does not matter which number is on top or bottom. Regroup if necessary and bring the decimal straight down into the answer line. This method is known as the **standard algorithm**.

$$\begin{array}{r} {}^{1\,1}\phantom{.00} \\ 27.50 \\ +\ \ 4.65 \\ \hline \$32.15 \end{array}$$

The standard algorithm is also useful for subtraction scenarios. For example, if a piece of ribbon measures 132.1 centimeters, and 27.76 centimeters are cut off and removed, how many centimeters of ribbon are left?

Stack the values vertically and line up the decimals. Make sure the larger number, 132.1, is on the top. Sometimes it is helpful to fill in any empty spaces with a zero. Regroup if necessary, and again bring the decimal straight down into the answer line.

$$\begin{array}{r} 11\ \ \ 10\phantom{0} \\ 2\ \cancel{1}\ \ \ \cancel{0}\,10 \\ 1\ \cancel{3}\,\cancel{2}\,.\ \cancel{1}\,\cancel{0} \\ -\ \ \ 2\ 7\ .\ 7\ 6 \\ \hline 1\ 0\ 4\ .\ 3\ 4 \end{array}$$

There are 104.34 centimeters of ribbon left.

**Review Video: Adding and Subtracting Decimals**
Visit mometrix.com/academy and enter code: 381101

### EXAMPLE

Solve using the standard algorithm: $40.03 - 26.12 =$ ____

Line up the decimals when adding and subtracting decimals. Regrouping is required for this problem.

```
   9
  3 10  10
  40. 03
 -26. 12
 -------
  13. 91
```

$$40.03 - 26.12 = 13.91$$

Check for accuracy using addition: $13.91 + 26.12 = 40.03$.

### EXAMPLE

Solve using the standard algorithm: $63.04 + 99.09 =$ ____.

```
  1   1
  63. 04
 +99. 09
 -------
 162. 13
```

Line up the decimals when adding and subtracting decimals: $63.04 + 99.09 = 162.13$.

## MULTIPLYING BY 10 AND 100

When multiplying by 10, the decimal point moves **one place** to the **right**. When multiplying by 100, the decimal point moves **two places** to the **right**. The pattern continues for each multiple of 10. This is a convenient way to multiply numbers by powers of 10. For example, notice the decimal movement in the following examples:

$$45.62 \times 10 = 456.2$$

$$45.62 \times 100 = 4{,}562.0$$

The same pattern can be seen when multiplying whole numbers. Any whole number can be expressed as a decimal. Think about where the decimal point is in the number 50. Sometimes the decimal point is not written for whole numbers, but it's technically there. 50 has a "decimal" to the right of the ones place. Remember, a decimal separates the ones place from the tenths place. 50 is equal to 50.0.

$$50.0 \times 10 = 500.0$$

Notice how the decimal moves one place to the right.

$$50.0 \times 100 = 5{,}000.0$$

Notice how the decimal moves two places to the right.

## Representing Problems

### Strip Diagrams

Strip diagrams can be used to solve addition, subtraction, multiplication, and division problems.

#### Addition and Subtraction

$$50 + a = 200$$

Set up a diagram.

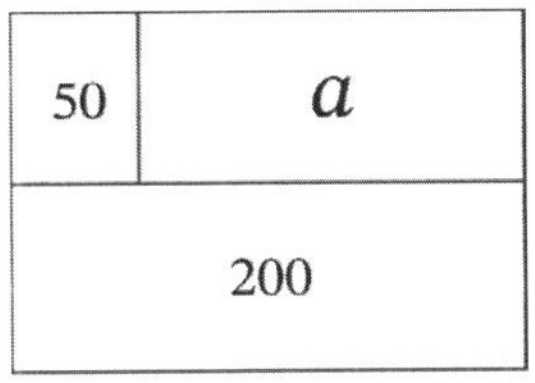


$$a = 150$$

$$28 - b = 16$$

Set up a diagram.

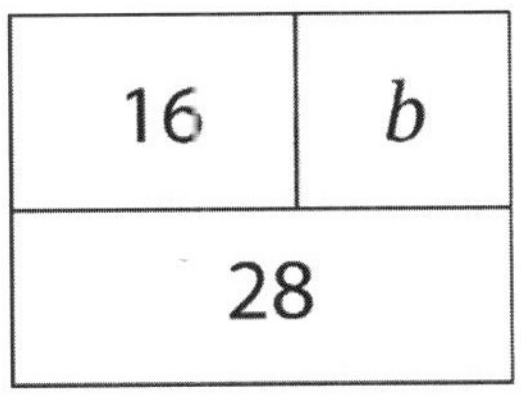


$$b = 12$$

#### Multiplication and Division

$$c \times 8 = 40$$

Set up a diagram.

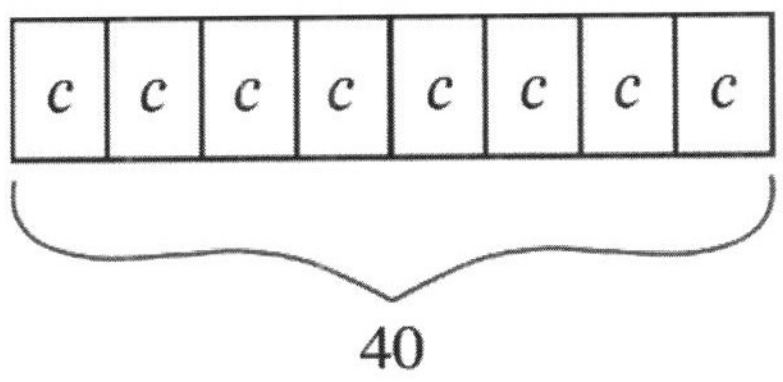


$$c = 5$$

$$25 \div d = 5$$

Set up a diagram.

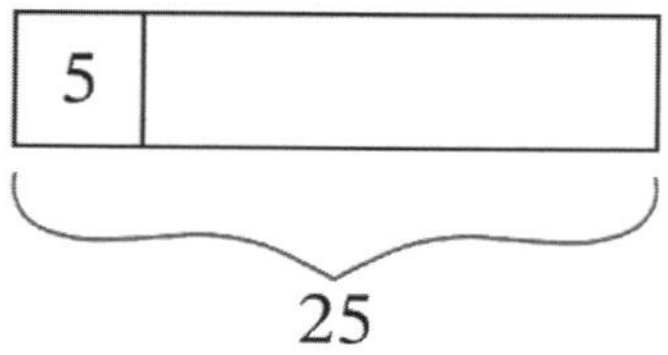


$$d = 5$$

## Multi-Step Problems

$$100 - (45 \div 9)$$

Start by solving the section inside the parentheses.

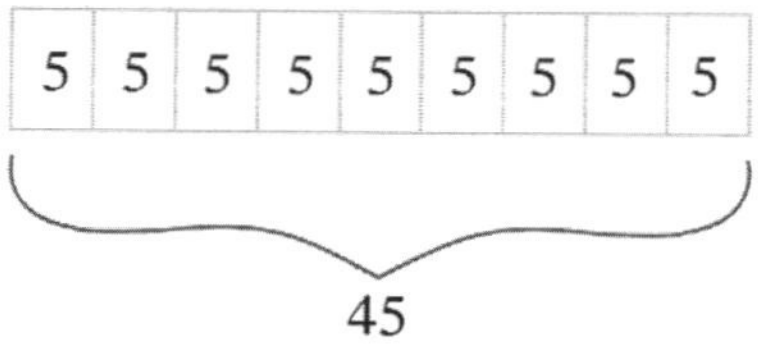


$$45 \div 9 = 5$$

Now subtract 5 from 100.

$$100 - 5 = 95$$

## Example

Juniper Middle School has 330 students in 7th grade. There are a total of 11 classrooms, all with an equal number of students in each classroom. If each student needs 3 textbooks, how many textbooks are needed for the students in one classroom?

To figure out how many textbooks are needed for the students in one classroom, start by finding the number of students in each classroom. Since there are 330 total students and 11 classrooms, either of the following equations can be used to find the number of students in each classroom ($s$).

$$330 \div 11 = s$$

$$11 \times s = 330$$

In either case, $s = 30$, so there are 30 students in each classroom.

The next part of the question says that each student needs 3 textbooks, so to find the number of textbooks needed for all the students in one classroom, set up the following equation:

$$t = 3 \times 30$$

$$t = 90$$

This means that 90 textbooks are needed for the students in one classroom.

## EXAMPLE

Write two multiplication and division equations that can be represented by the tape diagram below.

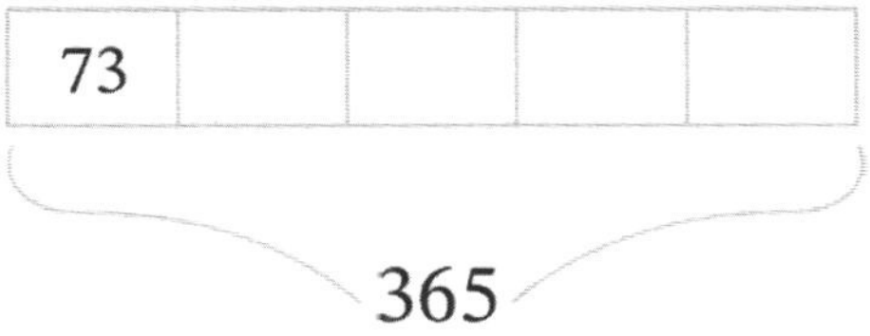


The tape diagram shows 5 equal sections of 73, with a total of 365. Two multiplication equations and two division equations can represent the model. Use fact families to create the following four equations:

$$365 \div 5 = 73$$
$$365 \div 73 = 5$$
$$5 \times 73 = 365$$
$$73 \times 5 = 365$$

### *INPUT-OUTPUT TABLES*

**Expressions**, such as $5m$, can be displayed in an **input-output table**. For example, in the expression $5m$, when $m = 1$, the expression becomes $5(1)$ which simplifies to 5. When $m = 2$, the expression becomes $5(2)$ which simplifies to 10. The pattern continues.

This can be shown with an input-output table. The **input value** is $m$, and the **output value** is determined when the expression is evaluated.

| **Input ($m$)** | 1 | 2 | 3 | 4 | 5 |
|---|---|---|---|---|---|
| **Output ($5m$)** | 5 | 10 | 15 | 20 | 25 |

Notice how each input value increases by 1, and each output value increases by 5.

When an input-output table represents a consistent pattern, the pattern is referred to as a **rule**. The rule in this example is, "multiply by five." A rule makes it possible to determine unknown values in an input-output table. For example, if $m = 15$, the output is determined by multiplying 15 and 5: $15 \times 5 = 75$. When $m = 5$, the output is 75.

EXAMPLE

Complete the input-output table relating the number of bikes and the total number of wheels. Write a rule to describe the relationship.

| Number of Bikes | Number of Wheels |
|---|---|
| 1 | 2 |
| 2 | |
| 4 | |
| 6 | |
| 10 | |

The relationship between the number of bikes and the number of wheels can be described with the following "rule": $w = 2b$, where $w$ represents the total number of wheels, and $b$ represents the number of bikes. The total number of wheels is calculated by multiplying the number of bikes by 2.

| Number of Bikes | Number of Wheels |
|---|---|
| 1 | 2 |
| 2 | 4 |
| 4 | 8 |
| 6 | 12 |
| 10 | 20 |

EXAMPLE

Complete the input-output table based on the following rule. RULE: Add 19 to the input.

| Input | Output |
|---|---|
| 4 | |
| 9 | |
| 16 | |
| 19 | |
| 25 | |

The rule states "add 19 to the input". This means that 19 will be added to every input value to calculate the corresponding output value.

| Input | Output |
|---|---|
| 4 | 23 |
| 9 | 28 |
| 16 | 35 |
| 19 | 38 |
| 25 | 44 |

# Measurement and Geometry

## Relative Sizes of Measurements

The **metric system** is a system of measurement used for identifying mass, volume, and length. Most countries in the world use the metric system when making calculations in math and science. However, the United States has another measurement system called the **customary system**. The customary system also measures mass, volume, and length, but it uses different units.

For example, the metric system has base units of meters, liters, and grams. Meters measure length, liters measure volume, and grams measure mass. The metric system is convenient in math and science because it follows the base-ten number system. This means that quick calculations and conversions can be done simply by multiplying or dividing by a power of ten. For example, 10 millimeters is equivalent to 1 centimeter.

The customary system has much more than three units. For example, when measuring volume, options include ounces, cups, pints, quarts, and gallons. Converting between units is more challenging because each unit has a different conversion factor. For example, there are 4 quarts in a gallon, but 16 ounces in a pint. Distance is measured in inches, feet, yards, and miles. Mass is similar to weight, and is measured in ounces, pounds, and tons. It is important to become familiar with units in the metric and customary systems.

### *Customary Units*

- **1 ounce**: about the weight of a candy bar
- **1 pound**: about the weight of a football
- **1 ton**: about the weight of a car

- **1 inch**: about the width of a quarter
- **1 foot**: about the height of a 2 liter soda bottle (12 inches)
- **1 yard**: about the width of a door (3 feet)
- **1 mile**: about 4 laps on an outdoor running track

- **1 ounce**: the amount of liquid in two tablespoons
- **1 cup**: the amount of liquid in a coffee cup (8 ounces)
- **1 pint**: the amount of liquid in a small water bottle (16 ounces)
- **1 quart**: the amount of liquid in a jug of juice (2 pints)
- **1 gallon**: the amount of liquid in a large container of milk

### *Metric Units*

- **Meter:** about the width of a door frame
- **Liter:** about the volume of a large water bottle
- **Gram:** about the mass of a paperclip

## Converting Between Units

### Metric System

When converting units within the metric system, simply multiply or divide by a factor of 10. Notice the base unit is bolded (1 meter, 1 gram and 1 liter).

| Length | Weight | Volume |
|---|---|---|
| 1 km = 1,000 m | 1 kg = 1,000 g | 1 kL = 1,000 L |
| 1 m = 0.001 km | 1 g = 0.001 kg | 1 L = 0.001 kL |
| **1 m** = 100 cm | **1 g** = 100 cg | **1 L** = 100 cL |
| 1 cm = 0.01 m | 1 cg = 0.01 g | 1 cL = 0.01 L |
| 1 m = 1,000 mm | 1 g = 1,000 mg | 1 L = 1,000 mL |
| 1 mm = 0.001 m | 1 mg = 0.001 g | 1 mL = 0.001 L |

For example, 2.56 meters is equivalent to 256 centimeters because meters are 100 times larger than centimeters. 3,366 millimeters is equivalent to 3.366 meters because millimeters are 1,000 times smaller than meters. Conversions in the metric system are quick because all it requires is knowing where to move the decimal point. Remember, each decimal movement to the right represents multiplication by 10. Each decimal movement to the left represents division by 10.

**Review Video: Metric System Conversion**
Visit mometrix.com/academy and enter code: 163709

### Customary System

Converting within the customary system is more complicated. For this reason, the metric system is generally the system used in math and science. Notice how there is not really any pattern to follow when converting from one unit to the next. For example, there are 5,280 feet in a mile, but there are 12 inches in a foot.

| Length | Weight | Volume |
|---|---|---|
| 12 in = 1 ft | 16 oz = 1 lb | 128 fl. oz = 1 gal |
| 3 ft = 1yd | 2,000 lb = 1 ton | 2 pt = 1 qt |
| 5,280 ft = 1 mi | | 8 pt = 1 gal |
| 1,760 yd = 1 mi | | 4 qt = 1 gal |

## Solving Problems Involving Measurements

When solving problems involving units for mass, length, or volume, first identify whether the units are metric or customary. Once this has been determined, think about how much you will need to multiply or divide by to make the **conversion**. For example, consider the following scenario.

James is pouring 4 gallons of juice into pints. How many pints can James pour if he pours out all the juice?

Ask yourself, "are these customary or metric units?" These are customary units.

Now, consider how many pints are in 4 gallons. There are 4 quarts in a gallon, so there are 16 quarts total.

There are 8 pints in a quart, so there are $16 \times 8$ total pints.

$$16 \times 8 = 128$$

James can pour 128 pints of juice.

### *Example*

A baseball game started at 7:10. The game ended at 9:15. How long did the game last?

Count up by hours and then count up by minutes. 7:10 to 8:10 is one hour. 8:10 to 9:10 is one hour. 9:10 to 9:15 is 5 minutes. Altogether, this is 2 hours and 5 minutes.

### *Example*

A tablet weighs 265 grams. Does a stack of 8 of these tablets have a mass that is more or less than 1 kilogram? (1 kg = 1,000 g)

Each tablet has a mass of 265 grams, so 8 tablets have a mass of $8 \times 265$ g = 2,120 kg. The mass of 8 tablets is 2,120 grams. 1 kilogram consists of 1,000 grams. $2{,}120 > 1{,}000$, so the tablets have a mass greater than 1 kilogram.

## Solving Using the Area and Perimeter of Rectangles

The **area** of a rectangle is calculated by multiplying the **length** and the **width**. For example, the rectangle below has a length of 8 yards and a width of 3 yards. So, the area of the rectangle is $8 \times 3 = 24$ square yards.

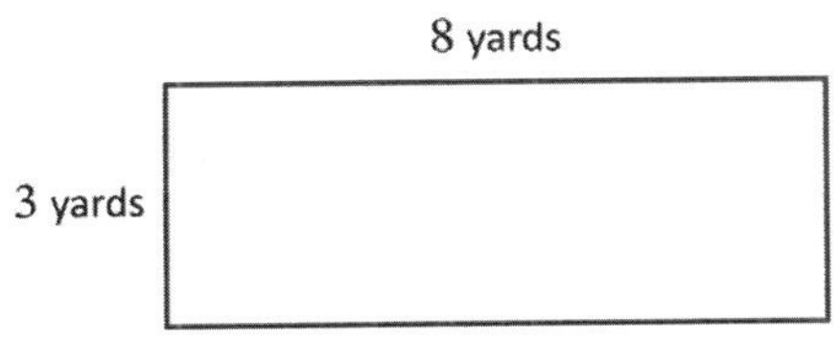


The **perimeter** of a rectangle is calculated by adding all four **side lengths**.

$$\text{Perimeter} = \text{length} + \text{length} + \text{width} + \text{width}$$

Another way to calculate perimeter: $P = 2l + 2w$.

A rectangle has 2 lengths and 2 widths, and the sum of these 4 sides is the perimeter. For example, the rectangle below has a length of 32 meters and a width of 20 meters.

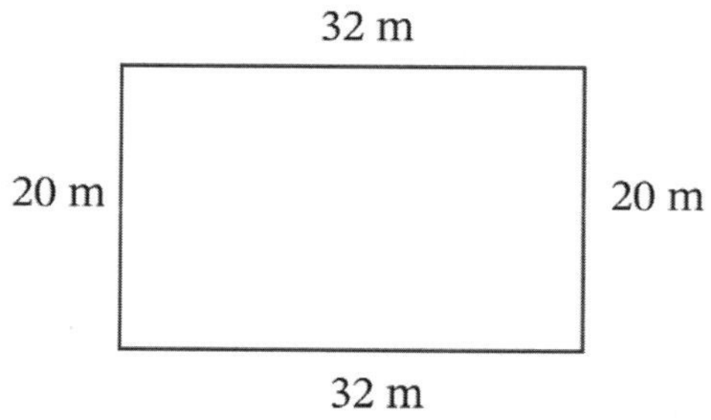


$$P = 32 + 32 + 20 + 20$$

$$P = (2 \times 32) + (2 \times 20)$$

Both equations simplify to 104, so the perimeter of the rectangle is 104 meters.

### *Variation in Rectangle Construction*

A group of rectangles can have the same area but different perimeters. For example, consider a rectangle with an area of 20 square feet. How can this rectangle be built?

The rectangle may have a length of 1 foot and a width of 20 feet.

The rectangle may have a length of 2 feet and a width of 10 feet.

The rectangle may have a length of 4 feet and a width of 5 feet.

All three of these rectangles have an area of 20 square feet. However, each rectangle has a unique perimeter.

1 foot by 20 feet: Perimeter of 42 feet.

2 feet by 10 feet: Perimeter of 24 feet.

4 feet by 5 feet: Perimeter of 18 feet.

Now, consider a rectangle with a perimeter of 10 meters. There is more than one correct way to build this rectangle. For example, a 3-meter by 2-meter rectangle has a perimeter of 10 meters and an area of 6 square meters. However, a 4-meter by 1-meter rectangle also has a perimeter of 10 meters but it has an area of 4 square meters.

**Review Video: Area and Perimeter of Rectangles and Squares**
Visit mometrix.com/academy and enter code: 428109

### Example

A city planner is creating a model design for new green space. The model has an area of 96 square centimeters and a length of 12 centimeters. What is the width of the model?

The area of a rectangle is calculated by multiplying the length by the width: $A = l \times w$. In this scenario, the area and the length are provided. Substitute $A$ and $l$ into the formula.

$$A = l \times w$$

$$96 = 12 \times w$$

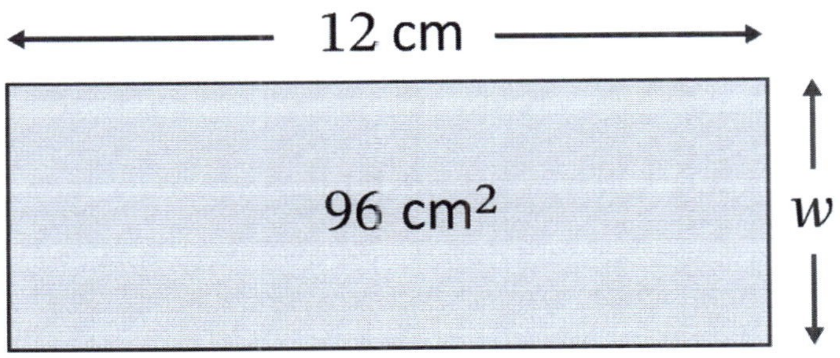


Divide 96 by 12 to find the width.

$$w = 96 \div 12 = 8$$

The width of the model is 8 centimeters.

### Example

Student $A$ says there is only one way to draw a rectangle with a perimeter of 14 units. Student $B$ says there is more than one way do draw a rectangle with a perimeter of 14 units. Which student is correct? Support your answer with a model.

Option 1: 2 by 5. This rectangle has an area of 10 square units and a perimeter of 14 units.

Option 2: 1 by 6. This rectangle has an area of 6 square units and a perimeter of 14 units.

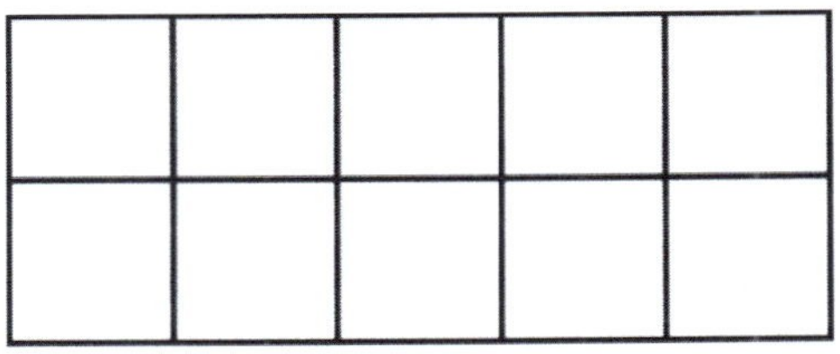

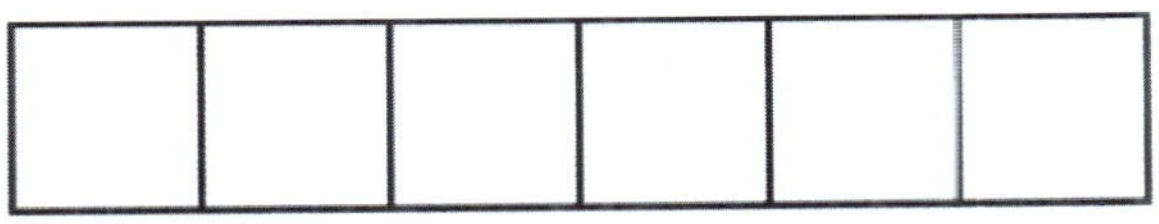

Student $B$ is correct. There is more than one way to draw a rectangle with a perimeter of 14 units.

## Geometry Terms

**Geometry**, or the study of shapes, is filled with unique terminology and vocabulary. It is important to become familiar with this math vocabulary to be able to precisely classify and identify two- and three-dimensional shapes.

The most basic terms include points, lines, line segments, rays, angles, perpendicular lines, and parallel lines.

A **point** is an exact location with no size. This often appears as a dot, and is usually labeled with a letter, such as Point $A$.

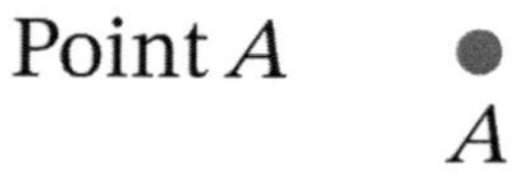


A **line** is a straight path that extends in opposite directions. A line does not have a width, and it extends indefinitely in both directions. Lines are labeled with letters representing points on the line, such as $\overleftrightarrow{AB}$.

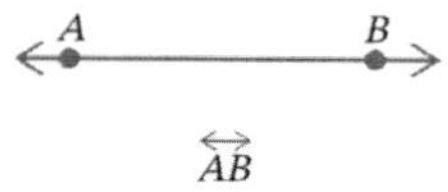


A **line segment** is a part of a line. A line segment has endpoints, beginning and ending at a point labeled with a letter, such as $\overline{AB}$.

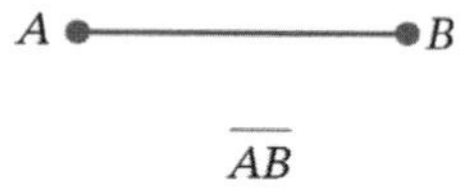


A **ray** is a part of a line that starts at an endpoint and then extends out indefinitely. Rays are labeled starting with a letter at the endpoint and ending with a letter representing another point on the ray, such as $\overrightarrow{AB}$.

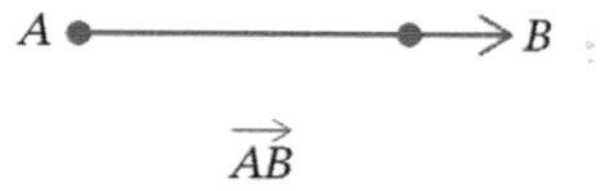


An **angle** is formed when two straight lines or rays meet at a common endpoint. The two rays below form an angle.

**Parallel lines** extend side-by-side and never intersect. To help visualize parallel lines, think of train tracks.

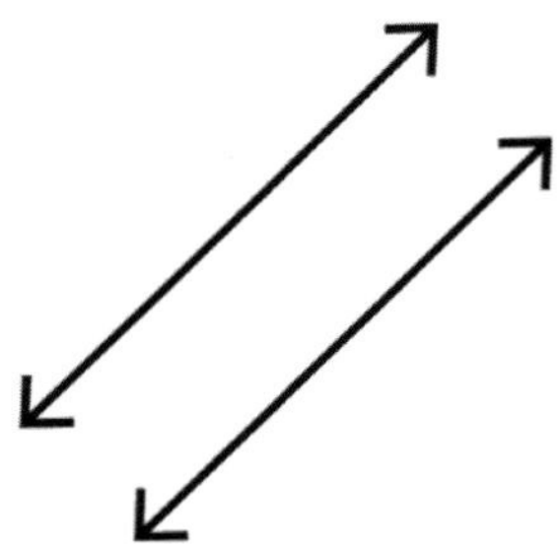

**Perpendicular lines** intersect to form a right angle. To help visualize perpendicular lines, think of a corner or a T-shape.

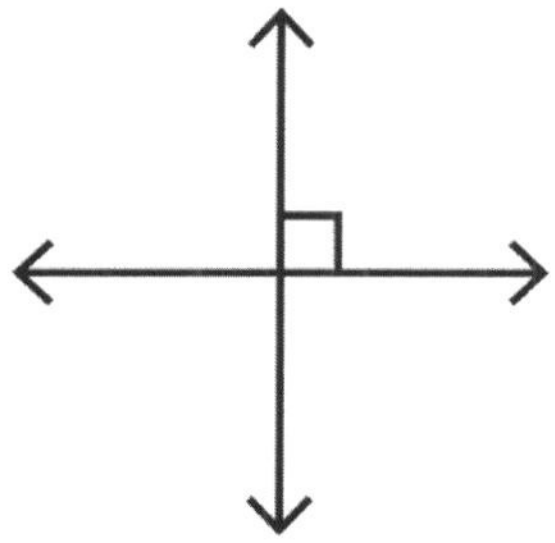

**Review Video: Parallel and Perpendicular Lines**
Visit mometrix.com/academy and enter code: 815923

## Parallel and Perpendicular Lines

When two lines are **parallel**, they **never intersect**. Parallel lines are like railroad tracks, extending side by side, but never crossing. **Perpendicular** lines **intersect** to form a **90-degree angle**. Perpendicular lines form **right angles**.

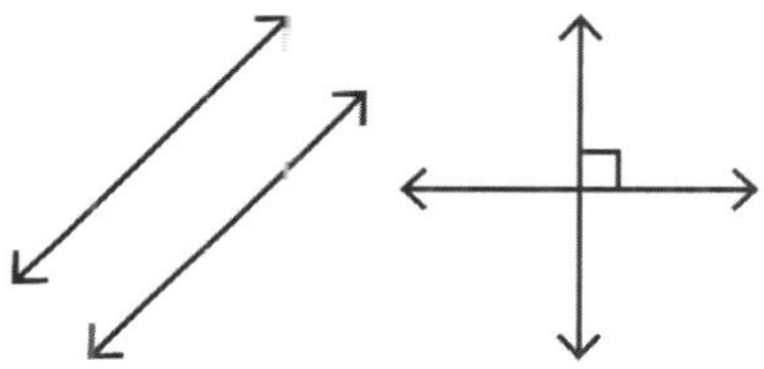

Two-dimensional figures can be classified based on their number of sides, their angle measures, and by the presence of parallel or perpendicular side lengths.

## Right, Acute, and Obtuse Angles

A **right angle** consists of 90 degrees and forms a corner. Angles that are less than 90 degrees are considered **acute angles**. Angles that are wider than 90 degrees but less than 180 degrees are considered **obtuse angles**.

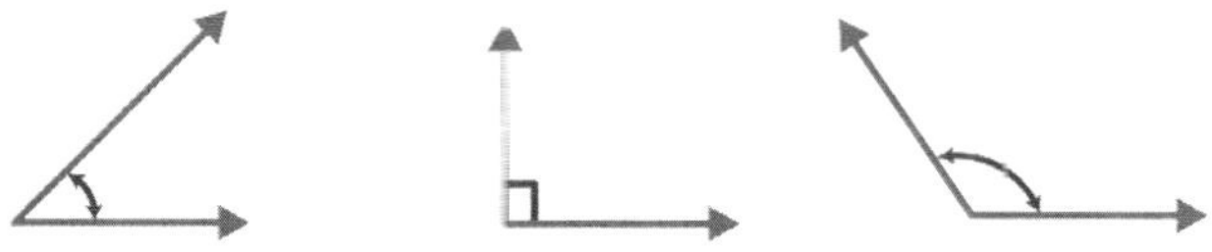

## Classifying and Sorting Figures

A **quadrilateral** is a four-sided shape. The table below shows 4 common quadrilaterals. Notice how trapezoids have exactly one pair of parallel sides, but parallelograms and rhombi have two pairs of parallel sides. Rectangles and squares have two pairs of parallel sides and four right angles formed by perpendicular side lengths.

| | | |
|---|---|---|
|  | Exactly one pair of parallel sides | Trapezoid |
| 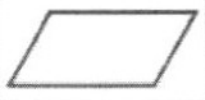 | Two pairs of parallel sides | Parallelogram |
| 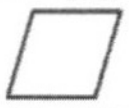 | Parallelogram with congruent sides | Rhombus |
| 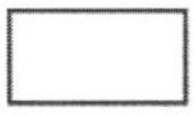 | Parallelogram with right angles | Rectangle |
|  | Rectangle with congruent sides | Square |

### *Two-Dimensional Figures*

Two-dimensional shapes can be classified by the number of sides they have. Polygons are considered **regular polygons** if all the sides are the same length. For example, a regular pentagon has 5 sides, and all of the sides are the same length. Side lengths that are the same are considered **congruent**. For example, a square has 4 congruent side lengths.

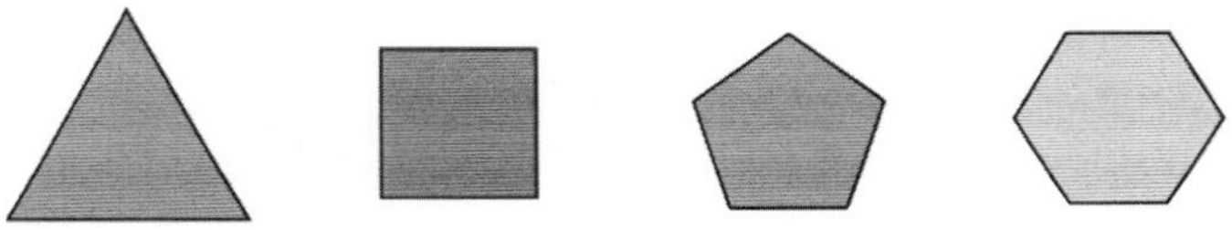

Triangle 3 Sides | Quadrilateral 4 Sides | Pentagon 5 Sides | Hexagon 6 Sides

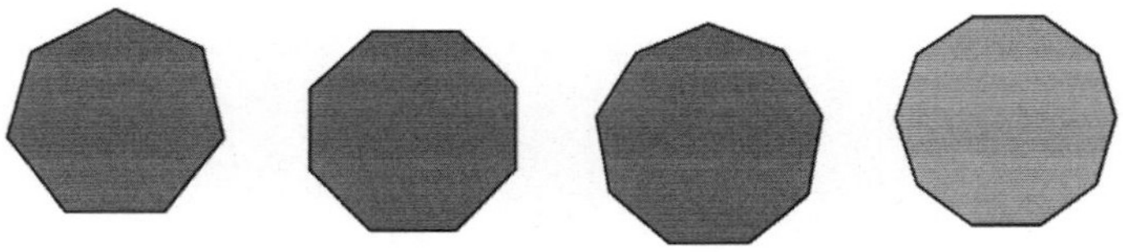

Heptagon 7 Sides | Octagon 8 Sides | Nonagon 9 Sides | Decagon 10 Sides

Not all polygons will have parallel or perpendicular side lengths. Consider the regular polygons above. The triangle, pentagon, hexagon, heptagon, octagon, nonagon, and decagon have no right angles and no perpendicular sides. Some of the polygons do contain side lengths that are parallel. For example, the bottom side length and the top side length of a hexagon are parallel. Notice how the angle measures of the triangle are all acute, the angles in the quadrilateral are right, and the angle measures for all the other polygons are obtuse. When classifying two-dimensional shapes, it is important to look for characteristics such as parallel lines, perpendicular lines, acute angles, obtuse angles, and right angles.

**EXAMPLE**

A quadrilateral with exactly one pair of parallel sides is classified as a ____________.

A trapezoid is defined as a four-sided shape with only one set of parallel sides.

**EXAMPLE**

Student A states that all squares are rectangles, but not all rectangles are squares. Student B states that all rectangles are squares, but not all squares are rectangles. Which student is correct?

All squares are rectangles, but not all rectangles are squares. The definition of a rectangle is a 4-sided figure with 4 right angles. A square qualifies as a rectangle because it has 4 sides and 4 right angles. However, a square has 4 equal sides. Not all rectangles have 4 equal sides, so not all rectangles are squares. Student A is correct.

### *QUADRILATERALS*

A **quadrilateral** is a 4-sided shape. There are many subcategories of quadrilaterals. The most common are parallelogram, rhombus, rectangle, square, and trapezoid.

**Parallelogram**: A parallelogram has two pairs of parallel sides. It sometimes looks like a leaning rectangle.

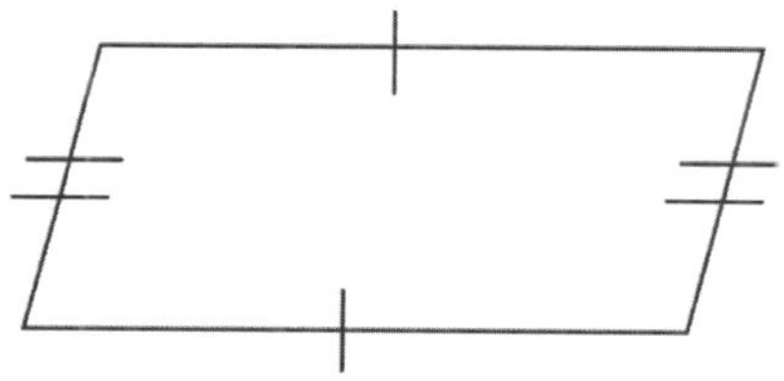

**Rhombus**: A rhombus is a parallelogram with four equal sides. It has no 90° angles.

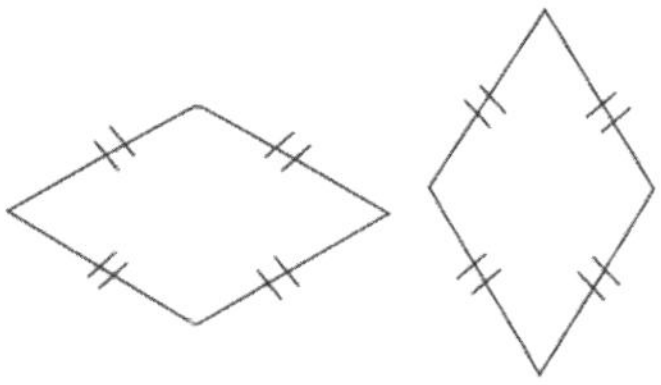

**Rectangle**: A rectangle has two equal parallel long sides, two equal parallel short sides, and four 90° angles.

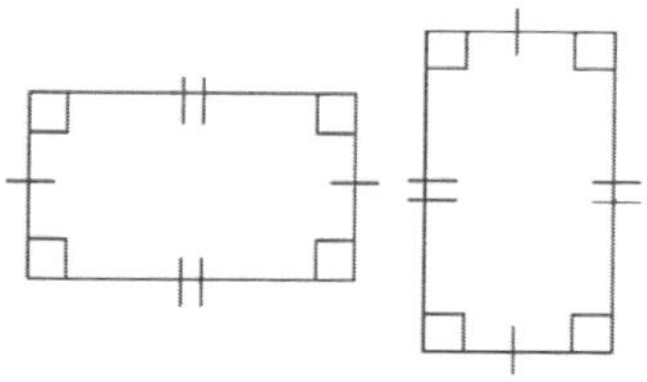

**Square**: A square has four equal sides. Its opposite sides are parallel, and it has four 90° angles.

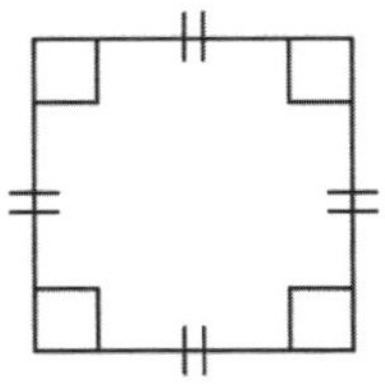

**Trapezoid**: A trapezoid has one pair of parallel sides and one pair of non-parallel sides.

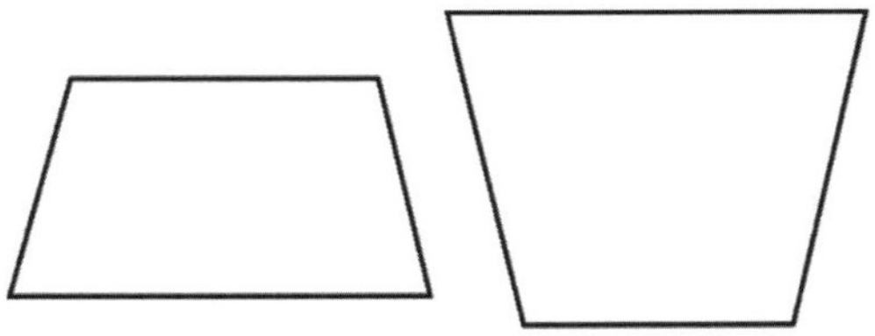

Not all 4-sided shapes fall into these categories. For example, the shapes below are quadrilaterals, but they do not fall into any of the subcategories mentioned above. They are simply referred to as quadrilaterals.

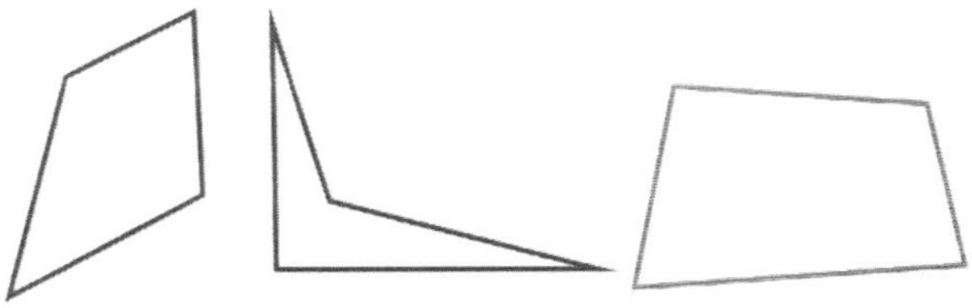

EXAMPLE

All the shapes below can be classified as ________. The top two shapes can also be classified as ________ or as ________.

Quadrilateral: 4-sided polygon
Parallelogram: A quadrilateral that has 2 pairs of parallel sides
Rhombus: A parallelogram with 4 congruent side lengths

All the shapes below can be classified as quadrilaterals. The green and yellow shapes can also be classified as rhombi or as parallelograms.

### *THREE-DIMENSIONAL FIGURES*

The most common three-dimensional figures include cones, cylinders, spheres, triangular and rectangular prisms, and cubes. When identifying and classifying three-dimensional figures it is important to be aware of the number of faces, edges, and vertices. **Faces** are the flat surfaces, **edges** are where two faces come together, and **vertices** are like corners, where more than two faces come together. For example, a rectangular prism has 6 faces, 12 edges, and 8 vertices.

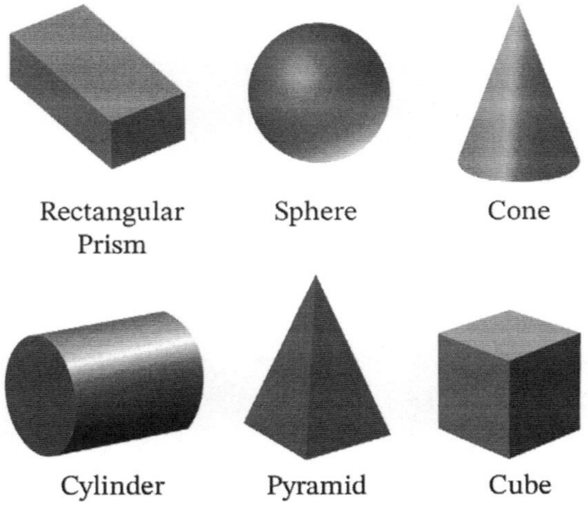


Three-dimensional figures can be identified based on their faces, edges, and vertices. For example, a **sphere** is a round shape where every point on the surface is an equal distance from the center. A sphere is shaped like a ball, and has no faces, no edges, and no vertices. **Cylinders** have two circular faces, and one curved surface. Cylinders have no edges and no vertices. **Cones** have one circular face and one curved surface. Cones consist of one face, one vertex, and no edges. Triangular prisms and rectangular prisms are in a similar family of shapes to each other. Remember, **prisms** have two ends that are the exact same shape and size, and the sides are rectangular. **Triangular prisms** have two triangular base shapes and rectangular sides. **Rectangular prisms** have two rectangular base shapes and rectangular sides. **Cubes** are similar to rectangular prisms, but with cubes, each of the six faces on a cube are identical. Cubes have six identical faces, twelve edges, and eight vertices. **Pyramids** have one base shape, and triangular sides that all come together at the *vertex*.

Another way to sort three-dimensional shapes is to identify whether the shape can roll, slide, or both. For example, a cube can slide, but a cylinder can roll and slide.

**Review Video: 3D Geometric Shapes**
Visit mometrix.com/academy and enter code: 738045

## Example

List the shapes from least to greatest based on the number of vertices.

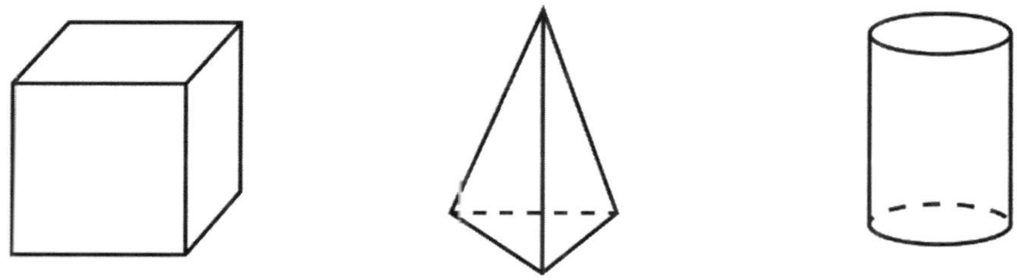

Vertices are like corners, where more than 2 faces meet.
A cylinder has 0 vertices.
A triangular pyramid has 4 vertices.
A cube has 8 vertices.

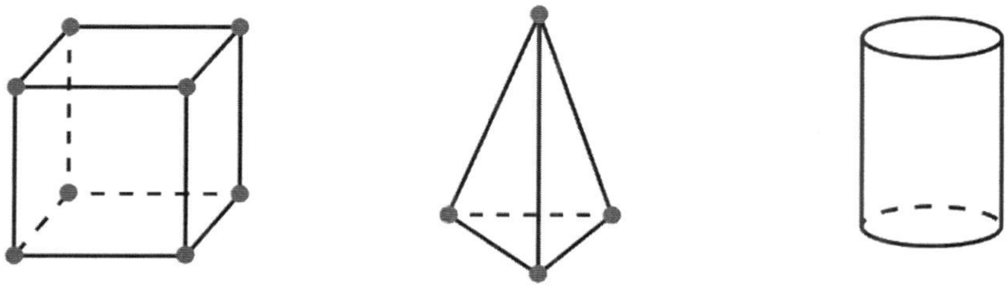

From least to greatest: Cylinder, Triangular Pyramid, Cube.

## Time

Draw the time 7:20 on an analog clock and a digital clock.

On the analog clock, the small hand will be just after the 7, showing it is just after 7 o'clock. The big hand will be at 20 minutes, which is at 4.

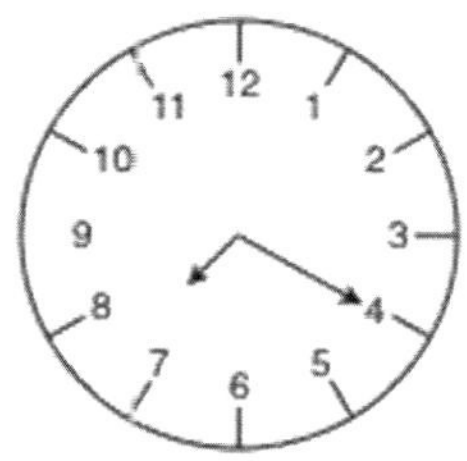


On a digital clock, the time will be written in the order: hours, then minutes. Since the hour is only one digit, there may be a 0 before the 7.

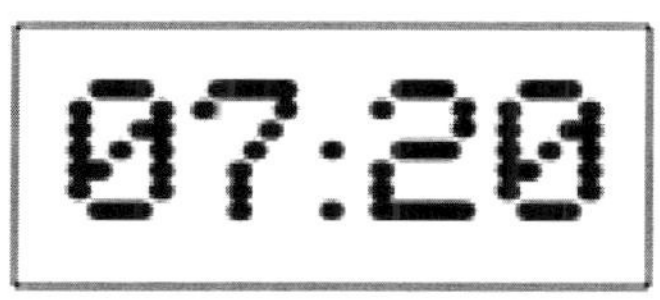

Find the time on the clock below.

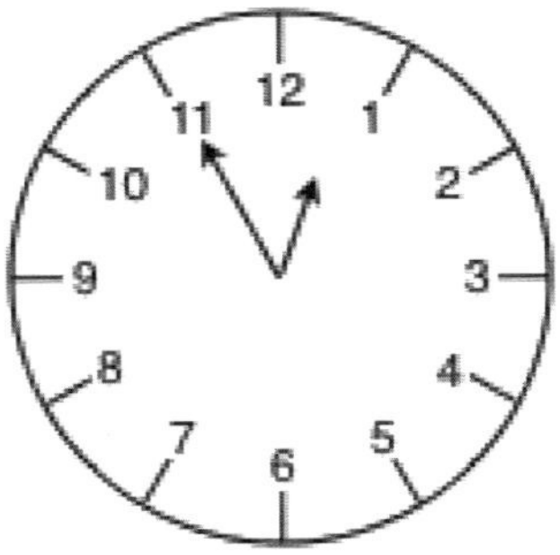


The big hand is on the 11, so the minutes is 55. The small hand is just before the 1, which means that it is close to 1 o'clock, but it is not yet 1 o'clock. It is still 12 o'clock. The time is 12:55.

## Time Intervals

### Things to remember:

There are 60 seconds in 1 minute.

There are 60 minutes in 1 hour.

There are 24 hours in 1 day.

There are 365 days in 1 year.

### *Adding and Subtracting Time*

When adding or subtracting time in minutes, an hour can be visualized as 4 sections of 15 minutes.

$\frac{1}{4}$ of an hour: 15 minutes

$\frac{2}{4}$ of an hour: 30 minutes

$\frac{3}{4}$ of an hour: 45 minutes

$\frac{4}{4}$ of an hour: 60 minutes

### STRATEGIES FOR ADDING AND SUBTRACTING TIME

For example, if a student practices the piano for 15 minutes a day, for 4 days, how long have they practiced in all?

Use a model. Each 15-minute session represents $\frac{1}{4}$ of an hour. $15 + 15 + 15 + 15 = 60$. So, the student has practiced for 60 minutes, which is 1 hour.

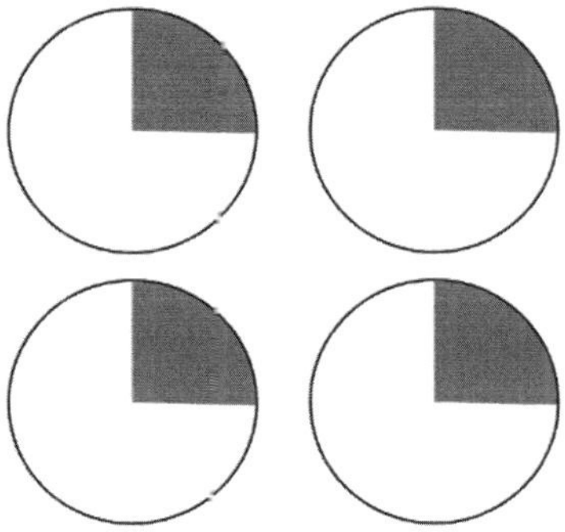

Using sections of the clock to add or subtract is a great way to solve problems mentally. Remember, one quarter of an hour is 15 minutes, and one half of an hour is 30 minutes. Skip counting by 15 or 30 is an efficient way to solve problems involving elapsed time. This also works for subtraction problems.

Consider the following scenario: A student studied 45 minutes for a math test, and 15 minutes for a science test. How much longer did the student study for the math test than the science test?

Math: 45 minutes

Science: 15 minutes

Subtract the time between studying for math and studying for science: $45 - 15 = 30$. This represents half an hour. The student spent 30 minutes more studying for the math test than the science test.

## Probability, Statistics, Patterns, Functions, and Algebra

### PROBABILITY

**Probability** is the likelihood of a certain outcome occurring for a given event. An **event** is any situation that produces a result. It could be something as simple as flipping a coin or as complex as launching a rocket. Simple probability can be found using the formula below.

$$P = \frac{\text{Number of desired outcomes}}{\text{Number of total possible outcomes}}$$

### EXAMPLE

Darla is going to make 24 cookies total. 5 of them will be chocolate chip, 15 of them will be sugar, and 4 of them will be snickerdoodles. If she randomly selected a cookie off the trays, what would be the likelihood that she selects a sugar cookie?

Since 15 out of the 24 total cookies are sugar cookies, the probability is $\frac{15}{24}$ which simplifies to $\frac{5}{8}$. The likelihood that she selects a sugar cookie is very high since majority of her cookies on the trays are sugar cookies.

## REPRESENTING DATA

Data comes from a collection of facts or information. **Data** can be collected by observing, questioning, or measuring. It is common for data to be displayed using a **chart**, **table**, or **graph**. Three commonly used displays are frequency tables, dot plots, and stem-and-leaf plots. These displays can consist of whole number values or fractional values.

### *BAR GRAPHS*

**Bar graphs** use horizontal or vertical bars to represent the total amount for each category. For example, this bar graph shows the number of votes for a variety of snacks. The length of the bar represents the number of votes. Notice how the red popcorn bar represents 5 votes, the green crackers bar represents 2 votes, and so on. The interval should always be scaled and consistent when displaying data graphically. For example, the number of votes on this bar graph increases by 2 consistently.

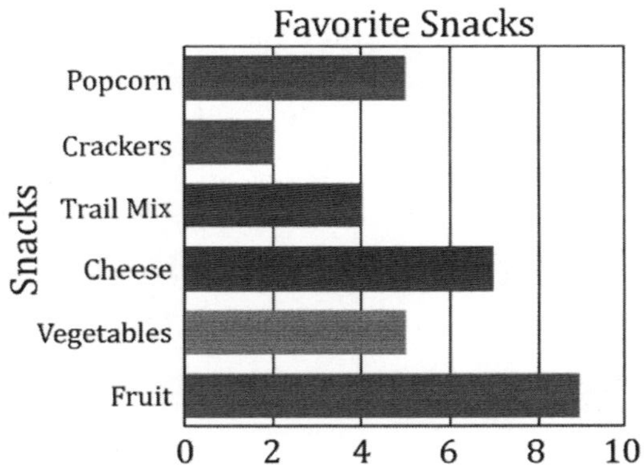

### *Line Graphs*

**Line graphs** have one or more lines of varying styles (solid or broken) to show the different values for a set of data. The individual data are represented as ordered pairs, much like on a Cartesian plane. In this case, the $x$- and $y$-axes are defined in terms of their units, such as dollars or time. The individual plotted points are joined by line segments to show whether the value of the data is increasing (line sloping upward), decreasing (line sloping downward), or staying the same (horizontal line). Multiple sets of data can be graphed on the same line graph to give an easy visual comparison. An example of this would be graphing achievement test scores for different groups of students over the same time period to see which group had the greatest increase or decrease in performance from year to year (as shown below).

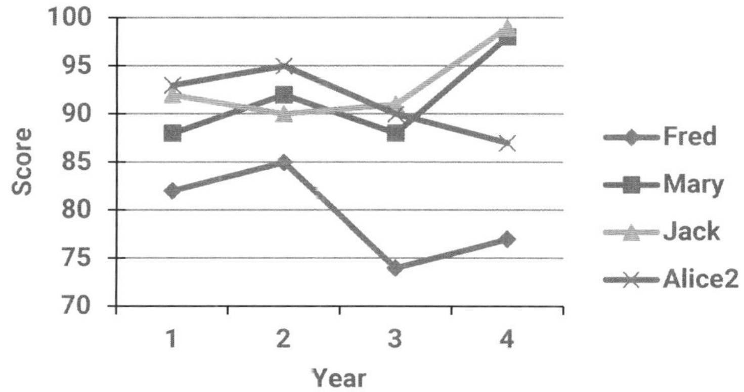


**Review Video: How to Create a Line Graph**
Visit mometrix.com/academy and enter code: 480147

### *Frequency Table*

**Frequency tables** are similar to dot plots because they show how often a data point occurs. Frequency tables list each value that appears in a data set, followed by the number of times it appears. Many frequency tables also include tally marks.

| Favorite Subject | Tally Marks | Number of Students |
|---|---|---|
| Art | IIII | 4 |
| Mathematics | ~~IIII~~ II | 7 |
| Science | ~~IIII~~ | 5 |
| English | IIII | 4 |

### *Pictographs*

Data can be summarized by studying graphical displays such as these. Consider the pictograph below. The **pictograph** uses pictures to represent the value for each category. In this pictograph, each picture represents 1 student. The pictograph shows the variety of ways students in a 3rd grade class commute to school each day. The graph can be used to summarize the data that was collected. For example, since each picture represents 1 student, we know there are 20 students in the class. We also know the most common mode of transportation is taking the bus, and the least common mode of transportation is walking on foot.

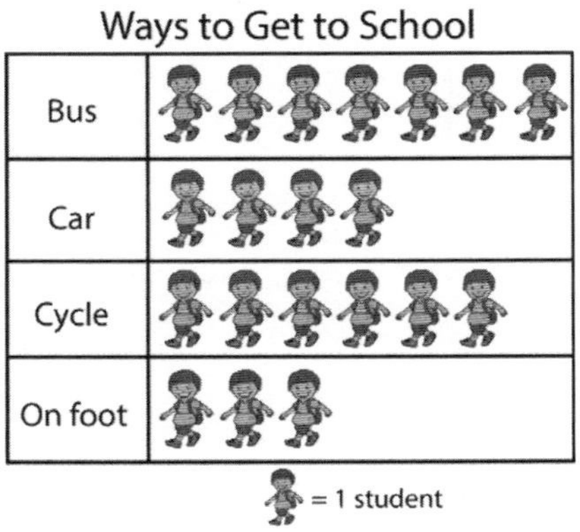


**Review Video: Pictographs**
Visit mometrix.com/academy and enter code: 147860

## Patterns

A pattern is a particular arrangement of shapes, colors, pictures, numbers, objects, and other various things that repeats. Each pattern has a specific rule to follow. Patterns can also be referred to as sequences.

### Example 1

Find the next number in each pattern:

1) 2, 4, 6, 8, ...

2) 5, 10, 15, 20, ...

3) 60, 50, 40, 30, ...

1) The numbers are increasing by 2. Add 2 to the last number to find the next number: 2, 4, 6, 8, 8 + 2 = 10.

2) The numbers are increasing by 5. Add 5 to the last number to find the next number: 5, 10, 15, 20, 20 + 5 = 25.

3) The numbers are decreasing by 10. Subtract 10 from the last number to find the next number: 60, 50, 40, 30, 30 − 10 = 20.

### EXAMPLE 2

Draw the next figure in this pattern:

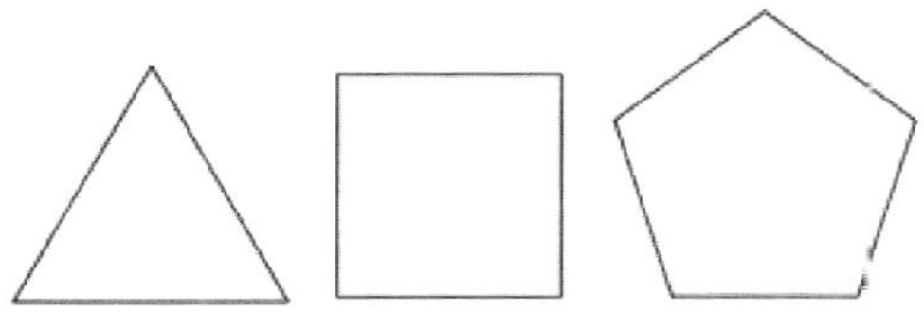

Look at the sides of each figure.

Figure 1: 3 sides

Figure 2: 4 sides

Figure 2: 5 sides

The number of sides on each figure is increasing by 1. The next figure will have 6 sides.

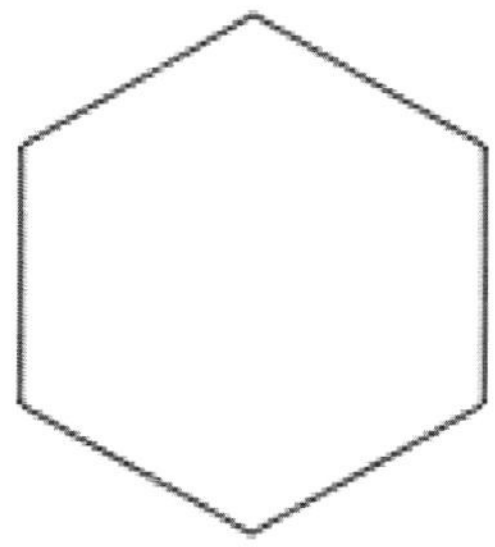

### EXAMPLE 3

Find the next figure in the pattern.

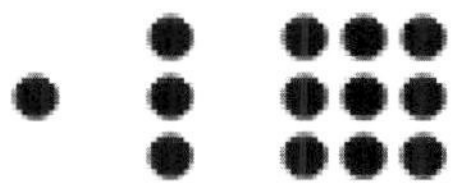

The first figure has 1 dot. The second has 3 dots. The third has 9 dots. Each figure is 3 times the size of the figure before it. The next figure will be three of the last figure:

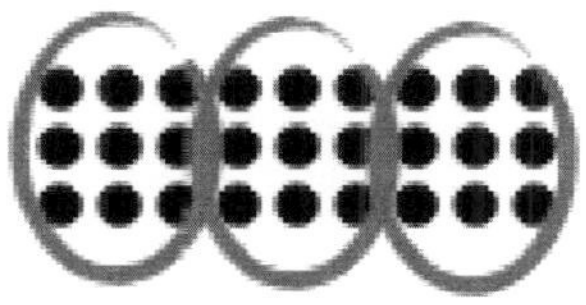

A figure that includes three of the last figure has $3 \cdot 9 = 27$ dots.

## Equivalent Mathematical Relationships

Equations can be used to represent equivalent mathematical relationships. Equations consist of two equivalent expressions joined together by an equal sign. The equal sign signifies that one side of the equation is balanced with or the same as the other side of the equation. For example, look at the equation below.

$$2 + 4 = 6$$

This equation signifies that $2 + 4$ is the same as or balanced with 6. A good way to visualize this concept is by using a number balance. This is a balance that allows weighted tags to be hung on different number values to compare the values of each number. On one side of the number balance, a weighted tag would be placed on 2 and an additional weighted tag would be placed on 4. On the opposite side of the number balance, a weighted tag would be placed on 6. Since the values are equivalent, the number balance should be balanced and straight across. However, if the values were not equivalent to each other, the greater value side of the number balance would move down towards the ground, and the lesser value side of the number balance would move up towards the sky.

# Reading Practice Test #1

*Refer to the following for questions 1–11:*

The Tournament

(1) The sun was warm as Keith and Joe walked home from school.

(2) "Tomorrow will be a perfect day to skateboard," Keith said. "Let's meet at the park at ten o'clock."

(3) "I can't," Joe said. "I have a karate tournament. I've been doing it since I was six."

(4) "Can't you get out of it?" Keith complained. "This will be the first sunny Saturday of spring."

(5) "I have a better idea. Come with me to the tournament." said Joe.

(6) "It sounds boring," Keith said.

(7) "It won't be boring," Joe promised. "Will you come?"

(8) "I'll ask my mom," Keith said.

(9) Later, Keith called Joe. "Mom said I can go. When will we meet?"

(10) "We'll pick you up at nine o'clock," Joe said. "See you tomorrow!"

(11) On the drive to the tournament, Joe told Keith that karate was a tradition in his family. Joe's father started studying karate when he was six, just like Joe. His grandfather learned karate as a boy in Okinawa.

(12) "Where's Okinawa?" Keith asked.

(13) "It's an island off the tip of Japan," Joe told him. "That's where my grandfather grew up."

(14) "Is your grandfather your karate teacher?" Keith asked.

(15) Joe laughed. "No. He's too old to teach anymore. I study with Master Lee in a dojo downtown."

(16) Joe explained that a dojo was a karate school. Master Lee taught many students in his dojo. In the tournament, Joe would compete against friends from his dojo and students from other dojos. He was nervous and excited.

(17) When they arrived at the tournament, Master Lee met them near the door. Joe introduced Keith to Master Lee. Master Lee smiled and bowed to Keith. Keith bowed back, even though he felt a little funny.

(18) Master Lee led them into the arena. The wide floor was divided into several rings. In each ring, students competed. Around the rings, family and friends cheered and offered encouragement. Joe waved to friends from his dojo.

(19) "I have to get dressed," Joe told Keith. "I'll be back in a few minutes."

(20) Joe disappeared into a locker room. When he came back, he wore a white top and pants. A green belt was tied around his waist.

(21) Keith grinned. "Nice outfit. Why is your belt green? It seems like everyone here has a different color of belt."

(22) Joe explained that belt color showed the skill level of a student. Beginners had white belts. After passing some tests, they earned a yellow belt. Then they earned a green belt. That was the skill level Joe had achieved. His next step was to earn a brown belt. Someday Joe hoped to earn a black belt like his father and grandfather and Master Lee. Then he could teach karate to others.

(23) Master Lee called Joe to a nearby ring. It was almost time for Joe to compete. He did some stretching exercises to prepare his body for competition. When Joe's name was called, he bowed to Master Lee and walked to the center of the ring.

(24) Keith felt worried. "What if he gets hurt?" Keith asked Joe's dad.

(25) Joe's dad explained it was a light contact competition. Students made only gentle, controlled contact with each other. They were judged on speed and accuracy rather than force or power. Keith was relieved.

(26) As the match began, Keith cheered for Joe as he punched, kicked, and blocked against his opponent's attacks. Joe was really good at karate! Keith's and Joe's dads yelled and clapped as the match came to an end.

(27) Joe was breathless when he came to stand beside them. They waited anxiously for the judges' decision. The four judges conferred quietly at their table. Finally, they announced their decision: all four points went to Joe. Joe won the match!

(28) As the tournament continued, Joe kept winning matches. Keith cheered louder and louder with every win. He felt proud that someone as talented as Joe was his friend. He also admired the way his friend used his karate skills to honor his family's heritage. Keith hoped he could attend another tournament with Joe very soon!

**1. In what season is the story set?**

a. Spring
b. Summer
c. Fall
d. Winter

**2. Why can't Joe go skateboarding with Keith?**

a. Joe hates skateboarding
b. Joe has a class at Master Lee's dojo
c. Joe has to go to a karate tournament
d. Joe doesn't like Keith anymore

**3. According to the story, what does a karate student's belt color represent?**

a. The student's favorite color
b. The student's karate teacher
c. The form of karate the student studies
d. The student's skill level

**4. In paragraph 27, what is the definition of the word "conferred"?**

a. Argued
b. Joked
c. Decided
d. Discussed

**5. Based on the story, why does Joe want Keith to come to the karate tournament with him?**

a. Joe wants Keith to understand that karate is important to him
b. Joe does not want Keith to go skateboarding without him
c. Joe wants Keith to meet Master Lee and Joe's dad
d. Joe wants Keith to be jealous of his karate skills

**6. What point of view is used to tell this story?**

a. First person
b. Second person
c. Third person
d. All of the above

**7. Which of the following best describes how Keith's attitude toward the karate tournament changes between paragraph 6 and paragraph 28?**

a. Keith's attitude does not change at all.
b. Keith goes from thinking the tournament is boring to hoping to attend another one.
c. Keith goes from thinking that karate is an awesome sport to thinking that karate is boring.
d. Keith decides he doesn't want to skateboard anymore; he wants to study karate.

**8. What is the primary purpose of this story?**

a. To show how important karate is to Joe
b. To show how much Keith likes skateboarding
c. To show how long Keith and Joe have been friends
d. To show what a good teacher Master Lee is

**9. Based on the information given in the story, how likely is Joe to keep practicing karate?**

a. Very unlikely
b. Somewhat unlikely
c. Somewhat likely
d. Very likely

**10. Which of the following statements about the story is a fact, rather than an opinion?**

a. By the end of the story, Keith wants to take karate.
b. Because Joe wins all his matches, Master Lee is obviously an excellent teacher.
c. Joe's father and grandfather both practice karate.
d. None of the other students in Master Lee's dojo are as good as Joe.

**11. Based on the story, how does practicing karate honor Joe's family heritage?**

a. Karate is taught in Okinawa, and Joe's grandfather is Okinawan.
b. Karate is a tradition in Joe's family, practiced by three generations.
c. Karate is popular in the town where Joe and his family live.
d. Many Asians practice karate, and Joe is Asian.

*Refer to the following for questions 12–17:*

**Gabby Douglas: Star of the Olympics**

(1) She stands at the chalk bowl, whitening her hands, her determined face staring at the uneven bars. She moves to the bars, salutes the judges, and mounts. Over the next few minutes, she performs an almost perfect routine, hailed by some experts as one of the most amazing performances by anyone at the 2012 Olympic Games. She moves through each maneuver of the routine with the confidence of a mature competitor, while the watching world holds its collective breath. As she sticks her dismount, she flashes that beautiful, contagious smile, and we jump out of our seats, cheering. She's done it again!

(2) Gabby, born on December 31, 1995, in Virginia Beach, Virginia, began her formal gymnastics training at the age of 6 years old. By the time she was 8 years old, she had won a state championship. So, when Gabby turned 14, she left her hometown and family to move to West Des Moines, Iowa, to train with Liang Chow. Chow is a trainer known all over the world for turning American gymnasts into Olympic champions and gold medalists. Travis and Missy Parton, who have a daughter who is also a student of Chow's, offered to be Gabby's host family. Gabby very quickly became close to the Parton family and even considers herself to be a "big sister" to the Parton's four daughters.

(3) Leaving her home and family was difficult for Douglas but soon proved to be a strategic move. In 2010, at the Nastia Liuken SuperGirl Cup, Gabby made her debut on the national level, winning fourth all-around. She continued to compete throughout the rest of 2010, winning fifth all-around at the 2010 Pan American Championships, earning her a place on the US team. In 2011, the US team won the gold medal in the team finals at the World Artistic Gymnastics Championships in Tokyo, Japan. When she won the 2012 Olympic Trials in San Jose, California, Gabby earned a place on the US national team that would represent the United States at the 2012 Summer Olympics in London.

(4) Gabby Douglas arrived at the 2012 Olympic Games in London, England, as an underdog, but she left the competition as not only a world champion, but also America's sweetheart. The 4'11", 16-year-old young lady mesmerized the world with her power, flexibility, and form. Many who were familiar with her career were concerned that Gabby would crack emotionally under the great pressure of participating in the world's most prestigious athletic event, but her nerves appeared to be made of steel. Even in the most intense moments of the competition, Gabby seemed focused and calm, ready to help Team America bring home the gold. Not only is she the first African American female to win gold in the individual all-around event, but she has also been nicknamed "Flying Squirrel" because of the way she seems to fly through the air when competing on the bars.

(5) During the London Olympics, Gabby stood out as a star, not only for her gymnastic skills, but also for her fun personality and support of the other members of the US team. Since the Olympics, she has received much attention from the media and has appeared on the cover of several magazines, such as Sports Illustrated and Time. In 2012, she was named Sportswoman of the Year by the Women's Sports

Foundation. She has received several endorsement deals with companies such as Kellogg's and Procter & Gamble.

(6) For Gabby, it's all been about a dream. "I think when you have a dream, you won't let anyone stop you," she said. And her dream has definitely come true.

**12. Which word is a good synonym for *prestigious* in paragraph 4?**

a. Crowded
b. Normal
c. Impressive
d. Televised

**13. What is the main idea of this passage?**

a. Gabby Douglas was not well known before she competed at the Olympics.
b. Gabby Douglas had to make sacrifices, but they led her to become a skilled Olympian.
c. People were afraid that Gabby Douglas be affected by the pressure of the Olympics.
d. Gabby Douglas had to leave her home in order to train for the Olympics.

**14. Why did the author include paragraph 3 in this passage?**

a. To explain why Gabby Douglas moved away from home
b. To describe how Gabby Douglas practices for competitions
c. To show how Gabby Douglas made it to the Olympics
d. To tell why Gabby Douglas wanted to go to the Olympics

**15. Which sentence from the passage shows that Gabby Douglas had to make sacrifices to pursue a career in gymnastics?**

a. She stands at the chalk bowl, whitening her hands, her determined face staring at the uneven bars.
b. By the time she was 8 years old, she had won a state championship.
c. Leaving her home and family was difficult for Douglas but soon proved to be a strategic move.
d. Even in the most intense moments of the competition, Gabby seemed focused and calm, ready to help Team America bring home the gold.

**16. Why did the author include paragraph 2, which provides an anecdote about Gabby Douglas's life?**

a. To show where Gabby Douglas lived when she was a child
b. To show what kind of town Gabby Douglas grew up in
c. To show how Gabby Douglas made friends during her training
d. To show the steps Gabby Douglas took to become a great gymnast

**17. Which of the following is the best summary of paragraph 3?**

a. Even though it was hard for Gabby to leave her family, the training she received made her a great and successful gymnast.
b. Gabby Douglas had to compete before she could go to the Olympics, but she eventually earned a spot on the US national team.
c. Gabby Douglas's decision to seek better training helped her improve, succeed in several competitions, and earn a place on the US national team.
d. Gabby Douglas won several medals as she worked to earn a spot on the US national team, which competes at the Olympics.

*Refer to the following for questions 18–29:*

A Lesson Learned

(1) Beautiful melodies floated from Uncle Eddie's guitar. Kari listened with wonder. The way Uncle Eddie made the guitar sing filled Kari with a desire to learn to play. She wanted to make beautiful music too.

(2) "Teach me to play, Uncle Eddie," Kari begged.

(3) Uncle Eddie looked intently at Kari. "Learning to play isn't easy, Kari. It takes hard work and practice. Are you ready for that?"

(4) "I am! I promise." Kari was thrilled. She was sure playing the guitar would come easily for her. "When can we start?"

(5) "I'll come by at two o'clock on Saturday," Uncle Eddie said. "Be ready to work hard."

(6) Kari laughed. "I will," she promised. "Thanks, Uncle Eddie. See you Saturday!"

(7) Kari could hardly wait for Saturday to come. She dreamed about the songs she would play. She imagined impressing her friends with her skills. Kari was sure she would be a guitar expert in no time. She was so excited.

(8) On Saturday afternoon, Uncle Eddie rang the doorbell. Kari ran to let him in.

(9) "Ready to learn?" Uncle Eddie greeted her.

(10) Kari nodded. She followed him into the family room. She waited for him to get out his guitar and teach her a song, but he didn't even open the case. Instead, he took a book from his music bag.

(11) "We'll start with a history of the guitar," Uncle Eddie said. "Did you know stringed instruments have been around for thousands of years?"

(12) Kari was unimpressed. "Wow," she said.

(13) Uncle Eddie said guitars came from Spain more than 500 years ago. He said they could be used to play a variety of music styles and were one of the most popular instruments.

(14) Kari sighed. "That's great, Uncle Eddie, but I just want to play. When can I start playing songs?"

(15) Uncle Eddie laughed. "Patience, Kari. There's a lot to learn about the guitar before you're ready to play one."

(16) "Like what?" Kari asked.

(17) Uncle Eddie handed her a diagram of a guitar. He explained the two basic guitar parts were the body and the neck. These were made up of other parts.

(18) "The tuning pegs are tightened and loosened so the strings make the right notes," Uncle Eddie told Kari.

(19) Then he showed her the nut at the top and the bridge at the bottom that held the strings in place. He pointed out the fingerboard all along the neck and the frets that helped with finger placement. Finally, he described the top of the body—the sounding board—with a hole in the middle to produce a sweet sound.

(20) Uncle Eddie told Kari to learn the names of the guitar parts as her homework for the next lesson.

(21) "But I don't want homework," Kari protested. "I want to play songs! I didn't even play one note."

(22) With a sigh, Uncle Eddie opened his guitar case and took out his instrument. He played a simple folk song. When he played the song three times, Kari grinned.

(23) "I've got it! I can do this," Kari insisted.

(24) Uncle Eddie showed her how to hold the guitar. Kari started to play, but the notes were all wrong. It didn't sound at all like Uncle Eddie's beautiful music. Kari handed the guitar back to Uncle Eddie with frustration.

(25) "Maybe the guitar isn't for me," she said.

(26) Without a word, Uncle Eddie took out a CD and put it in the player behind him. Tuneless, horrible music filled the room. Kari laughed.

(27) "Hey! That person is worse than I am," she said.

(28) Uncle Eddie smiled. "That's me at my first lesson."

(29) "No way!" Kari said.

(30) "Yep," said Uncle Eddie. "Kari, I've played for 15 years. It took time and practice to get this good."

(31) "Do you think I could play like you someday?" Kari asked.

(32) "If you work hard," answered Uncle Eddie.

(33) "Maybe I should start with my homework for our next lesson," Kari said.

(34) Uncle Eddie hugged her. "That sounds like a great place to start."

**18. What is the setting for Kari's guitar lessons?**

a. Uncle Eddie's house
b. Kari's house
c. A music school
d. The community center

**19. Based on the story, which of the following best qualifies Uncle Eddie to teach guitar lessons to Kari?**

a. He is Kari's uncle
b. He has taught many guitar students before
c. He is looking for work
d. He knows how to play the guitar very well

**20. When did Uncle Eddie say he would come to give Kari her first guitar lesson?**

a. Friday at two o'clock
b. Saturday at noon
c. Saturday at two o'clock
d. Sunday at noon

**21. In paragraph 3, what does the word "intently" mean?**

a. In a focused way
b. In a disinterested way
c. In a happy way
d. In a disgusted way

**22. Which of the following belongs in the empty box according to the sequence of the story?**

| Kari wants to learn to play the guitar. | Uncle Eddie agrees to teach her. | | Kari becomes bored and frustrated. | Kari learns it takes hard work to play guitar. |
|---|---|---|---|---|

a. Kari plays well on her first try
b. Uncle Eddie begins the lesson with the history and structure of the guitar
c. Uncle Eddie does not show up for the lesson
d. Kari's friends decide they want Uncle Eddie to teach them too

**23. What is the main theme of this story?**

a. To show that Uncle Eddie is not a good teacher
b. To show that Kari is not a good student
c. To show that learning to play the guitar is boring
d. To show that learning to play the guitar takes hard work

**24. In what point of view is this story written?**

a. First person
b. Second person
c. Third person
d. All of the above

**25. What is the difference between Uncle Eddie's feelings and Kari's feelings about learning to play the guitar?**

a. Uncle Eddie feels it will be hard, while Kari feels it will be easy
b. Kari feels it will be hard, while Uncle Eddie feels it will be easy
c. Both Kari and Uncle Eddie feel it will be hard
d. Both Kari and Uncle Eddie feel it will be easy

**26. How does the author show in paragraph 14 that Kari is unhappy with Uncle Eddie's history lesson on guitars?**

a. By saying, "Kari was unhappy."
b. By having Kari say something unkind to Uncle Eddie
c. By writing, "Kari sighed."
d. By having Kari leave the room

**27. Who is playing the "horrible music" Kari hears in paragraph 26?**

a. Uncle Eddie's first student
b. Uncle Eddie
c. Kari
d. Kari's father

**28. Based on what was discussed in the story, what does it take to play the guitar well?**

a. A very expensive guitar
b. A very skilled guitar teacher
c. A thorough knowledge of guitar history
d. Hard work and a lot of practice

**29. Based on the information presented in the story, which of the following is a fact instead of an opinion?**

a. Uncle Eddie has been playing guitar for 15 years
b. Kari will never learn to be a good guitar player
c. Playing the guitar is a boring hobby
d. Everyone who plays the guitar knows a lot about guitar history

*Refer to the following for questions 30–35:*

**Less Litter**

(1) Have you ever been riding in the car and looked outside at the scenery? The scenery, whether it is a landscape or the middle of a city, can be beautiful, but it can also be spoiled by litter. When people litter, they can cause harm to the areas around them. It is very important to make sure you dispose of trash properly rather than dropping or tossing it on the ground.

(2) One reason to avoid littering is that litter can harm animals. When litter is thrown into the grass, left on the beach, or dropped on walking trails, animals may find it and try to eat it. Animals cannot always tell what they are eating, and if they eat trash, it can injure them or make them sick.

(3) Litter can also hurt plants. Plants use their roots to absorb nutrients from the soil. When trash is left on the ground, it may get buried in the dirt. This means that plants' roots will be blocked by the trash, and they may absorb chemicals from the buried trash. The trash can also prevent water from soaking into the ground, which also hurts plants. When trash is placed in a trashcan, it is less likely to harm plants and animals.

(4) In addition to causing harm to plants and animals, litter can also harm people and the environment. When litter is thrown out, no matter where it lands, strong winds or animals may carry it to bodies of water. When litter gets in the water, it pollutes it. Some trash may be decorated using dye or ink. Dye and ink can dissolve in the water and become difficult to remove from it. Over time, plastic will break down in water, so it also becomes difficult to take out of the water. When polluted water flows through an area, it affects nearby plants, animals, and soil.

(5) This water is also brought into water treatment centers, where it is filtered, or cleaned, so it can be used in houses and other buildings. However, when water is very polluted, not all of the things polluting the water can be removed from it. This means they can end up in our drinking water. The chemicals and debris that may be left in drinking water can be harmful to humans. Litter is not the only thing that pollutes water, but reducing the amount of litter can help decrease water pollution.

(6) Litter also distracts from the beauty of the scenery around us. Wildflowers that grow by the side of the highway are beautiful. However, when people toss trash from their cars, then cans, wrappers, and other trash surround and cover these flowers. This is also true of sand on the beach or plants in the forest. Litter often takes people's attention away from the natural scenes around them.

(7) Urban areas like cities can also be beautiful, but only when they are kept clean. Litter on sidewalks is unpleasant to see, may smell bad, and can get in the way of people walking through a city. Whether litter is left in nature or in a town or city, it is often upsetting to see. Litter can disrupt people who want to focus on the beauty around them.

(8) Litter can have a negative impact on both our health and the world around us. Even though we cannot always avoid having trash, we can be careful about what we do with it. Next time you are outside and have something to throw away, hold onto

it until you can find a trash can and throw it away properly. Reducing litter is an important way to help keep the areas around us clean, healthy, and beautiful.

**30. What is the main claim the author has made in this passage?**

a. Litter is a big source of water pollution.
b. Any area can be affected by litter.
c. People should stop littering.
d. Litter can make landscapes ugly.

**31. Who did the author most likely write this essay for?**

a. Anyone who spends a lot of time outside
b. People who volunteer to pick up litter
c. People who clean the water we drink
d. Anyone who may have trash

**32. Why did the author write this passage?**

a. To persuade readers not to litter
b. To tell readers how to avoid littering
c. To show readers the effects of litter
d. To inform readers about the causes of litter

**33. Why did the writer organize this passage using a cause-and-effect structure?**

a. To tell readers about events caused by littering
b. To tell readers the common effects of littering
c. To tell readers what will happen if they stop littering
d. To tell readers how to prevent others from littering

**34. How does the author support the main claim in this passage?**

a. By explaining what can happen when people litter
b. By showing how easy it is to throw things away
c. By sharing anecdotes about people who littered
d. By summarizing the laws that forbid littering

**35. Which of the definitions below matches the meaning of the word *spoiled* in paragraph 1?**

| **spoiled** (adjective) |
| --- |
| 1. given too many privileges<br>2. expired or rotten<br>3. messed up or ruined<br>4. taken from its owner |

a. Definition 1
b. Definition 2
c. Definition 3
d. Definition 4

*Refer to the following for questions 36–40:*

**The Alligator and the Squirrel**

(An adaptation of Aesop's Fable, The Lion and the Mouse)

(1) Once, in a lush African forest, there lived an old alligator. Being a very old alligator indeed, he kept to himself, spending his days swimming, sleeping, and sunning himself. Most of the other forest animals were wise enough to leave the old reptile alone, but, one day, an astonishing thing happened.

(2) Alligator was just dozing off one morning after a lazy swim, when he felt movement on his tail. "Say, who is that running along my tail?

(3) It was Squirrel. At the sound of Alligator's big, booming voice, Squirrel froze in his tracks. *Oh no*, thought Squirrel, *now, what will I do*? Truthfully, Squirrel had made quite a habit of running up and down Alligator's tail. The bumps on Alligator's tail were quite large to a small animal like Squirrel, and running over them helped keep him in tip-top shape. Thus, Squirrel could beat all the other squirrels to the tastiest nuts! Normally, Squirrel made sure that Alligator was completely asleep before beginning his workout ritual, but, today, he'd been impatient. Now, he was in trouble. Just then, Alligator, with one powerful swish of his mighty tail, tossed Squirrel into the air, placing him on Alligator's chin.

(4) "Well," said Alligator, "it's little Squirrel. How are you today, my silly little friend?"

(5) Squirrel looked into Alligator's big, bulging eyes. He had to think fast, so he mustered up all the courage he had, smiled his friendliest smile, and said, "Why, good morning, dear Alligator! Isn't it a lovely morning?"

(6) Alligator chuckled to himself. What luck! Since he had begun his day with a swim, he'd neglected to come up with any breakfast for himself. And now, it seemed his breakfast had come to him. "Oh, yes, dear Squirrel," said Alligator, "it is a beautiful morning. And how wonderful for you, since it will be the last morning you will ever see."

(7) Squirrel swallowed hard. "The last morning I will ever see? Whatever do you mean, Alligator?"

(8) Alligator smiled. "Well, it just so happens, Squirrel, that I have not yet had my breakfast this morning. And since you were so foolish as to run along my tail, I cannot help but think that you will be as good a breakfast as any." And, with that, Alligator opened his huge mouth and started to swallow the little animal. Squirrel grabbed one of Alligator's sharp teeth and held on for dear life.

(9) "Wait, I beg you to let me live! I may be able to help you someday in the near future," said Squirrel.

(10) At this, Alligator laughed out loud. "You, tiny Squirrel, help me? I think not. But you do amuse me, Squirrel, so I will let you live. Go, be on your way, and do not let me catch you running on my tail again."

(11) Just a few days later, Alligator fell into a trap set by some hunters. He was caught in a large net, and no matter how hard he swished his tail, he could not seem to break free. "Alas, my life is over!" said Alligator.

(12) About that time, Squirrel happened by and saw poor Alligator caught in the trap. He immediately ran over and began gnawing the ropes of the net. After a while, Squirrel had gnawed a hole in the net big enough for Alligator to escape.

(13) "Thank you, dear Squirrel! It seems that you were right. You and I will be friends forever," said Alligator.

(14) "Little friends may prove great friends," said Squirrel.

**36. Why did the author write this story in the third person?**

a. The author wanted the reader to know Alligator's thoughts.
b. The author wanted to make Squirrel the narrator of the story.
c. The author wanted to show both Alligator's and Squirrel's thoughts.
d. The author wanted the reader to know how Alligator feels about Squirrel.

**37. Which two qualities of the story show the reader that this story is a fable? Select all that apply.**

a. This story is based on something that actually happened.
b. This story has a beginning, middle, and end.
c. This story only has two characters.
d. This story uses events to teach a lesson.
e. The main characters in this story are animals.

**38. Which of the following is a theme found in this story?**

a. No one can be trusted.
b. Squirrels are helpful creatures.
c. The point of being nice is to earn favors from others.
d. Friends come in all shapes and sizes.

**39. Which of the following events is most likely to happen after the events in the story?**

a. Squirrel will avoid Alligator at all costs.
b. Alligator will eat Squirrel for dinner.
c. Alligator will help Squirrel in the future.
d. Squirrel will get caught in a hunter's trap.

**40. How does the event in paragraph 10 affect the rest of the story?**

a. It makes Alligator afraid of Squirrel.
b. It teaches Squirrel to stay away from Alligator.
c. It causes Alligator to get caught in a trap.
d. It allows Squirrel to help Alligator later.

# Answer Key and Explanations for Reading Test #1

**1. A:** is the best choice because paragraph 4 indicates that the story is set in spring. B, C, and D are not the best choices because the story is set in spring.

**2. C:** is the best choice: In paragraph 3 Joe tells Keith that he can't go skateboarding because he has a tournament to attend. A, B, and D are not the best choices because they are not true statements according to the story.

**3. D:** is the best choice because the color of a student's karate belt indicates the student's skill level. A, B, and C are not the best choices because they do not represent the true meaning of the belt color.

**4. D:** is the best choice because the correct definition of "conferred" is "discussed." A, B, and C are not the best choices because they are not proper definitions of "conferred."

**5. A:** is the best choice because Joe invites Keith to the tournament so that Keith will understand that karate is important to Joe. B and D are not the best choices because they do not accurately represent Joe's attitude in the story. C is not the best choice because it does not represent Joe's main motivation for inviting Keith to the tournament.

**6. C:** is the best choice because this story is written from the third person point of view. A, B, and D are not the best choices because they represent points of view not used in this story.

**7. B:** is the best choice because Keith's attitude changes from thinking karate is boring to hoping to attend another tournament. A is not the best choice because Keith's attitude does change throughout the story. C and D are not the best choices because they do not accurately represent the change in Keith's attitude.

**8. A:** is the best choice because the primary purpose of the story is to show that karate is important to Joe. C is a good answer, but it is not the best choice because it does not reflect the primary purpose of the story. B and D are not the best choices because they do not represent themes or purposes from the story.

**9. D:** is the best choice because karate is very important to Joe, so he is very likely to keep practicing it. A, B, and C are not the best choices because they do not accurately represent Joe's likelihood of continuing to practice karate.

**10. C:** is the best choice because it is a fact that Joe's father and grandfather both practice karate. A, B, and D are not the best choices because they are all statements of opinion instead of fact.

**11. B:** is the best choice because karate is part of Joe's family heritage, as three generations of his family practice karate. A and D are good answers, but they are not the best choices because they do not demonstrate how Joe's family heritage involves karate. C is not the best choice because it does not express how karate honors Joe's family heritage.

**12. C:** Paragraph 4 states that Gabby Douglas participated "in the world's most prestigious athletic event." This is referring to the Olympics. The passage shows that Gabby Douglas had to work hard and compete against many other gymnasts to get a chance to compete in the Olympics. This shows that the people who participate in the Olympics are especially skilled and talented. This means they are also impressive, which is a synonym for *prestigious,* so choice C is correct. This also shows that the Olympics are not normal, so choice B is incorrect. The passage does not give any information about how many people attended the Olympics, so choice A is incorrect. While the Olympics are televised, this is not related to the other ideas in the sentence or paragraph. This makes choice D incorrect.

**13. B:** This passage gives information about how Gabby Douglas worked her way up to the Olympics, how well she did at the Olympics, and what happened after she competed at the Olympics. The passage explains that she had to leave her family in order to get the training she needed. It also describes how much she competed, which shows how much time she put into improving her skills. This shows that she had to make sacrifices, but those sacrifices allowed her to compete in the Olympics. This means choice B is correct. The passage does not mention whether or not Gabby Douglas was well known before the Olympics, so choice A is incorrect. Choices C and D both reference a supporting detail from the passage. However, neither of these choices show the main idea of the whole passage. This makes choices C and D incorrect.

**14. C:** Paragraph 3 describes the events that led to Gabby Douglas earning a chance to compete in the Olympics. These events show how Gabby Douglas made it to the Olympics, so choice C is correct. Gabby Douglas's decision to move away from home is described in paragraph 2, not paragraph 3. Paragraph 3 shows the effects of this decision, but not what caused it, so choice A is incorrect. Gabby Douglas's practices are not described in the passage, so choice B is incorrect. The reason Gabby Douglas wanted to go to the Olympics is also not mentioned in the passage. Because of this, choice D is incorrect.

**15. C:** Choice C shows that Gabby Douglas sacrificed living with her family to become a better gymnast. This means choice C is correct. Choice A describes what Gabby Douglas does right before starting her routine. This does not show that she made a sacrifice, so choice A is incorrect. Choice B shows that Gabby Douglas had talent at a young age. However, this sentence describes Gabby Douglas's early accomplishment, not a hard decision she had to make. This makes choice B incorrect. Choice D shows that Gabby Douglas stayed cool under pressure. This also describes Gabby Douglas, but it does not show what she had to sacrifice, so choice D is incorrect.

**16. D:** Paragraph 2 explains that Gabby Douglas moved away from home so that she could train with Liang Chow. She hoped that training with Chow would help her become a better gymnast. Moving and training with Chow are steps Gabby Douglas took to become a better gymnast, so choice D is correct. Gabby Douglas's childhood hometown is a detail mentioned in paragraph 2, but this is not what the paragraph is about. This means choices A and B are incorrect. The paragraph shows that she got along well with her host family, but it does not say she made other friends. This is also not the focus of this paragraph, so choice C is incorrect.

**17. C:** Choice C is the best summary because it gives the key points from the paragraph. Choice A is incorrect because it leaves out the key point that Gabby Douglas was chosen for the US national team. Choices B and D are incorrect because they do not show that Gabby Douglas had to go to many competitions and perform well to be chosen for the US national team.

**18. B:** is the best choice because the story indicates that the setting is Kari's house. A, C, and D are not the best choices because they do not represent the correct setting for the story.

**19. D:** is the best choice: Uncle Eddie is qualified to teach guitar because he plays very well. A, B, and C are not the best choices because they do not represent Uncle Eddie's best qualification to teach guitar.

**20. C:** is the best choice because in paragraph 5, Uncle Eddie says he will come by on Saturday at two o'clock. A, B, and D are not the best choices because they indicate times not referenced in the story.

**21. A:** is the best choice because "intently" means "in a focused way." B, C, and D are not the best choices because they do not represent accurate definitions of "intently."

**22. B:** is the best choice because it best completes the sequence of the story. A, C, and D are not the best choices because they do not complete the sequence according to the progression of the story.

**23. D:** is the best choice because the main theme of the story is to show that learning to play the guitar takes hard work. A, B, and C are not the best choices because they do not represent the main theme of the story.

**24. C:** is the best choice because this story is written in third person. A, B, and D are not the best choices because they represent incorrect points of view for this story.

**25. A:** is the best choice because Uncle Eddie feels playing the guitar will be hard, but Kari feels it will be easy. B, C, and D are not the best choices because they represent inaccurate perspectives for Uncle Eddie and Kari according to the story.

**26. C:** is the best choice because paragraph 14 says "Kari sighed" as the author's way of indicating Kari's displeasure. A, B, and D are not the best choices because they do not reference details included in paragraph 14.

**27. B:** is the best choice because Uncle Eddie is playing the "horrible music" Kari hears in paragraph 26. A, C, and D are not the best choices because they do not represent the correct person who is playing the "horrible music."

**28. D:** is the best choice because the story points out that it takes a lot of practice and hard work to play the guitar well. A, B, and C are not the best choices because they do not include what it takes to play the guitar well.

**29. A:** is the best choice because it is the only statement of fact from the story. B, C, and D are not the best choices because they are all statements of opinion instead of fact.

**30. C:** The author states that it is important for people to throw trash away rather than allowing it to become litter. The author also explains why l.itter is harmful. This shows that the author's main claim is that people should stop littering, so choice C is incorrect. Only paragraphs 4 and 5 mention water pollution. This is not a topic that the whole body of the passage supports, so choice A is incorrect. While the statement in choice B is true, the passage focuses on the effects of litter, not the places where litter tends to be found. This makes choice B incorrect. Choice D is a supporting detail that the author uses to show why people should stop littering, so choice D is incorrect.

**31. D:** People who have trash can litter if they choose to drop or throw their trash on the ground instead of throwing it away in a trash can. The purpose of the passage is to persuade anyone with trash to throw it away instead of littering, so choice D is correct. People who do not go outside often can still litter. Also, people who often go outside are more likely to see litter and understand why it is bad. This makes choice A incorrect. People who volunteer to clean up litter are not likely to create more litter and, therefore, do not need to hear this passage's message, so choice B is incorrect. People who work to clean the water that people use indoors are not the only people who may litter. This means choice C is incorrect.

**32. A:** The purpose of this passage is to persuade readers to throw trash away instead of littering. The author does this by sharing several negative effects of littering. However, the main purpose of the passage is not only to show the effects of litter. In the introduction, the author states that it is important to throw things away instead of littering. This shows that the author's purpose is to persuade the reader not to litter. This means choice C is incorrect. The passage mentions that throwing things away is better than littering, but this is only one way to avoid littering. This means choice B is incorrect. The passage does explain what litter is and where it comes from, but this is a supporting detail. It is not the purpose of the passage, so choice D is incorrect.

**33. B:** The passage uses a cause-and-effect structure to show the effects that littering causes. Each body paragraph explains how litter can cause a negative effect, so choice B is correct. The passage does not describe specific events that littering has caused, so choice A is incorrect. The passage also does not clearly explain what will happen if people stop littering or stop others from littering. This means that choices C and D are incorrect.

**34 .A:** Each body paragraph in this passage describes possible effects of littering, so choice A is correct. The passage does not explain how to avoid littering, so choice B is incorrect. The passage also does not contain stories about people who have littered, so choice C is incorrect. Laws that forbid littering are also not mentioned in the passage, so choice D is incorrect.

**35. C:** Paragraph 1 explains that scenery can be spoiled by litter. Since litter can prevent someone from seeing the scenery as it is when it is clean, litter messes up, or ruins, scenery. This matches the third definition, so choice C is correct. Litter cannot give scenery privileges or permission, so choice A is incorrect. Litter cannot take scenery from its owner or cause it to expire, so choices B and D are also incorrect.

**36. C:** Both Squirrel's thoughts and Alligator's thoughts are shown in this story. Paragraph 3 shows Squirrel's thoughts when Alligator asks who is running on his tail. Paragraph 6 describes Alligator's thoughts about eating Squirrel for breakfast. The reader can know the thoughts of both characters, so choice C is correct. Since the author did not want to only show Alligator's thoughts, choices A and D are incorrect. Squirrel is not the narrator of the story. If Squirrel was the narrator, the story would be written in the first person. This means choice B is incorrect.

**37. D, E:** The author of this story used the events to teach a lesson, or a moral. Fables are used to teach moral lessons. Fables also usually include characters that are animals. Since this story has a moral and animal characters, choices D and E are correct. Fables are not based on true events. They are fictional, so choice A is incorrect. A fable does have a beginning, middle, and end, but so do most other stories. The beginning, middle, and end show that this is a complete story, but not that it is specifically a fable. This makes choice B incorrect. Fables can have more than two characters, so the fact that this story only has two characters does not make it a fable. This means choice C is incorrect.

**38. D:** In this story, Squirrel and Alligator become friends, even though they are very different from each other. They are completely different animals, and Alligator even almost eats Squirrel.

However, they become friends after they show kindness to each other. In paragraph 14, Squirrel even says that little friends can make good friends. This shows that friends can come in all shapes and sizes, so choice D is correct. In the story, Squirrel tells Alligator that if he lets him go free, he may be able to help him later. Squirrel does keep his word and helps Alligator escape from a trap. This shows that he is trustworthy, so choice A is not supported by the passage. The statement in choice B is not a theme. The statement is too specific to be a theme. It is not proven by the story since there is only one squirrel, and he only helps once. This means choice B is incorrect. Alligator does not believe that Squirrel will help him, so he does not show him kindness in order to earn a favor. This makes choice C incorrect.

**39. C:** Since Squirrel and Alligator are now friends, they will likely be kind and helpful to each other. It is very likely that Alligator will help Squirrel if he can, so choice C is correct. Alligator tells Squirrel that they will be friends, which means he will probably not try to eat Squirrel again. This means choice B is incorrect. Since Alligator is no longer dangerous to Squirrel, there is no need for Squirrel to avoid him, so choice A is incorrect. The hunters were hunting large animals like Alligator. There are no details in the story that show that the hunters want small animals like Squirrel, so choice D is incorrect.

**40. D:** In paragraph 10, Alligator expresses that he thinks what Squirrel said is funny. Because of this, he lets Squirrel go free. Since Alligator let Squirrel go, Squirrel is able to return to help Alligator later in the story. This means choice D is correct. Alligator does not show that he fears Squirrel at any point in the story, so choice A is incorrect. Squirrel rescues Alligator the next time he sees him, so he does not avoid Alligator. This means choice B is incorrect. Squirrel does not help the hunters catch Alligator or do anything that would cause Alligator to get caught, so choice C is correct.

# Reading Practice Test #2

*Refer to the following for questions 1–10:*

<u>That Was Then, and This Is Now</u>

(1) Becca slumped on Grandma's flowered sofa. She loved Grandma, but her house was so dull. Becca was bored.

(2) "Grandma, there's nothing to do!" Becca whined.

(3) "You could watch TV," Grandma suggested.

(4) "There's nothing to watch on your channels. Why don't you have cable?" Becca asked.

(5) "I don't need cable," Grandma said. "When I was little, there were only three television stations available. In fact, we didn't even have a TV until I was 12 years old. And even then, it was black-and-white."

(6) "That sounds awful," Becca said.

(7) "Actually, we thought it was wonderful," Grandma said. "But that was then, and this is now."

(8) "Well, what about getting a game system or a computer. That would give me something to do when I'm here," Becca said.

(9) "We didn't have computers or game systems when I was young," Grandma said. "But we always managed to keep ourselves quite busy."

(10) "You must have been so bored all the time," Becca said. "What did you do to keep busy?"

(11) "Oh, we played outside. We rode our bikes, and sometimes we stuck playing cards in the spokes of the wheels to make them sound like motorcycles. We went fishing and built forts out of blankets or scrap wood or whatever else we could find. Yes, we kept busy." Grandma smiled, remembering.

(12) "I guess that doesn't sound so bad," Becca said. "But what if it was raining, like today? Then you couldn't do any of those things."

(13) "On rainy days, we played inside games," Grandma said. "We played checkers and solitaire and other games. We read books for hours. We made paper dolls and designed whole wardrobes for them. But I guess that was then, and this is now."

(14) "Wow," said Becca. "That sounds kind of fun. What else was different way back then?"

(15) Grandma laughed. "It wasn't all that long ago, Becca. But many things were different."

(16) Grandma told Becca about having fresh milk delivered to her doorstep in glass bottles instead of buying it in plastic jugs at the supermarket. She talked about wearing dresses to school every day instead of jeans and T-shirts. She talked about using pay phones instead of cell phones. She talked about listening to soap operas on the radio instead of watching them on TV. She talked about playing records and dancing the twist.

(17) "But that was then," Grandma said, "and this is now."

(18) Becca was amazed. "You're right, Grandma. Practically everything is different now. It seems like the whole world has changed since you were my age."

(19) Grandma shook her head. "Not everything has changed, Becca. Some things will never change."

(20) "Like what?" Becca asked.

(21) "Well," Grandma answered, "back then grandmas loved their granddaughters, just like I love you now."

(22) Becca leaned over and hugged Grandma tightly. "I love you, too," she said. "Now, how about a game of checkers?"

(23) Grandma smiled. "Sounds good. Maybe things haven't changed so much after all!"

(24) They played checkers, and Grandma beat Becca all three games. Then they used pillows and blankets and all six dining room chairs to build a massive fort in the living room. They sat in the dim fort and had a picnic lunch of sandwiches and chocolate chip cookies. After lunch, Grandma showed Becca how to make paper dolls and design clothes for them. The afternoon flew past.

(25) When Becca's mom came to pick her up, Becca did not want to go home.

(26) "But I thought you were bored," Grandma said.

(27) Becca grinned. "Oh, Grandma," she said, "I was bored. But that was then, and this is now!"

**1. Where does this story take place?**

a. At Becca's house
b. At Grandma's house
c. At a vacation house
d. At Becca's mom's house

**2. Which of the following best represents the main theme of this story?**

a. There are many different ways to have fun
b. Becca is bored all the time
c. Grandma is old and dull
d. Activities from the past are not exciting

**3. How does Becca feel at the beginning of this story?**

a. Happy
b. Sad
c. Angry
d. Bored

**4. What word does the author use in paragraph 1 to describe Becca's feelings about Grandma's house?**

a. Exciting
b. Tolerable
c. Dull
d. Boring

**5. What is the difference between Becca's attitude at the beginning of the story and her attitude at the end?**

a. There is no difference in her attitude
b. She is bored at the beginning of the story and not bored at the end
c. She is angry with Grandma at the beginning of the story and happy with her at the end
d. She is excited at the beginning of the story and bored at the end

**6. Which of the following does the story say Grandma did to keep busy when she was young?**

a. Watch color TV
b. Use a computer
c. Play outside
d. Go to the mall

**7. What is the author's main purpose in writing this story?**

a. To entertain
b. To inform
c. To persuade
d. To influence

**8. Which of the following is a statement of fact?**

a. Black-and-white TV is boring
b. Grandma is a dull person
c. Milk used to be delivered in glass bottles
d. Playing outside is exciting

**9. Where do Grandma and Becca eat their lunch in this story?**

a. Outside on the lawn
b. In a blanket fort
c. At the dining table
d. At a restaurant

**10. Which of the following does Becca ask Grandma to get in this story?**

a. A dog
b. A TV
c. A car
d. A computer

*Refer to the following TWO passages for questions 11–22:*

## The Tradition of Dance

(1) It is estimated that there are over 300 Native American tribes, and each of them uses dancing to communicate culture. Native American dances date back hundreds of years and come in many different forms. Different tribes use dance for different purposes and to convey different messages.

(2) Although each dance is different, they all have meanings that are rooted in ancient tradition. The Iroquois performed a corn husk dance to bring good crops and many healthy babies to the tribe. The Choctaw women danced with medicine men to bring their tribe victory in sporting events. The Plains Indians offered thanks to the gods through their Sun Dance, and the Cherokee celebrated both peace and war with the Eagle Dance. During the Snake Ceremonial, Hopi dancers even held live snakes in their mouths before releasing them into the desert to bring rain and a good harvest.

(3) Each of the many different dances also requires a unique costume. These costumes vary widely, but—just like the dances—each has a special meaning. Most dance costumes include a headdress and special ceremonial clothing. Some also include a wand, jewelry, and even body paint. In addition, feathers are often used in costumes to symbolize human traits. One of the most common feathers used is the eagle feather, which represents strength in many tribes.

(4) Though many of the Native American dances are now performed only in ceremonies and at powwows, they remain an important element of Native American culture. These dances are a language, rich in history and meaning. They are passed from generation to generation and will always be a vital part of Native American tradition.

## The Story of My People

(1) As we pulled into the community college parking lot, I felt my excitement rising. Powwows were one of my favorite things. I loved the talking, the laughing, the music, and—most of all—the dancing. I loved seeing and hearing and feeling my Cherokee heritage.

(2) Inside the large gymnasium, the powwow was just getting started. My father and grandfather went to join the men who had gathered in the far corner. Around the edges of the gym, women sat behind long tables draped with vibrant cloths. On the tables were items for sale. I wandered around and looked at the leather vests, beaded belts, and beautiful jewelry.

(3) As I came to the end of the tables, I heard behind me the low, pulsing beat of a single drum. It made a hollow, echoing sound. Soon other drums joined the rhythm, filling the air with their deep sound. High-pitched rattles joined in, and a group of men drifted to the center of the floor. The dancing had begun.

(4) I found a seat on some bleachers and watched with wonder. Synchronized steps beat out a perfect rhythm while voices chanted high and low in beautiful unison. Feathers and beads and shiny black braids flashed past as the intensity increased. It was magical to me.

(5) Some dances were for the children; some were for the men or women; some were for everyone. Sometimes tribes danced separately, and sometimes they all danced together. Some dances offered thanks, and others asked for blessings; some were celebrations, and others were prayers. But although each dance was different, they all told a story. It was an ancient story: the story of my people.

*Questions 11–15 pertain to the passage "The Tradition of Dance":*

**11. What is the main purpose of dance in the Native American culture?**

a. To provide exercise
b. To communicate a message
c. To entertain children
d. To prepare for battle

**12. According to paragraph 2, what is the similarity between the Iroquois corn husk dance and the Hopi Snake Ceremonial?**

a. They were both intended to bring good crops
b. They both involved women and medicine men
c. They both involved the use of snakes
d. They both involved the use of corn husks

**13. Which of the following is a statement of fact?**

a. Eagle feathers are the best feathers
b. Native American costumes are beautiful
c. Ceremonial headdresses make dancers look important
d. Many Native American costumes include a wand and jewelry

**14. What does the eagle feather represent in many Native American tribes?**

a. Power
b. Wealth
c. Strength
d. Authority

**15. What was the author's main purpose in writing this article?**

a. To inform
b. To entertain
c. To influence
d. To persuade

*Questions 16–20 pertain to the passage: "The Story of My People"*

**16. What tribe represents the heritage of the narrator of this story?**

a. Hopi
b. Cherokee
c. Iroquois
d. Choctaw

**17. In what point of view is this story written?**

a. First person
b. Second person
c. Third person
d. None of the above

**18. What is the primary reason the narrator enjoys going to powwows so much?**

a. They are very exciting
b. There are many people there
c. There are interesting things to buy
d. They represent the narrator's heritage

**19. Which of the following is a statement of opinion?**

a. Some dances are designed to bring a blessing
b. Each dance is different, but each has a meaning
c. Many dances involve synchronized steps, music, and chanting
d. Native American dancing is emotionally powerful

**20. What does the narrator do before the dancing begins?**

a. Buys snacks at the snack bar
b. Looks at the tables of items for sale
c. Takes a walk around the campus
d. Practices different dancing steps

*Questions 21–22 pertain to both passages "The Tradition of Dance" and "The Story of My People"*

**21. Which main theme is central to both stories?**

a. The value of powwows in Native American culture
b. The focus on family in Native American culture
c. The importance of dancing in Native American culture
d. The power of medicine men in Native American culture

**22. What is Native American dancing compared to in both stories?**

a. Language
b. Music
c. Cooking
d. Art

*Refer to the following for questions 23–34:*

In Abuela's World

(1) In June, just after school ended, Marianna and her family went to see her abuela—her grandmother—in Tampico, Mexico. By the time they reached Abuela's small house by the sea, Marianna was exhausted. Abuela put a thick mat on the floor for a bed, and Marianna stretched out and went to sleep.

(2) When Marianna awoke the next morning, the sun was already high in the sky. The air was warm and sticky. Marianna rubbed her eyes and wandered into Abuela's kitchen. Delicious smells bubbled up from a pot on the stove.

(3) "Buenos dias, sleepyhead," Abuela said with a grin. "You must have been tired. You slept half the day away."

(4) Marianna stretched and yawned as her mother came into the kitchen. "What are we doing today, Mami?" Marianna asked.

(5) "Papi and Jorge and I are going down to the beach soon," Mami answered. "You can come with us or stay here with Abuela."

(6) Marianna chose the beach. As she lay in the sun, she listened to the waves. Sea birds called overhead, and the gentle sea breeze kissed her face. It was a perfect afternoon.

(7) The next day, Abuela joined them as they drove south to visit some Aztec ruins. Although the Aztec people once ruled the area of Mexico where Abuela lived, they were conquered by the Spaniards long ago. Crumbling ruins were all that remained of their ancient civilization. Marianna had read about the Aztecs in school. It was amazing to think these stones were once part of the great Aztec empire.

(8) On her third full day in Mexico, Marianna saw her cousins. The three boys shyly greeted Marianna. Then they turned to her younger brother, Jorge.

(9) "Want to play some futbol, Jorge?" they asked.

(10) Jorge nodded. He knew futbol meant soccer in Spanish, and he loved soccer. Marianna went out to watch the boys play. She liked soccer, too, but it was too hot to play in the blazing sun.

(11) Marianna sat on the shady porch and watched the boys kick the ball in the dusty street. The boys played hard, and Marianna found herself cheering for Jorge's team. As the sun went down, they called it a tie and finally headed inside.

(12) The visit to Abuela's world flew by. On the day before she had to leave, Marianna found Abuela in the kitchen.

(13) "I don't want to go home," Marianna said. "I love you, and I love Mexico."

(14) Abuela smiled. "I love you, too. But you would eventually miss your life in America. And you can always come to visit."

(15) "I guess so," said Marianna. "But I'll miss Mexico."

(16) "I know," said Abuela, taking Marianna's hand. "So to help you take Mexico with you, we are having a grand fiesta tonight. Come shopping with me."

(17) They went to the open market where vendors spread their goods on blankets on the ground. Abuela selected items for the party, greeting many of the vendors by name. Then she bought Marianna some chicle, Mexican gum made from sapodilla pulp.

(18) That night, dozens of neighbors, friends, and family members came to the party. They talked and laughed and danced to the mariachi music. Abuela made incredible food for everyone. There was chicken with sweet and spicy mole, enchiladas with rich sauce, rice, fruit, and plenty of tortillas. It was a true feast.

(19) The party went late into the night. Marianna felt she had barely slept when Papi shook her awake and told her it was time to go. As they drove away, Marianna waved to Abuela. Although she was going home, Marianna knew her heart would always hold a special place for Abuela's world.

**23. What is the Spanish word for grandmother?**

a. Amiga
b. Abuela
c. Alla
d. Alegra

**24. Where is the main setting for this story?**

a. In the southwest
b. In Tampico, Mexico
c. At the ruins
d. In the open market

**25. Which choice best finishes the following chart of events on Marianna's vacation?**

| Marianna goes to the beach. | Marianna visits the ruins. | Marianna sees her cousins. | Marianna visits the open market. | |
|---|---|---|---|---|

a. Marianna visits a mountain
b. Marianna takes a road trip through Mexico
c. Marianna attends a big party at her grandmother's house
d. Marianna watches the boys play soccer

**26. Which paragraphs discuss Marianna's visit with her cousins?**

a. Paragraph 5 through paragraph 9
b. Paragraph 6 through paragraph 10
c. Paragraph 7 through paragraph 10
d. Paragraph 8 through paragraph 11

**27. Which word is the best English translation for the Spanish word "futbol"?**

a. Football
b. Soccer
c. Baseball
d. Kickball

**28. Why did the author tell this story from Marianna's point of view?**

a. So the reader can understand Marianna's thoughts and feelings
b. Because there was no other main character in the story
c. Because all good stories are written in third-person point of view
d. This story is not written from Marianna's point of view

**29. Why does the story say Marianna doesn't want to leave Mexico?**

a. She hates the long trip
b. She doesn't have to go to school in Mexico
c. She loves her grandmother, and she loves Mexico
d. She likes the weather at the beach

**30. In paragraph 6, which literary device is used to describe the wind?**

a. Simile
b. Personification
c. Metaphor
d. No literary device is used

**31. Which word best describes the relationship between Marianna and her grandmother?**

a. Tense
b. Distant
c. Polite
d. Loving

**32. Which of the following is a statement of opinion?**

a. Grandmother made chicken with mole for the party
b. Mariachi music was played at the party
c. The food at the party was incredible
d. Neighbors, friends, and famil y members attended the party

**33. Where did Marianna go with her grandmother on the day of the party?**

a. To the open market
b. To the beach
c. To the ruins
d. To the supermarket

**34. According to the story, what is the main ingredient of chicle?**

a. Chicken
b. Chocolate
c. Sugar and spices
d. Sapodilla pulp

*Refer to the following for questions 35–40:*

**Montana: Big Sky Country**

(1) Montana, the fourth largest state in America, is located in the northwest area of the US. It became the 41st state when it was admitted to the Union on November 8, 1889. Montana is bordered by four states – North Dakota, South Dakota, Wyoming, and Idaho. It is also bordered by Canada.

(2) Many people believe that Montana is one of the most scenic states in America. It certainly does have a lot of natural beauty. Its name means "mountain" in Spanish, and there are certainly lots of mountains there. Most mountains are on the western side of the state. The rest of the state is basically flat. Montana also contains many national and state parks. Part of Yellowstone National Park, one of the most famous natural attractions in the world, is in Montana. The state is also full of wildlife not found in most states. These animals include bighorn sheep, mountain lions, mountain goats, elk, bobcats, lynx, bison, black bears, and grizzly bears, to name just a few.

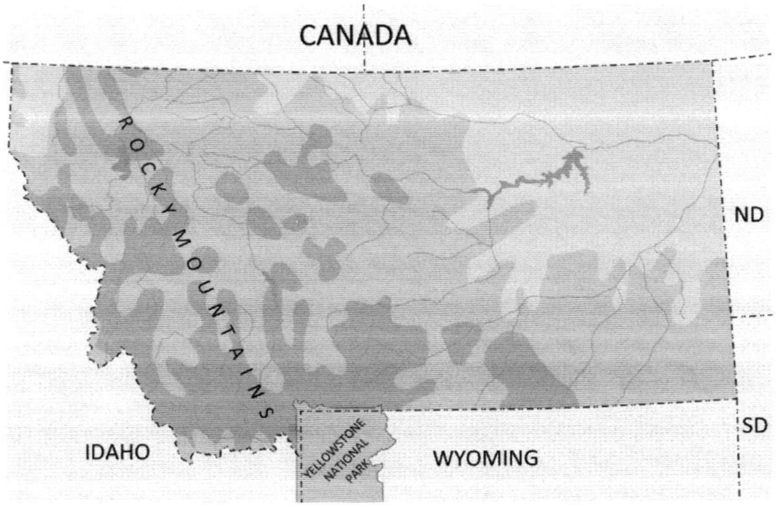


(3) Montana has several nicknames. One of them is "Big Sky Country," and another is "The Treasure State." The latter nickname refers to the fact that mining used to be a big industry in Montana, and that many people came to the area back in the 1800s searching for gold. These days, farming is the most common business in the state. Farmers in Montana raise lots of wheat, hay, barley and other crops. There are over two and a half million head of cattle in the state and hundreds of thousands of sheep.

(4) One of the most famous battles in American history took place in Montana. It's officially known as the Battle of the Little Bighorn, but many people call it Custer's Last Stand. Many Native Americans call it the Battle of the Greasy Grass. It took place in 1876, when Montana was still part of a territory and not yet a state. It was a battle between the US Army and two Native American tribes: the Lakota and the Cheyenne. The battle has become legendary because the Native Americans outnumbered the Army and defeated them badly. General George Custer and almost 300 soldiers died on the battlefield. The battlefield is now a national

monument. So, Montana is not only full of beauty and natural resources, but it's also rich in history.

**35. How does the map help the reader understand the information in the passage?**

a. The map shows the reader how much smaller Montana is than other states.
b. The map shows the reader how far apart the mountains in Montana are.
c. The map shows the reader where different crops and mines are found.
d. The map shows the reader the location of popular destinations and Montana's border states.

**36. What is true about the author's word choice and voice in paragraph 2?**

a. Words like *lots* and *basically* show that the author thinks Montana is boring.
b. Words like *beauty* and *famous* show that the author thinks Montana is great.
c. Words like *many* and *full* show that the author thinks Montana is crowded.
d. Words like *certainly* and *found* show that the author thinks Montana is mysterious.

**State** (*noun*)

1. A physical phase, such as liquid, solid, or gas
2. A section or part of a country
3. A strong expression of emotion
4. A governing group

**37. Which of the definitions above matches the way state is used in paragraph 1?**

a. Definition 1
b. Definition 2
c. Definition 3
d. Definition 4

**38. What is the main idea of paragraph 2?**

a. Montana has a beautiful landscape and is home to several parks and interesting wildlife.
b. Yellowstone National Park is in Montana, which brings in lots of tourists and gives wildlife a protected habitat.
c. Montana got its name because of the mountains found there, though they are only in the west.
d. There are many animals in Montana that are uncommon in other states.

**39. Which of the following is the best summary of paragraph 4?**

a. The Battle of Little Big Horn was a victory for the Lakota and Cheyenne Native American tribes. General Custer died in this battle, along with 300 members of the US Army.
b. Before Montana became a state, a famous battle occurred there. The battle has a few different names, including the Battle of Little Big Horn and the Battle of the Greasy Grass.
c. In 1876, a famous battle happened in what is now Montana. It was a victory for Native Americans, and the site is now a monument for the Americans that died in battle.
d. Montana has a unique landscape and produces a variety of resources. It has also been the home of many historical events, including the Battle of Little Big Horn.

**40. What would the author of this passage most likely think about the creation of another national park in Montana?**

a. The author would not want that to happen because there are already too many parks in Montana.
b. The author would support this so that more people can appreciate the natural areas in Montana.
c. The author would not support this because it would make the other parks in Montana less special.
d. The author would say this is a good idea because it would cause new kinds of animals to live in Montana.

# Answer Key and Explanations for Reading Test #2

**1. B:** is the best choice because this story is set at Grandma's house. A, C, and D are not the best choices because they do not accurately represent the setting for the story.

**2. A:** is the best choice because the main theme of this story is that there are many different ways to have fun. B, C, and D are not the best choices because they are not main themes of the story.

**3. D:** is the best choice because paragraph 1 says, "Becca was bored." A, B, and C are not the best choices because they do not accurately describe Becca's attitude.

**4. C:** is the best choice because paragraph 1 indicates that Becca thinks Grandma is "dull" A, B, and D are not the best choices because "dull" is the only word specifically used by the author to describe Becca's feelings about Grandma's house.

**5. B:** is the best choice because it most accurately represents the change in Becca's attitude between the beginning and end of the story. A, C, and D are not the best choices because they do not accurately describe the changes in Becca's attitude between the beginning and end of the story.

**6. C:** is the best choice because Grandma says she used to play outside. A, B, and D are not the best choices because they are not activities Grandma participated in to keep busy when she was young.

**7. A:** is the best choice because the author's main purpose in writing this story is to entertain the reader. B, C, and D are not the best choices because the purpose of the story is not to inform, persuade, or influence.

**8. C:** is the best choice because it is the only statement of fact. A, B, and D are not the best choices because they are all statements of opinion.

**9. B:** is the best choice because the story says Becca and Grandma ate lunch in a blanket fort. A, C, and D are not the best choices because they do not accurately describe where Becca and Grandma ate lunch.

**10. D:** is the best choice because in paragraph 8 Becca asked Grandma to get a computer. A, B, and C are not the best choices because Becca did not ask Grandma to get a dog, TV, or car.

**11. B:** is the best choice because the main purpose of dance in Native American culture is to communicate a message. A, C, and D are not the best choices because they do not accurately reflect the main purpose of dance in Native American culture.

**12. A:** is the best choice because the Iroquois corn husk dance and the Hopi Snake Ceremonial were both intended to bring good crops. B, C, and D are not the best choices because they do not represent the purpose of these dances.

**13. D:** is the best choice because it is the only statement of fact. A, B, and C are not the best choices because they are all statements of opinion.

**14. C:** is the best choice because in many Native American tribes the eagle feather represents strength. A, B, and D are not the best choices because they do not reflect the meaning of the eagle feather in many Native American tribes.

**15. A:** is the best choice because the author's main purpose in writing this article is to inform the reader. B, C, and D are not the best choices because the author's primary purpose in writing this article is not to entertain, to influence, or to persuade.

**16. B:** is the best choice because paragraph 1 indicates the narrator is of Cherokee heritage. A, C, and D are not the best choices because the narrator is not of Hopi, Iroquois, or Choctaw heritage.

**17. A:** is the best choice because this story is written in first person. B, C, and D are not the best choices because they do not accurately represent the point of view in which this story is written.

**18. D:** is the best choice because paragraph 1 indicates the narrator enjoys powwows because they represent the narrator's heritage. A, B, and C are not the best choices because they do not reflect the primary reason the narrator enjoys going to powwows.

**19. D:** is the best choice because it is the only statement of opinion. A, B, and C are not the best choices because they are all statements of fact.

**20. B:** is the best choice because the story indicates the narrator was looking at the items for sale on the tables before the dancing began. A, C, and D are not the best choices because they do not accurately reflect what the narrator was doing before the dancing began.

**21. C:** is the best choice because the importance of dancing in the Native American culture is a central theme in both stories. A, B, and D are not the best choices because they do not represent themes that are central to both stories.

**22. A:** is the best choice because both stories compare Native American dancing to language. B, C, and D are not the best choices because Native American dancing is not compared in these stories to music, cooking, or art.

**23. B:** is the best choice because the Spanish word for grandmother is "abuela". A, C, and D are not the best choices because none of these words mean grandmother.

**24. B:** is the best choice because this story is set in Tampico, Mexico. A, C, and D are not the best choices because they do not represent the true setting of this story.

**25. C:** is the best choice because it most accurately completes the chart of Marianna's vacation. A, B, and D are not the best choices because they do not accurately complete the chart of Marianna's vacation.

**26. D:** is the best choice because paragraphs 8 through 11 discuss Marianna's visit with her cousins. A, B, and C are not the best choices because they do not represent the correct range of paragraphs that discuss Marianna's visit with her cousins.

**27. B:** is the best choice because futbol means soccer. A, C, and D are not the best choices because they are incorrect translations of futbol.

**28. A:** is the best choice because the author wrote from Marianna's point of view to show her thoughts and feelings to the reader. B, C, and D are not the best choices because they do not represent the author's intentions in writing from Marianna's point of view.

**29. C:** is the best choice because paragraph 13 shows Marianna does not want to go home because she loves Abuela and loves Mexico. A, B, and D are not the best choices because they do not accurately reflect why Marianna does not want to leave Mexico.

**30. B:** is the best choice because paragraph 6 uses personification to describe the wind. A and C are not the best choices because simile and metaphor are not used to describe the wind in paragraph 6. D is not the best choice because personification is used, and personification is a literary device.

**31. D:** is the best choice because the relationship between Marianna and her grandmother is clearly loving. A, B, and C are not the best choices because they do not accurately describe the relationship between Marianna and her grandmother.

**32. C:** is the best choice because it is the only statement of opinion. A, B, and D are not the best choices because they are all statements of fact.

**33. A:** is the best choice because Marianna went to the open market with Abuela on the day of the party. B, C, and D are not the best choices because Marianna did not go to the beach, the ruins, or the supermarket with Abuela on the day of the party.

**34. D:** is the best choice because the main ingredient of chicle is sapodilla pulp. A, B, and C are not the best choices because they do not represent the main ingredient of chicle.

**35. D:** The map includes labels and markings that show the reader where the Rocky Mountains and Yellowstone National Park are. It also shows where other states border Montana. The map does not show any other state in full, so choice A is incorrect. The map only shows the Rocky Mountains and does not provide enough information to show the reader how far apart each mountain is. Choice B is incorrect. The map does not label or highlight crops and mines in Montana, so choice C is incorrect.

**36. B:** The author uses paragraph 2 to describe the natural beauty of Montana. In this paragraph, the author describes the mountains, parks, and wildlife that are found in Montana to show why many people enjoy the state. The author states that Montana has "natural beauty" and emphasizes that Yellowstone, the park it contains, is famous. These details suggest that the author also considers Montana to be great, so choice B is correct. The author uses paragraph 2 to show why Montana is special, so choice A is incorrect. The author uses the words *many* and *full* to describe the number of parks and the amount of wildlife in Montana. The author does not mention whether or not Montana is crowded with people, nor does he or she suggest that there is too much wildlife, so choice C is incorrect. The words *certainly* and *found* would most likely not be used to describe something mysterious. This is also not a topic that the author includes in paragraph 2, so choice D is incorrect.

**37. B:** Montana is a state in the United States of America. The author writes that Montana is the "fourth largest state in America" and describes where in the country it is located. This shows that Montana is a part of America, a country. This matches the meaning given in definition 2, so choice B is correct. The passage does not discuss science or types of matter, so choice A is incorrect. Montana is a place, so it cannot be or show an emotion. This means choice C is incorrect. Since Montana is a location, it also cannot govern or lead people like a person or group of people can. This means that choice D is also incorrect.

**38. A:** Paragraph 2 describes the landscape in Montana. It also tells the reader that it is home to parks and animals that are uncommon in other states. This paragraph focuses on the things that attract people to Montana's natural beauty, so choice A is correct. The location of Yellowstone, the mountains found in Montana, and the animals that live there are all supporting details. These details support the main idea, but none of them are the main idea. This means choices B, C, and D are incorrect.

**39. C:** Paragraph 4 describes the Battle of Little Big Horn, which occurred in Montana many years ago. The paragraph summarizes the battle and tells the reader that the site is now a memorial. This is best summarized in choice C, so it is correct. Choice C tells the reader that the battle happened in Montana, mentions who won the battle, and mentions the memorial. Choice A shares some details about the battle, but it does not mention that the battle happened in Montana. This summary does not show why the paragraph is in this passage and focuses on too many details, so choice A is incorrect. Choice B only says that there was a battle in what is now Montana and tells what names it has been called. This summary only summarizes the first few sentences of the paragraph. Since it does not summarize the whole paragraph, choice B is incorrect. Choice D summarizes paragraphs 2, 3, and 4. It is not an effective summary of paragraph 4, so choice D is incorrect.

**40. B:** The author mentions that people appreciate the natural, beautiful scenery in Montana. This is something that draws people to Montana. The author does not suggest that this is a bad thing. The author mentions it as something that makes Montana special. The author would most likely support more parks that would allow others to see and appreciate Montana, so choice B is correct. The author does not express an opinion about the number of parks in Montana, so choice A is incorrect. Additional parks would not make the current parks less special, so choice C is incorrect. The author does not say that the creation of parks caused uncommon animals to live in Montana, so choice D is incorrect.

# Mathematics Practice Test #1

**1. Which of the following is written in order from *greatest to least*, when reading from left to right?**

a.

| 44,982,016 | 5,221,415 | 782,498 | 586,301 | 69,309 |
|---|---|---|---|---|

b.

| 782,498 | 5,221,415 | 586,301 | 44,982,016 | 69,309 |
|---|---|---|---|---|

c.

| 782,498 | 69,309 | 5,221,415 | 586,301 | 44,982,016 |
|---|---|---|---|---|

d.

| 5,221,415 | 44,982,016 | 782,498 | 586,301 | 69,309 |
|---|---|---|---|---|

**2. A candy bowl contains 3 chocolates, 7 peppermints, and 4 lollipops. Adeline randomly draws a piece of candy from the bowl. Which of the following statements is true?**

a. The probability of her drawing lollipop is $\frac{4}{7}$.
b. The probability of her drawing a chocolate is $\frac{3}{4}$.
c. The probability of her drawing a peppermint is $\frac{1}{2}$.
d. The individual probabilities of her drawing each type of candy from the bowl are all equal.

**3. Which of the following models represents a fraction equivalent to $\frac{2}{5}$?**

a.
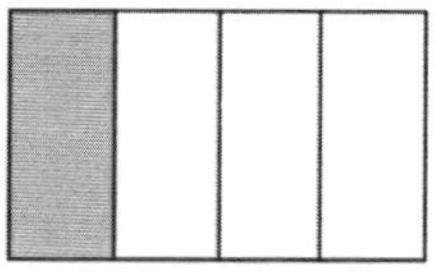

b.
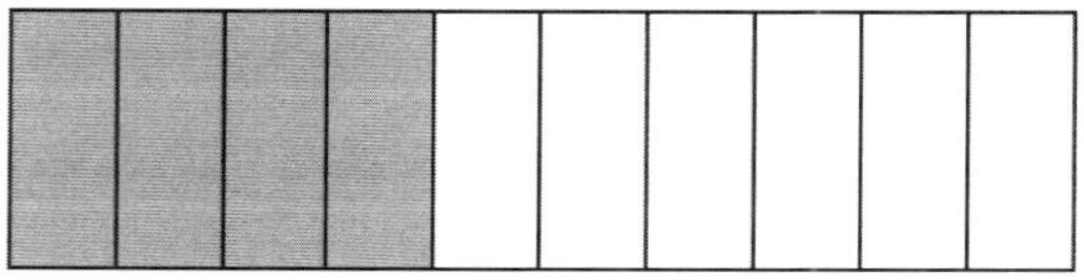

c.
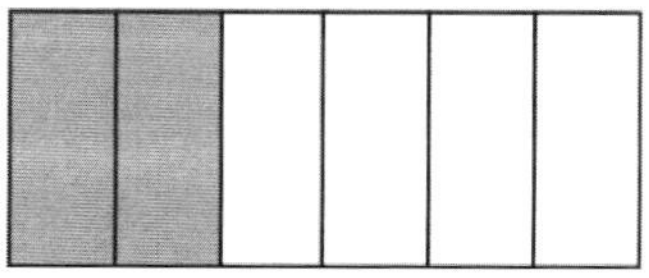

d.
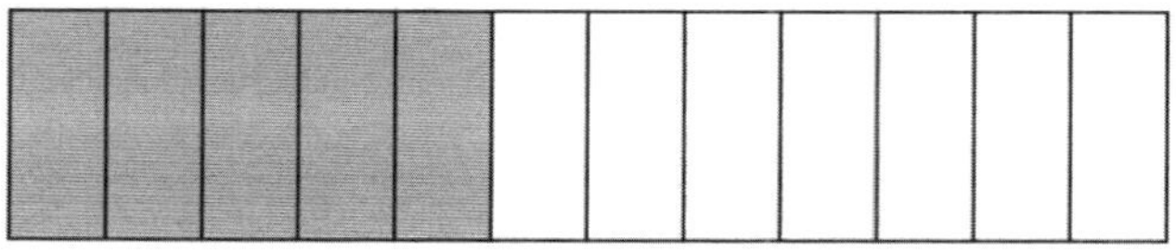

**4. Which fraction is represented by the diagram shown below?**

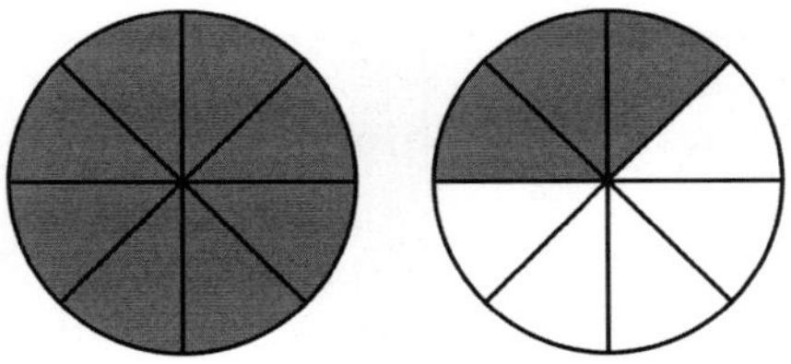

a. $1\frac{1}{8}$
b. $1\frac{1}{4}$
c. $1\frac{3}{8}$
d. $1\frac{1}{2}$

**5. Which of the following models represents a fraction less than the fraction shown below?**

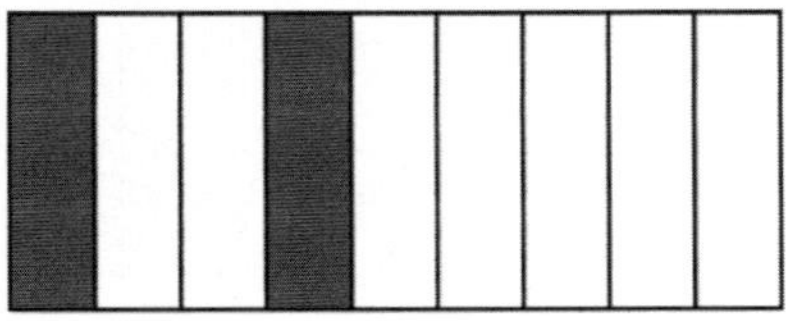

a. 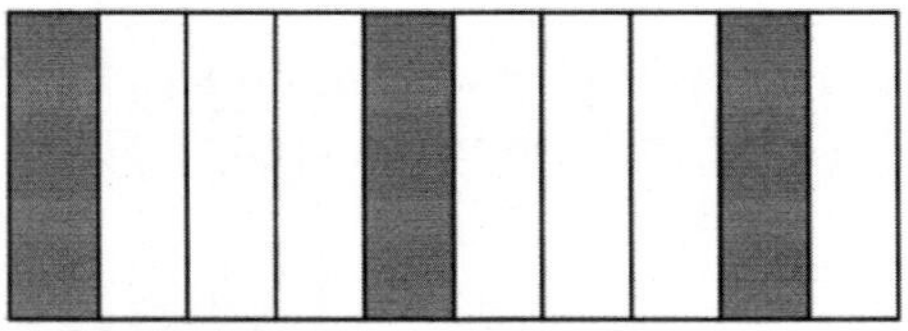

b. 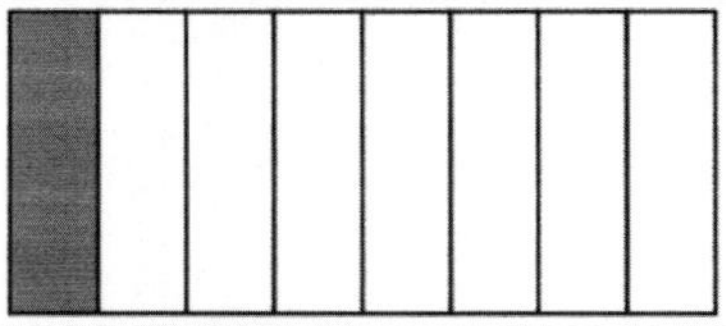

c. 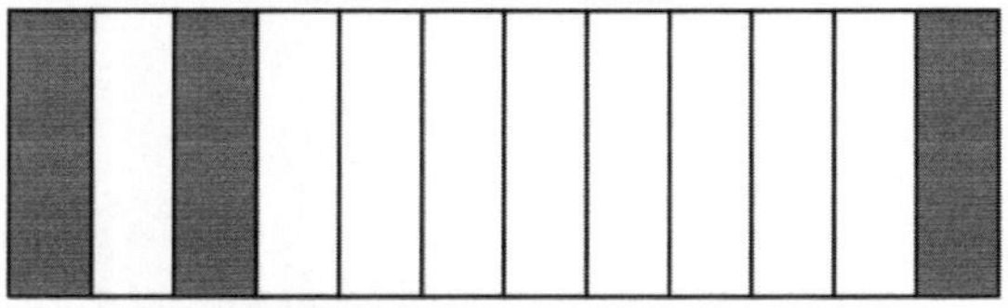

d. 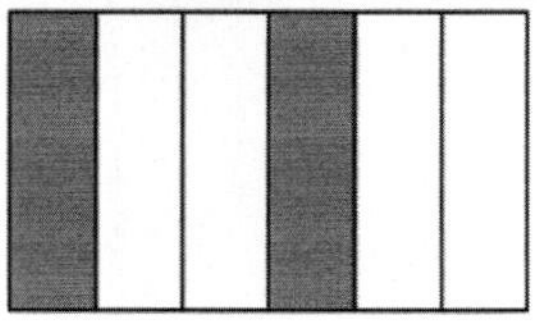

**6. Suppose each flat represents one unit. What number if represented below?**

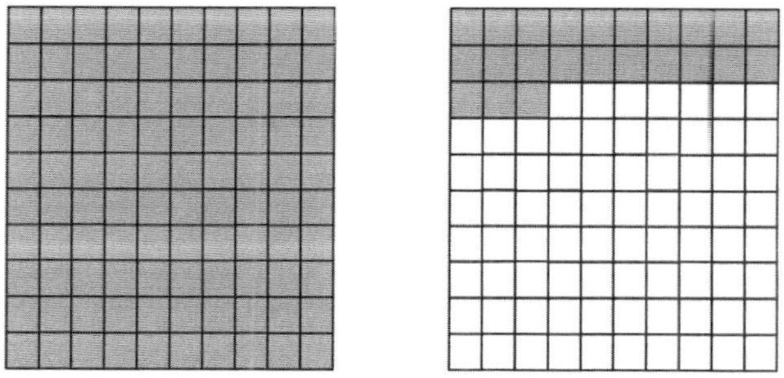

a. 12.3
b. 1.23
c. 0.123
d. 100.23

**7. Jasper collects 1,082 cans of food. He gives a certain number of cans to the first local charity he finds. He now has 602 cans of food. How many cans of food did he give to the first local charity?**

a. 430
b. 480
c. 682
d. 1,684

**8. Amanda creates the base of a picture frame, using 4.55 inches of red fabric and 6.25 inches of blue fabric. How many inches of fabric are used to create the base of the frame?**

a. 10.80 inches
b. 10.85 inches
c. 10.75 inches
d. 10.90 inches

**9. In multiplying 14 by 5, using the area model shown below, how many tens "rods" will be included in the product section of the model?**

a. 4
b. 5
c. 9
d. 10

**10. Which of the following number sentences is represented by the array shown below?**

X X X X X X
X X X X X X
X X X X X X
X X X X X X

a. $4 + 6 = 10$
b. $4 \times 6 = 24$
c. $24 - 6 = 18$
d. $24 \div 3 = 8$

**11. Which of the following number sentences is represented by the model shown below?**

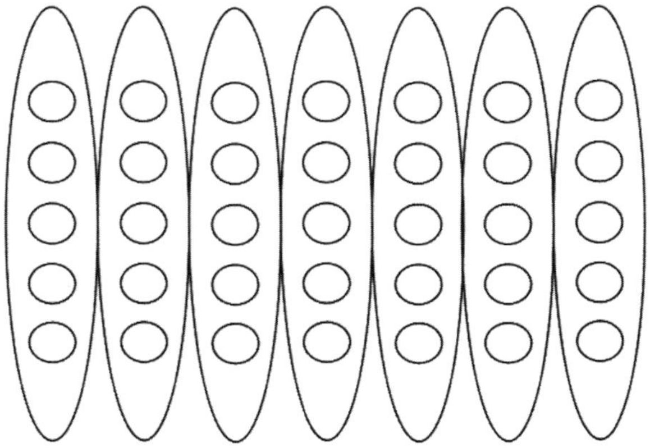

a. $7 \times 7 = 49$
b. $35 - 7 = 28$
c. $7 + 5 = 12$
d. $35 \div 7 = 5$

**12. Hannah ran 12 laps every day for 8 days. How many laps did she run in all?**

a. 108
b. 96
c. 84
d. 72

**13. Kevin approved 13 trees out of every group of trees he surveyed. He surveyed 15 groups of trees. How many trees did he approve?**

a. 155
b. 165
c. 195
d. 205

**14. Monique has $690 to spend on a 3-day trip. She plans to spend an equal amount of money per day. How many dollars can she spend per day?**

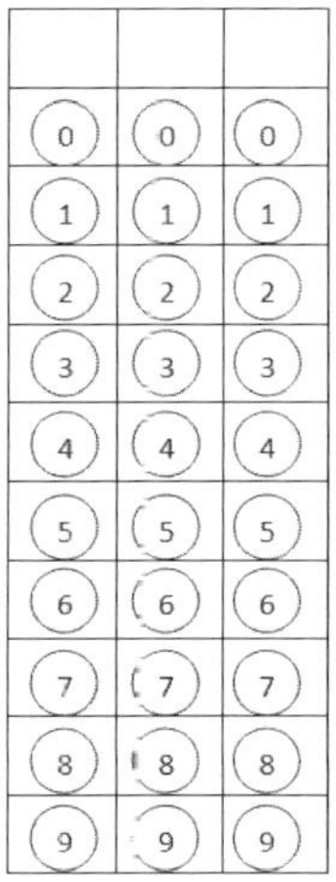

**15. Three friends sold cupcakes for a fundraiser. Eli sold 84 cupcakes, John sold 46 cupcakes, and Kim sold 72 cupcakes. Which of the following is the best estimate for the number of cupcakes the three friends sold in all?**

a. 180
b. 200
c. 210
d. 190

**16. Lynn has $316 to spend on groceries for the month. He plans to spend the same amount of money on groceries each week. Which of the following is the best estimate for the amount of money he can spend on groceries each week?**

a. $65
b. $75
c. $90
d. $95

**17. Carlisle charges $21.95 per hair cut and has completed 30 haircuts this week. Which of the following is the best approximation for the total charges for all haircuts?**

a. $450
b. $600
c. $750
d. $800

**18. Which of the following number sentences belongs in the fact family shown below?**

$7 \times 6 = 42$
$6 \times 7 = 42$
$42 \div 7 = 6$

a. $7 + 6 = 13$
b. $42 \div 6 = 7$
c. $42 + 7 = 49$
d. $42 - 6 = 36$

**19. What is the 11th number in the pattern shown below?**

10, 20, 30, 40, ...

a. 90
b. 100
c. 110
d. 120

**20. What is the 8th number in the pattern shown below?**

108, 96, 84, 72, ...

a. 48
b. 36
c. 24
d. 12

**21. Mrs. Thompson writes the number sentences shown below:**

$100 \times 13 = 1300$
$100 \times 14 = 1400$
$100 \times 15 = 1500$
$100 \times 24 =?$

**What is the product of the last number sentence?**

a. 2200
b. 2300
c. 2400
d. 2500

**22. The number of sit-ups Aisha has completed over a period of 3 days is shown in the table below.**

| Day | Number of Sit-ups |
|---|---|
| 1 | 35 |
| 2 | 70 |
| 3 | 105 |

**If this pattern continues, how many sit-ups will she have completed after 7 days?**

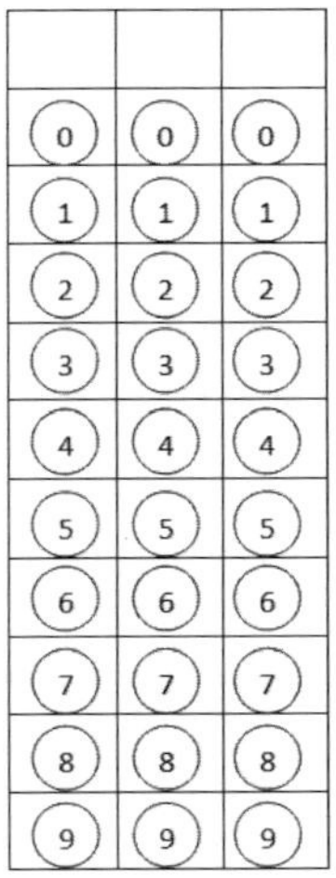

**23. What is the value of the underlined digit in 32$\underline{3}$,865,085?**

a. 300,000,000
b. 3,000,000
c. 300,000
d. 30,000

**24. Which of the following is largest?**

a. 0.55
b. 0.500
c. 0.505
d. 0.0555

**25. Which of the following pairs of lines are parallel?**

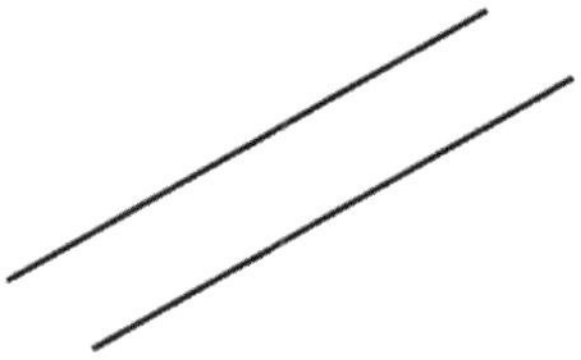
a.

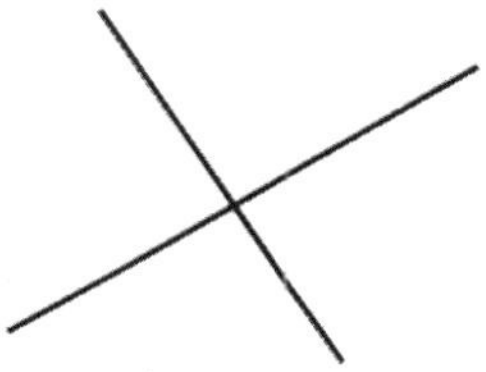
b.

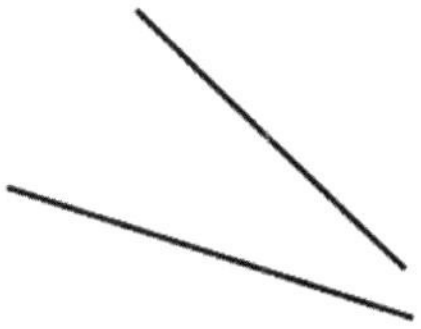
c.

d.

**26. Which of the following best describes the pair of lines shown below?**

a. perpendicular
b. parallel
c. intersecting and perpendicular
d. intersecting

**27. Which of the following figures has a square base and four triangular faces?**

a. cube
b. triangular prism
c. square pyramid
d. triangular pyramid

**28. Which of the following figures has 8 edges?**

a. triangular prism
b. cube
c. square pyramid
d. triangular pyramid

**29. Which shape has 5 sides?**

a. hexagon
b. pentagon
c. octagon
d. heptagon

**30. Which shape has 4 congruent sides and 4 right angles?**

a. square
b. rhombus
c. parallelogram
d. rectangle

**31. What number is represented by Point A, shown on the number line below?**

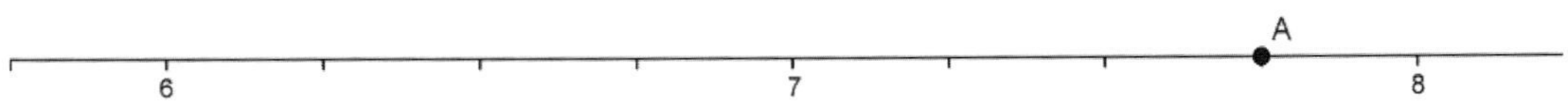


a. $7\frac{3}{8}$
b. $7\frac{1}{2}$
c. $7\frac{1}{4}$
d. $7\frac{3}{4}$

**32. Which point, on the number line below, represents $14\frac{2}{10}$?**

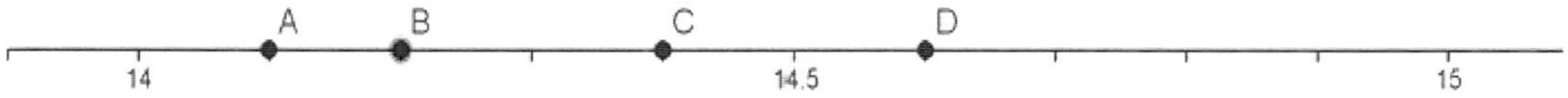


a. Point A
b. Point B
c. Point C
d. Point D

**33. A clock is shown below. Use the ruler from your mathematics chart to measure the width of the face of the clock, from one edge to the other. Which of the following best represents the width of the face?**

a. 4 centimeters
b. 7 centimeters
c. 9 centimeters
d. 11 centimeters

**34. Which of the following is the most reasonable estimate for the length of a book?**

a. $\frac{1}{2}$ meter
b. $11\frac{1}{2}$ inches
c. 8 millimeters
d. 2 yards

**35. Which of the following is the most reasonable estimate for the weight of a chair?**

a. 1 ton
b. 15 pounds
c. 3 kilograms
d. 6 grams

**36. Ana paints a line that is 14 feet, in length. How long is the painted line, in inches?**

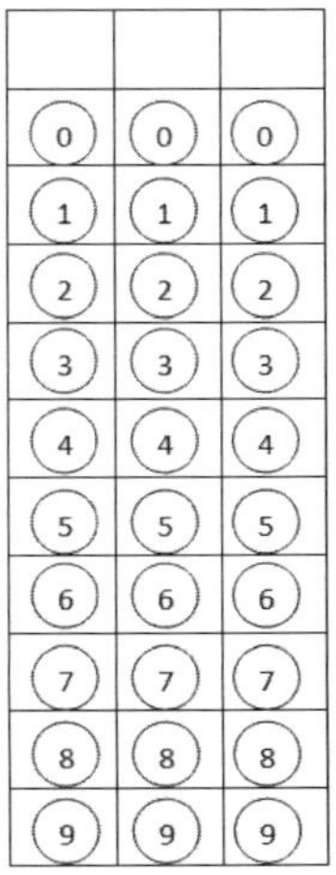

**37. Kevin's baby drinks 64 ounces of milk each day. How many pints of milk does his baby drink each day?**

a. 2
b. 4
c. 8
d. 12

**38. A sandbox has a length of 7.2 feet and a width of 3.98 feet. Which of the following best estimates the area of the sandbox?**

a. 21 $ft^2$
b. 32$ft^2$
c. 28 $ft^2$
d. 24 $ft^2$

**39. Which of the following units is used to measure mass?**

a. gram
b. inch
c. pound
d. centiliter

**40. Aubrey arrived at the party at the time shown on the clock below. It is now four-thirty. How much time has passed since she arrived at the party?**

| 2:15 |
|---|

a. 1 hour, 45 minutes
b. 2 hours, 5 minutes
c. 2 hours, 15 minutes
d. 2 hours, 30 minutes

**41. Kelsey surveys her classmates to determine their favorite types of music. The results are shown in the table below.**

| Type of Music | Number of Students |
|---|---|
| Classical | 7 |
| Rock | 8 |
| Blues | 11 |
| Country | 4 |
| Other | 10 |

**Which circle graph correctly represents the results?**

a.
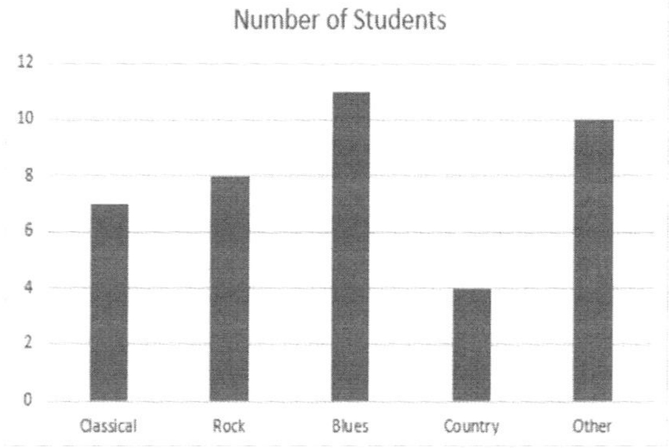


b.
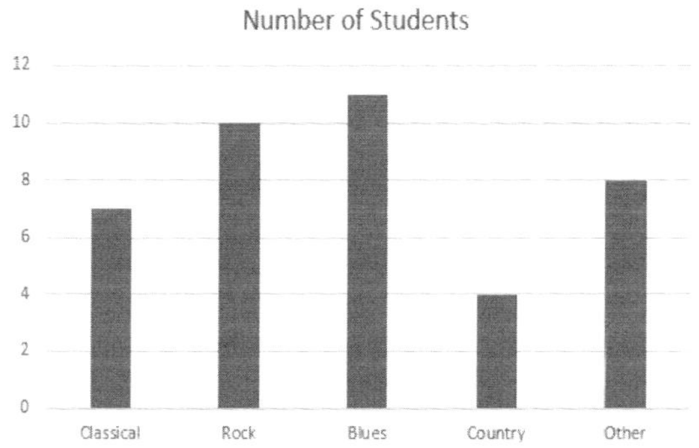


c.
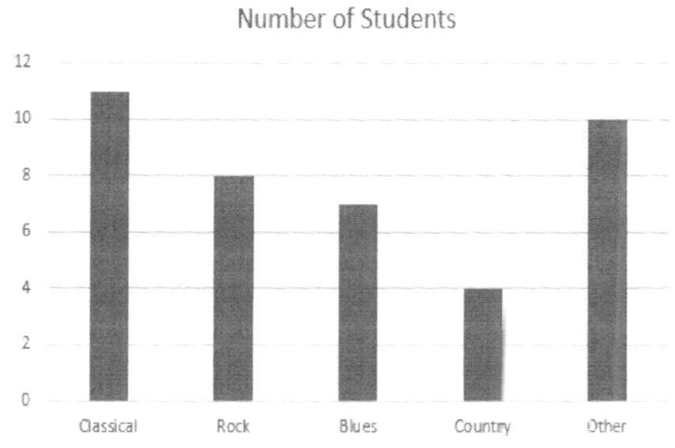


d.
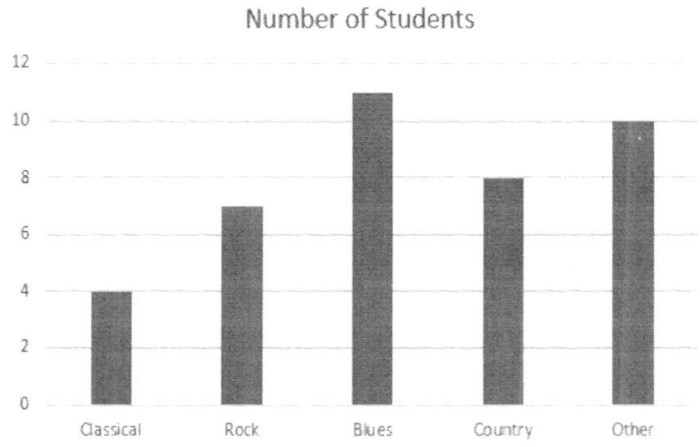

**42. The yearly earnings (in dollars) for a local business are represented by the line graph below.**

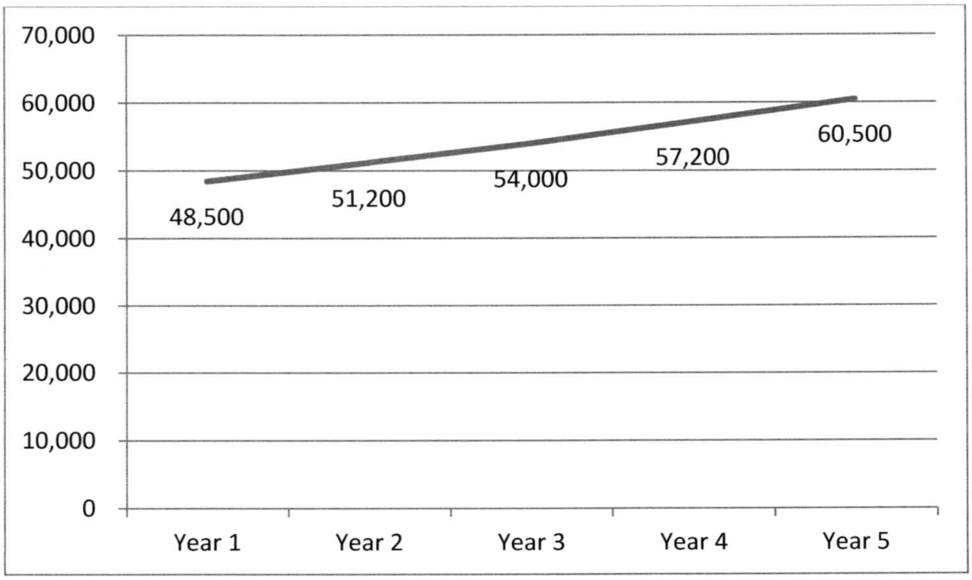


**Which of the following is the best estimate for the company's revenue in Year 8?**

a. $64,000
b. $69,000
c. $75,000
d. $78,000

**43. The bar graph below represents student preferences for different parks in Flagstaff, Arizona.**

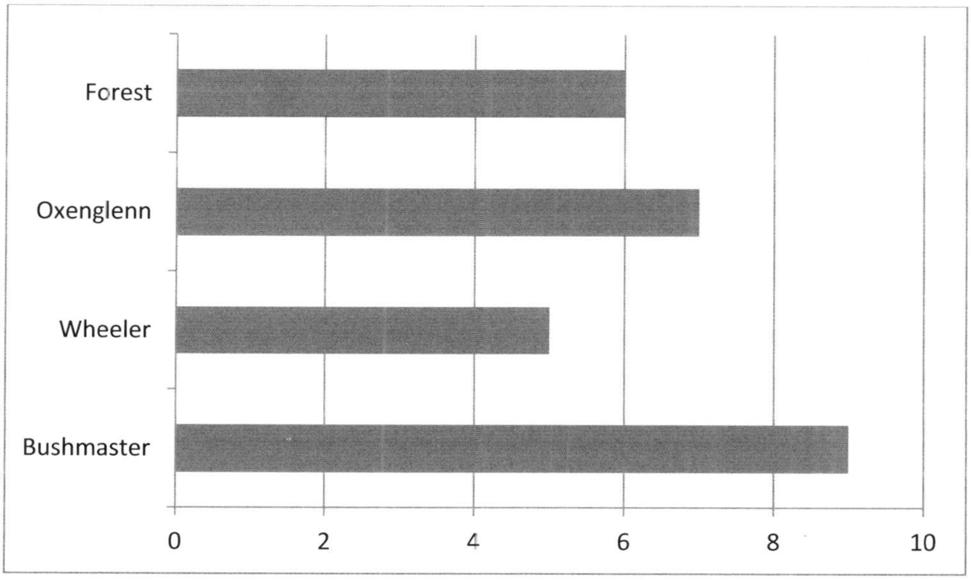


**Which park is preferred by the most students?**

a. Bushmaster
b. Wheeler
c. Oxenglenn
d. Forest

**44. A cafeteria offers 3 meats, 3 vegetables, 2 breads, and 2 desserts. How many possible meal combinations are there?**

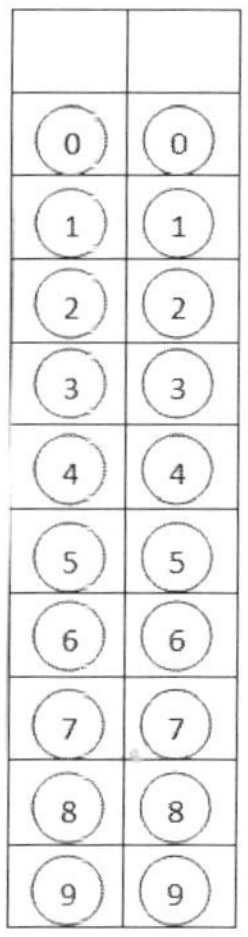

**45. What is the place value of the underlined digit in the following number: $706.39\underline{2}$**

a. Hundreds
b. Thousandths
c. Thousands
d. Hundredths

# Answer Key and Explanations for Mathematics Test #1

**1. A:** The number, 44,982,016, is the greatest because it has a value in the ten millions place. This number is followed by 5,221,415, which has a value in the millions place. The number, 782,498, is greater than 586,301 because the 7 in the hundred thousands of the first number is greater than the 5 in the hundred thousand place in the second number. The number, 69,309, is least because it only goes up to the ten thousands place value.

**2. C:** Since there are only 7 peppermint candies in the bowl and a total of 14 candies in the bowl, there are 7 out of 14 possibilities that she draws a peppermint candy. The probability of her drawing a peppermint is $\frac{7}{14}$. Once simplified, the probability is $\frac{1}{2}$. Answer choices A and B did not use the total amount of candies available in the bowl, so they are both incorrect. Answer choice D stated that each of the individual probabilities of selecting the candies would be the same. This is not true. Peppermint candy would have a probability of $\frac{1}{2}$. Chocolate candy would have a probability of $\frac{3}{14}$. Lollipops would have a probability of $\frac{2}{7}$. These are not equal.

**3. B:** The fraction, $\frac{2}{5}$, is equivalent to the fraction, $\frac{4}{10}$. The numerator and denominator of the given fraction are both multiplied by 2 to obtain the model for $\frac{4}{10}$; the fractions are proportional.

**4. C:** The diagram represents one whole, plus three-eighths of a second whole. Therefore, the diagram represents the fraction, $1\frac{3}{8}$.

**5. B:** The given model represents the fraction, $\frac{2}{9}$, which is approximately 0.22. The model for Choice B represents the fraction, $\frac{1}{8}$, which equals 0.125. This fraction is less than the given fraction. The fractions can also be compared by finding a least common denominator.

**6. B:** Since each flat represents one unit, the first flat represents 1, whereas the second flat represents $\frac{23}{100}$, or 0.23. Together, the diagram represents the number, 1.23.

**7. B:** In order to find the number of cans of food he gave to the first charity, the number of cans of food he has left needs to be subtracted from the number of cans he collected; $1{,}082 - 602 = 480$.

**8. A:** The sum of the two decimals is 10.80; the decimals are added just like whole numbers are, while aligning the decimal point.

**9. B:** Five tens "rods" will fit in the product section of the model. The rods will be placed to the right of the rod, shown in the diagram, underneath the five ones "units" at the top of the model.

**10. B:** The array represents the multiplication sentence, $4 \times 6 = 24$. Note. There are 4 rows and 6 x's in each row.

**11. D:** The model shows 35 counters, divided into 7 groups, with 5 counters in each group. Therefore, the model represents the number sentence, $35 \div 7 = 5$.

**12. B:** She runs $12 \times 8$ laps in all, or 96 laps.

**13. C:** Since he approved 13 trees out of every group of trees and surveyed 15 groups, he approved $13 \times 15$ trees, or 195 trees.

14. The correct answer is 230: In order to find the amount of money she can spend each day, 690 should be divided by 3; $690 \div 3 = 230$. Thus, she can spend 230 dollars per day.

**15. B:** The number of cupcakes sold can be rounded as follows: 80 cupcakes, 50 cupcakes, and 70 cupcakes, which sum to 200. Therefore, the best estimate for the number of cupcakes sold is 200 cupcakes.

**16. B:** The amount of money Lynn has to spend on groceries for the month can be rounded to \$300; $300 \div 4 = 75$. Thus, the best estimate for the amount of money he can spend per week is \$75.

**17. B:** The amount of money Carlisle charges per hair cut can be rounded to \$20; $20 \times 30 = 600$. Thus, his total charges are approximately \$600.

**18. B:** The missing number sentence in the fact family is the other division number sentence, which reads:$42 \div 6 = 7$.

**19. C:** The value of each number in the pattern is a multiple of 10. Therefore, the $11^{th}$ number represents the value of the product of 11 and 10; $11 \times 10 = 110$.

**20. C:** The pattern represents a sequence that subtracts 12 from each previous term. The first number in the pattern represents the product of 9 and 12; $9 \times 12 = 108$. The eighth number in the pattern is 7 numbers away from the first number of 108. Thus, the eighth number represents the product of 2 and 12, which equals 24. The eighth number in the pattern is 24. The eighth number in the pattern can also be found by subtracting 12 from the last given number in the pattern 4 more times; $72 - 12 = 60$; $60 - 12 = 48$; $48 - 12 = 36$; $36 - 12 = 24$.

**21. C:** As noted in the pattern, the product of 100 and 24 can be found by multiplying 24 by 1 and adding two zeros to the product. Thus, the product of 100 and 24 is 2400.

**22. 245.** Since she completes 35 each day, she has completed $35 \times 7$ situps after 7 days; $35 \times 7 = 245$.

**23. B:** The place value is assigned by the position of the digit. The places from left to right are ones, tens, hundreds, thousands, ten-thousands, etc. Since the digit 3 is in the seventh place from the left, it is in the millions place. The value of the digit is 3 X 1,000,000, which is 3,000,000.

**24. A:** When comparing decimals, compare them one decimal place at a time. First compare the part before the decimal point; whichever has the largest whole part is largest. If the whole parts are equal, compare the tenths place, the place just after the decimal point. If the digits in the tenths place are the same, compare the hundredths place, the second place after the decimal point, and so on. In this case, all the decimals have a zero before the decimal point, so we'll start by comparing the tenths place. 0.55, 0.500, and 0.505 all have a 5 in the tenths place, while 0.0555 has a zero in the tenths place. So, 0.55, 0.500, and 0.505 are larger than 0.0555. Now, compare the hundredths place of the remaining choices, discarding the 0.0555 that we now know is smallest. 0.55 has a 5 in the hundredths place, while 0.500 and 0.505 both have zeroes. So, 0.55 is the largest of the choices.

**25. A:** Parallel lines are lines that do not intersect and are the same distance apart.

**26. D:** The lines shown are intersecting, but they are not perpendicular; they do not form a right angle.

**27. C:** A square pyramid has a square base and four triangular faces.

**28. C:** A square pyramid has four edges on the base and one edge, coming from each vertex of the base.

**29. B:** A pentagon has 5 sides.

**30. A:** A square has four congruent sides and four right angles. A rhombus has four congruent sides, but is not required to have four right angles.

**31. D:** The number line is divided into fourths. Thus, between the whole numbers, 7 and 8, lie the fractions, $7\frac{1}{4}$, $7\frac{2}{4}$, and $7\frac{3}{4}$. Point A represents the fraction, $7\frac{3}{4}$.

**32. B:** The number line is divided into tenths. Thus, between the whole numbers, 14 and 15, lie the fractions, $14\frac{1}{10}$, $14\frac{2}{10}$ ... $14\frac{9}{10}$. The fraction, $14\frac{2}{10}$, lies two-tenths, or two intervals, to the right of 14.

**33. B:** The width of the face is approximately 7 cm, as measured from one edge of the face of the clock to the other edge.

**34. B:** The length of a book is possibly $11\frac{1}{2}$ inches; one-half of a meter is 50 centimeters, which would be almost 2 feet; 8 millimeters is less than 1 centimeter; and 2 yards is equal to 6 feet. None of the other measurements are likely for a book length.

**35. B:** A chair may possibly weigh 15 pounds; 1 ton is equal to 2,000 pounds; 3 kilograms is equal to 3,000 grams; and 6 grams is the weight of about 12 pencils.

**36. 168:** The length of the painted line, in inches, is equal to the product of 14 and 12; $14 \times 12 = 168$. Thus, the painted line is 168 inches, in length.

**37. B:** There are 8 ounces in each cup of milk, so 64 ounces is equal to 8 cups. Since there are 2 cups in a pint, there are 8 cups in 4 pints. Thus, his baby drinks 4 pints of milk each day.

**38. C:** The measurements of the sandbox can be rounded to 7 feet and 4 feet. The area of the sandbox is equal to the product of the measurements of the length and width of the box. Thus, the area is approximately $7 \times 4$, or 28 squared feet.

**39. A:** Mass can be measured in grams, whereas weight can be measured in pounds. Inches measure length, and centiliters measure capacity.

**40. C:** From 2:15 to 4:15, two hours have passed. From 4:15 to 4:30, 15 additional minutes have passed. Therefore, the elapsed time is 2 hours, 15 minutes.

**41. A:** The total number of students surveyed is 40, but the only information needed to make a bar graph is the number of students that like each music category. Thus, the classical category bar should be at 7 on the y-axis. The rock category bar should be at 8. The blues category bar should be at 11. The country category bar should be at 4, and the other category bar should be at 10. The bar graph, shown for Choice A, correctly represents these amounts.

**42. B:** The revenue, from year to year, increases by approximately $3,000. Thus, a good estimate for Year 6 would be $63,500, while a good estimate for Years 7 and 8 would be $66,500 and $69,500. The estimate for Choice B, of $69,000, is a good estimate for Year 8. Note. Some yearly changes were less than $3,000, while other yearly changes were more than $3,000.

**43. A:** There were 9 students who preferred Bushmaster Park; 9 students is more than any other number of students displayed on the bar graph.

**44. 36.** The possible meal combinations are equal to the product of the number of different types of each part of the meal. Thus, the possible meal combinations are equal to $3 \times 3 \times 2 \times 2$, or 36.

**45. B:** The first place to the right of the decimal point is the tenths place, the second place is the hundredths place, and the third place is the thousandths place. Since the underlined digit is three places to the right of the decimal point, it is in the thousandths place. It is important to distinguish between the thousands place and the thousandths place. The thousands place is four places to the left of the decimal point.

# Mathematics Practice Test #2

**1. The number of miles driven per year by five sales professionals is listed below.**

| 119,802 | 124,321 | 126,094 | 124,283 | 118,002 |
|---|---|---|---|---|

**Which of the following lists the number of miles driven per year, in order from least to greatest, when reading from left to right?**

a.

| 118,002 | 119,802 | 124,283 | 124,321 | 126,094 |
|---|---|---|---|---|

b.

| 124,283 | 124,321 | 118,002 | 119,802 | 126,094 |
|---|---|---|---|---|

c.

| 126,094 | 124,283 | 124,321 | 118,002 | 119,802 |
|---|---|---|---|---|

d.

| 119,802 | 124,283 | 124,321 | 118,002 | 126,094 |
|---|---|---|---|---|

**2. Which of the following numbers is less than 802,430,298?**

a. 802,428,986
b. 802,460,999
c. 802,431,304
d. 802,539,002

**3. What is the value of the underlined digit in <u>5</u>19,812,432?**

a. 500,000,000
b. 5,000,000
c. 500,000
d. 50,000

**4. Which of the following sets represents a fraction equivalent to $\frac{8}{12}$?**

a. 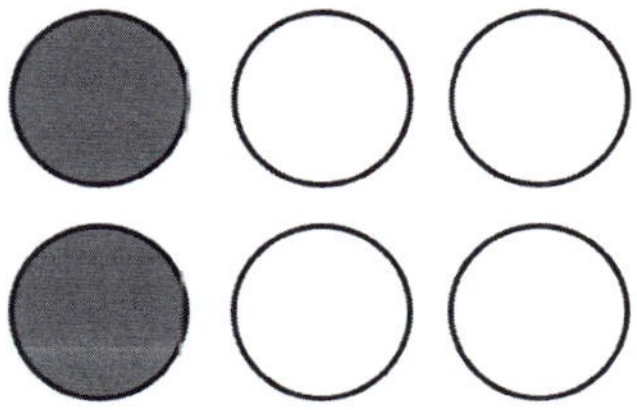

b. 

c. 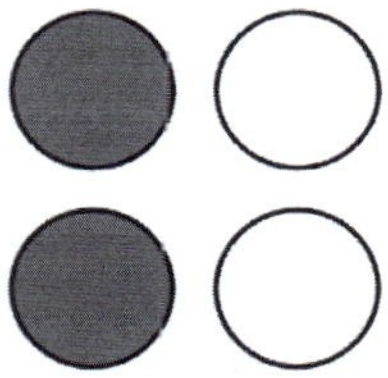

d. 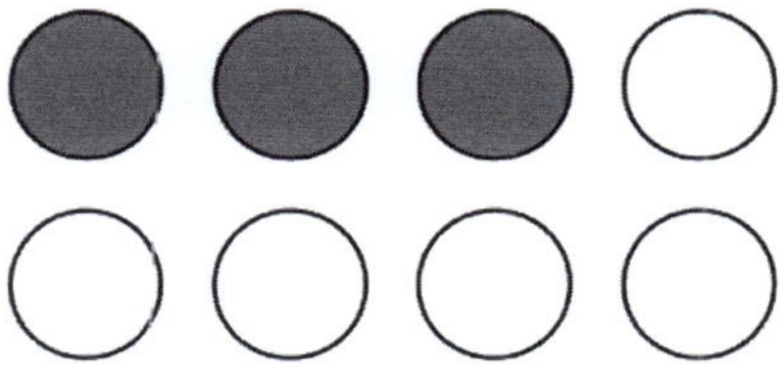

**5. Which of the following models represents a fraction equal to the fraction shown below?**

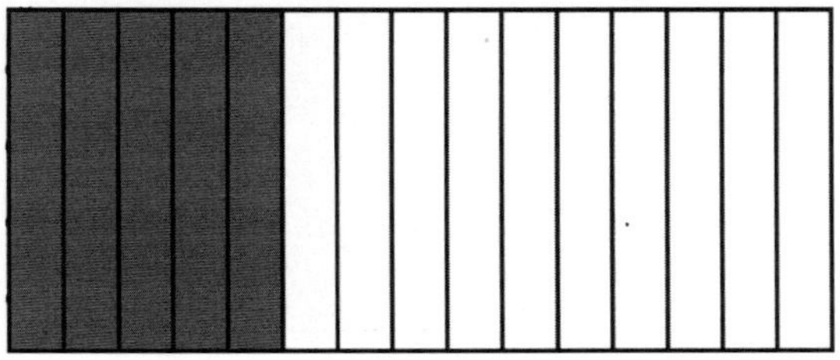

a. 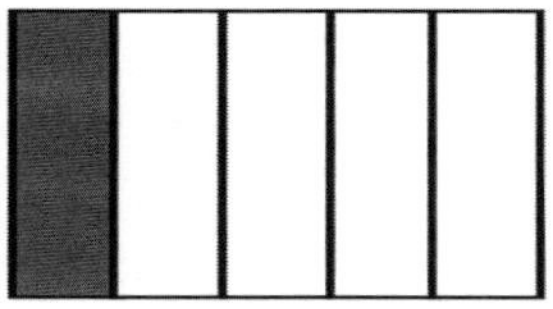

b. 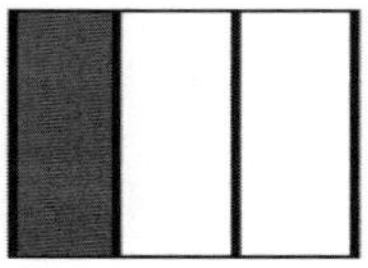

c. 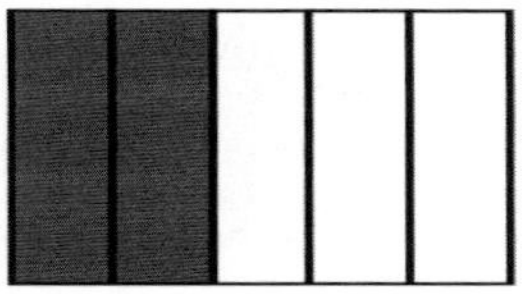

d. 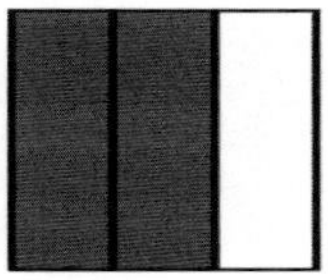

**6. Which fraction is represented by the diagram shown below?**

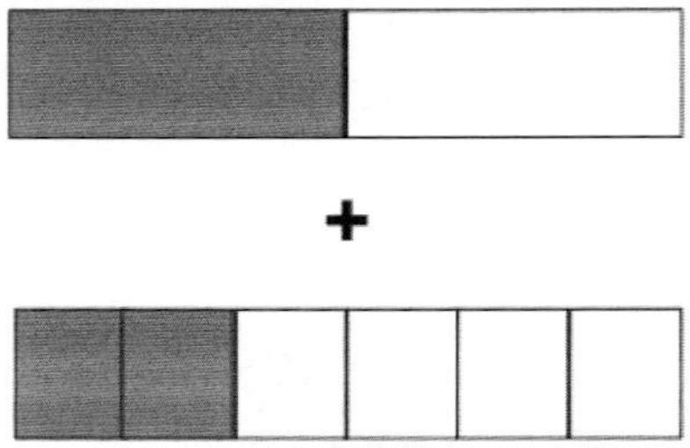

a. $\frac{1}{2}$
b. $\frac{1}{3}$
c. $\frac{3}{8}$
d. $\frac{5}{6}$

**7. How much of the flat shown below is shaded?**

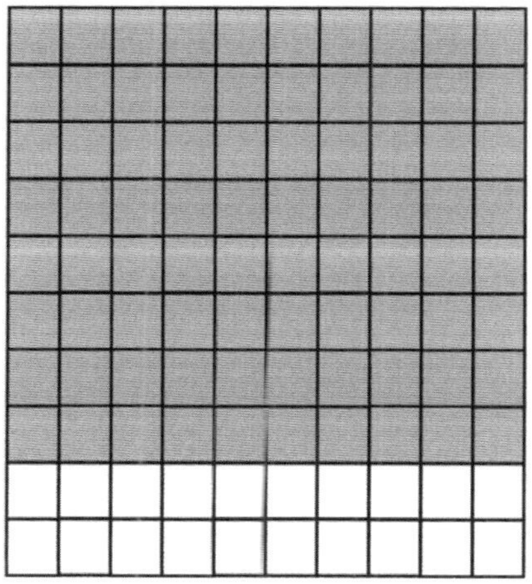

a. $\frac{3}{5}$
b. $\frac{3}{4}$
c. $\frac{4}{5}$
d. $\frac{2}{3}$

**8. Martin saved $156 in September, $173 in October, and $219 in November. How much money did he save during the three months?**

a. $538
b. $569
c. $548
d. $576

**9. Andrea pays $120 more in rent per month this year than she did last year. She pays $763 per month this year. How much did she pay per month last year?**

a. $663
b. $643
c. $863
d. $883

**10. Which sum is represented by the diagram shown below?**

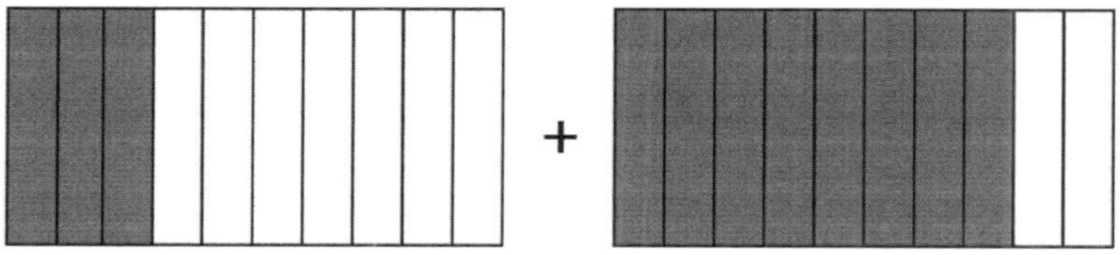

a. 1.08
b. 1.09
c. 1.10
d. 1.11

**11. Kelsey multiplies 18 by 6, using the area model shown below. How many unit "squares" will she include in the product section of the model?**

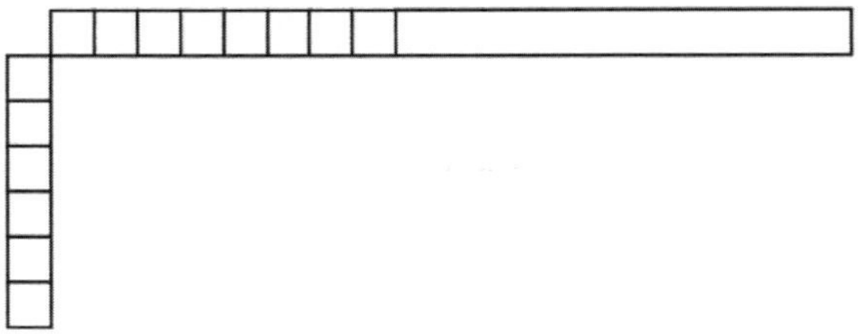

a. 40
b. 46
c. 48
d. 54

**12. Which fact is represented by the array shown below?**

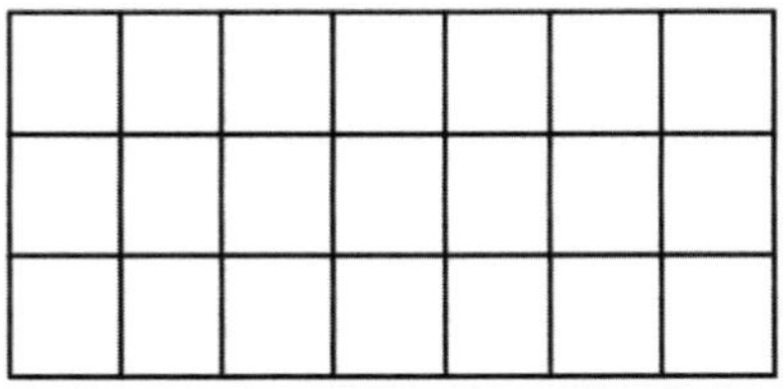

a. $3 + 7 = 10$
b. $21 - 7 = 14$
c. $3 \times 7 = 21$
d. $10 + 7 = 17$

**13. Eli has 42 crayons and plans to give the same number of crayons to each of his 6 friends. Which number sentence can be used to find the number of crayons he will give to each friend?**

a. $42 - 6 = 36$
b. $42 \div 6 = 7$
c. $42 \times 6 = 252$
d. $42 + 6 = 48$

**14. Alex buys 3 gallons of milk each week. How many gallons of milk does he buy in 12 weeks?**

a. 18
b. 24
c. 36
d. 48

**15. A candle-making shop sold 18 candles on Friday, 37 candles on Saturday, and 23 candles on Sunday. Which of the following is the best estimate for the number of candles sold during the three days?**

a. 60
b. 70
c. 80
d. 90

**16. Isabelle must drive 1,482 miles. She plans to drive approximately the same number of miles per day over the period of 5 days. Which of the following is the best approximation for the number of miles she will drive per day?**

a. 250
b. 300
c. 350
d. 400

**17. A consultant earned $17,850 over the course of 6 months. Which of the following is the best approximation for the amount of money the consultant earned each month?**

a. $2,500
b. $3,000
c. $3,500
d. $4,000

**18. Mr. Jacobsen writes the number sentences shown below:**

$8 \times 9 = 72$
$9 \times 8 = 72$
$72 \div 9 = 8$

**What is the fourth number sentence of this fact family?**

a. $8 + 9 = 17$
b. $72 - 8 = 64$
c. $72 \div 8 = 9$
d. $17 - 9 = 8$

**19. What is the 14th number in the pattern shown below?**

100, 200, 300, 400, ...

a. 1,200
b. 1,300
c. 1,400
d. 1,500

**20. What is the 12th number in the pattern shown below?**

11, 22, 33, 44, ...

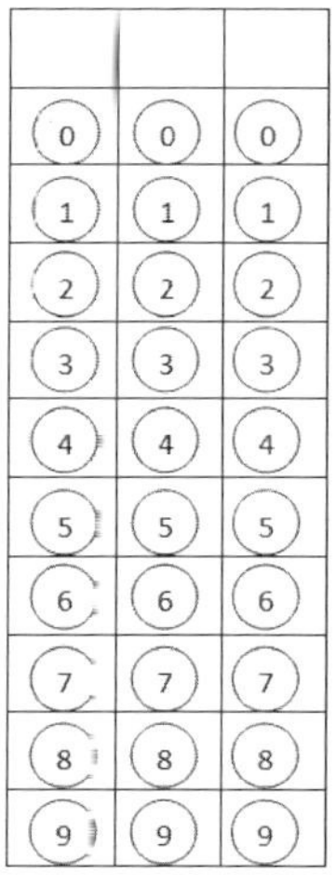

**21. The number of miles Brad has driven over a period of 3 days is shown in the table below.**

| Day | Number of Miles |
|---|---|
| 1 | 275 |
| 2 | 550 |
| 3 | 825 |

**If this pattern continues, how many miles will he have driven after 8 days?**

a. 2,000
b. 2,025
c. 2,075
d. 2,200

**22. Andrew displays the following sets of data to his colleagues. Which of the following represents the relationship between the first and second columns of data?**

| | |
|---|---|
| 4 | 16 |
| 7 | 19 |
| 12 | 24 |
| 14 | 26 |
| 19 | 31 |

a. The values in the second column are 12 more than the values in the first column.
b. The values in the first column are one-fourth of the values in the second column.
c. The values in the first column are 11 fewer than the values in the second column.
d. The values in the second column are 3 more than the values in the first column.

**23. A local citizen represents the total amount she has donated to a charity over the course of five years, using the table shown below.**

| **Year** | 1 | 2 | 3 | 4 | 5 |
|---|---|---|---|---|---|
| **Amount Donated** | $250 | $550 | $850 | $1,150 | $1,450 |

**If this pattern continues, how much will she have donated after 10 years?**

a. $2,850
b. $2,900
c. $2,950
d. $3,000

**24. How can the fraction $\frac{12}{4}$ be represented as a division problem?**

a. $4 \div 12$
b.

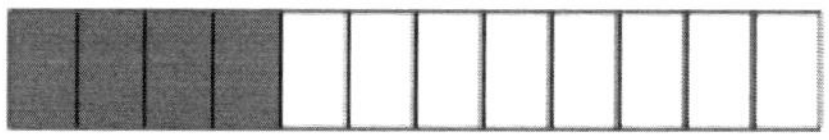

c. $12 \div 4$
d.

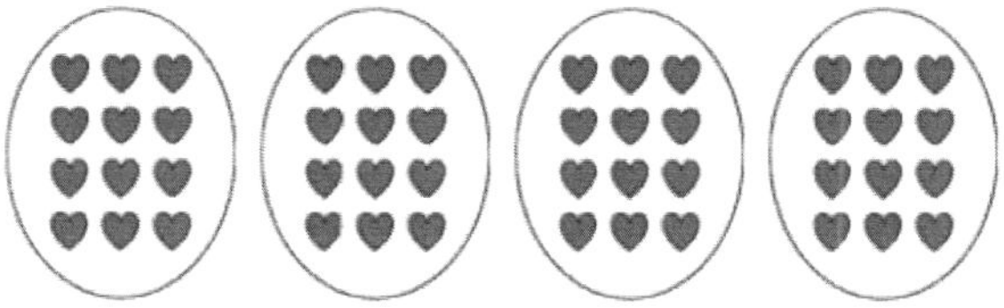

**25. What is the place value of the underlined digit in the following number: $314.\underline{6}57$**

a. Tens
b. Hundredths
c. Ones
d. Tenths

**26.Which of the following most accurately describes the pair of lines shown below?**

a. Lines that do not intersect
b. Lines that intersect
c. Lines that do not intersect and remain the same distance apart
d. Lines that are perpendicular

**27. Which of the following represents perpendicular lines?**

a. 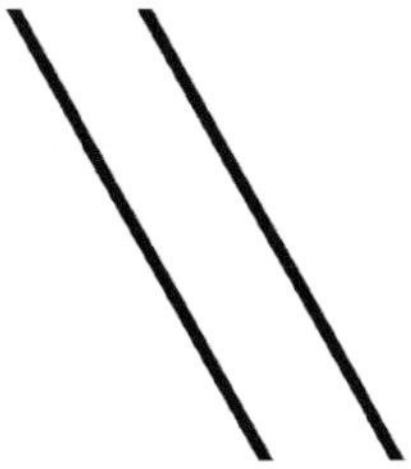

b. 

c. 

d. 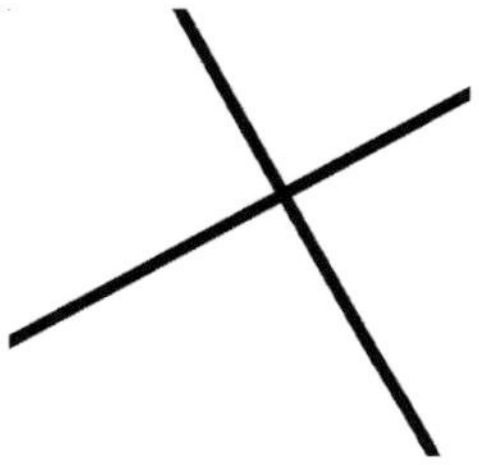

**28. Which of the following figures has 5 vertices?**

a. triangular prism
b. square pyramid
c. rectangular prism
d. triangular pyramid

**29. Which of the following figures has 4 faces?**

a. cube
b. triangular pyramid
c. triangular prism
d. square pyramid

**30. Which of the following figures has more than 6 vertices?**

a. triangular prism
b. cube
c. triangular pyramid
d. square pyramid

**31. Which of the following shapes has four sides and only one set of parallel sides?**

a. square
b. parallelogram
c. trapezoid
d. rectangle

**32. A bag contains 3 red cards, 7 blue cards, 9 green cards, and 6 yellow cards. Robert randomly draws a card from the bag. Which of the following represents the probability that Robert selects a blue card?**

a. $\frac{7}{9}$
b. $\frac{7}{12}$
c. $\frac{7}{15}$
d. $\frac{7}{25}$

**33. What decimal is represented by Point P, shown on the number line below?**

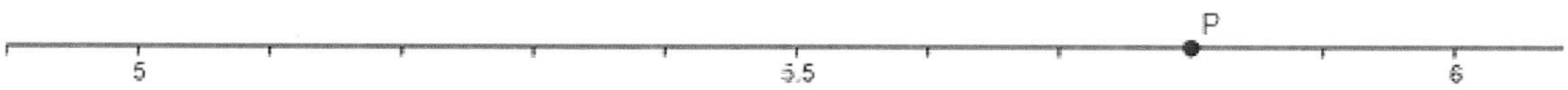


a. 5.6
b. 5.7
c. 5.8
d. 5.9

**34. What fraction is represented by Point A, shown on the number line below?**

a. $3\frac{1}{4}$
b. $3\frac{2}{3}$
c. $3\frac{1}{2}$
d. $3\frac{3}{4}$

35. **A scaled drawing of a barn is shown below. Use the ruler from your mathematics chart to measure the length of the barn. Which of the following best represents the length of the barn, in the drawing?**

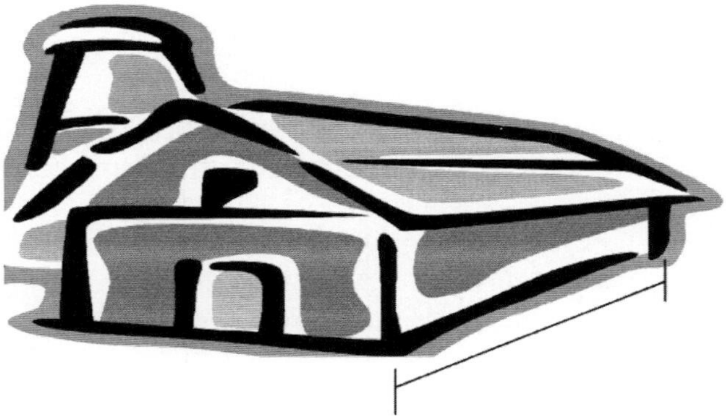

a. 1.5 inches
b. 2 inches
c. 2.5 inches
d. 3 inches

36. **Which of the following is the most reasonable estimate for the mass of a semi-truck?**

a. 8.164 milligrams
b. 8.164 grams
c. 8,164 kilograms
d. 8,164 centigrams

37. **Which of the following is the most reasonable estimate for the weight of a pencil?**

a. 12 ounces
b. 0.5 ounces
c. 2 pounds
d. 0.5 pounds

38. **Hannah weighs approximately 27 pounds. What is her approximate weight, in ounces?**

a. 432 ounces
b. 378 ounces
c. 324 ounces
d. 438 ounces

**39. Jamal drinks 2 quarts of water per day. How many cups of water does he drink?**

| | |
|---|---|
| 0 | 0 |
| 1 | 1 |
| 2 | 2 |
| 3 | 3 |
| 4 | 4 |
| 5 | 5 |
| 6 | 6 |
| 7 | 7 |
| 8 | 8 |
| 9 | 9 |

**40. A thank you card has a length of 4.12 inches and a width of 5.80 inches. Which of the following is the best estimate for the area of the card?**

a. 20 $in^2$
b. 24 $in^2$
c. 30 $in^2$
d. 27 $in^2$

**41. Elaine left for work at the time shown on the clock below. It is now 9:25. How much time has passed, since she left for work?**

| **7:35** |
|---|

a. 1 hour, 35 minutes
b. 1 hour, 40 minutes
c. 1 hour, 45 minutes
d. 1 hour, 50 minutes

**42. Anand surveys his classmates to determine their favorite season of the year. The results are shown in the table below.**

| Season | Number of Students |
|---|---|
| Fall | 7 |
| Winter | 3 |
| Spring | 12 |
| Summer | 18 |

Which bar graph correctly represents the results?

a.

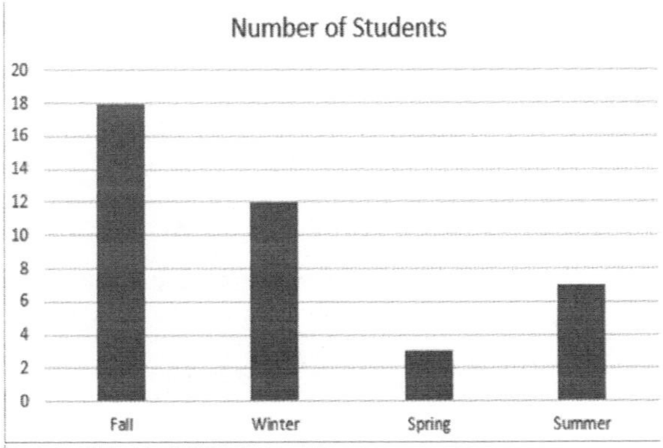


b.

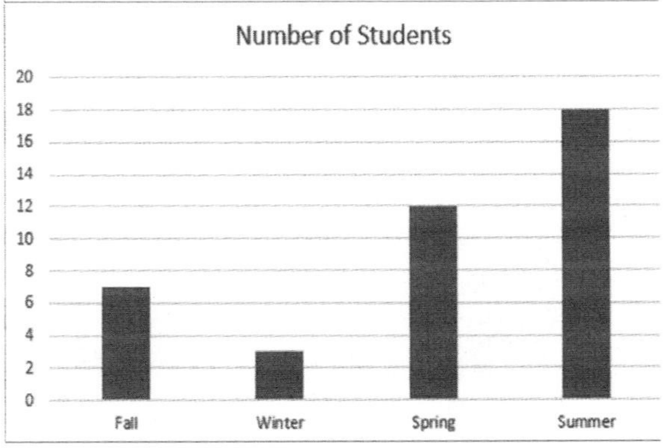


c.

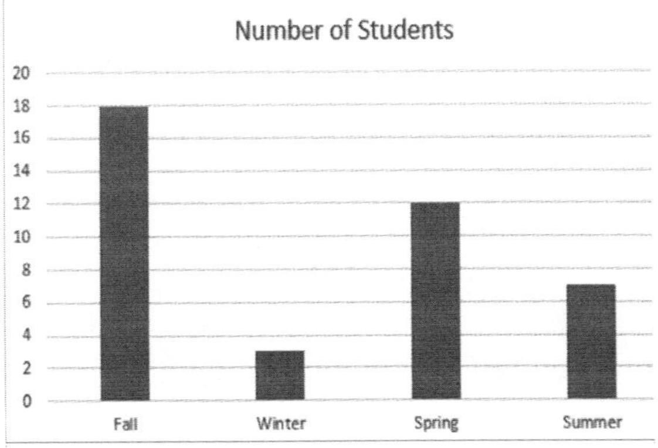


d.

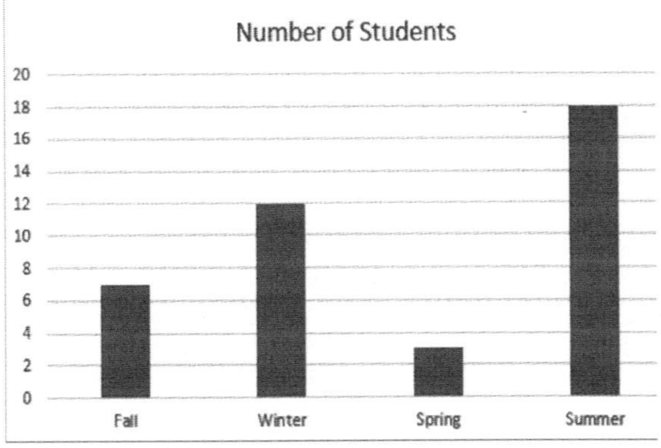

**43. The number of cars sold per year, by a local dealership, is represented by the line graph below.**

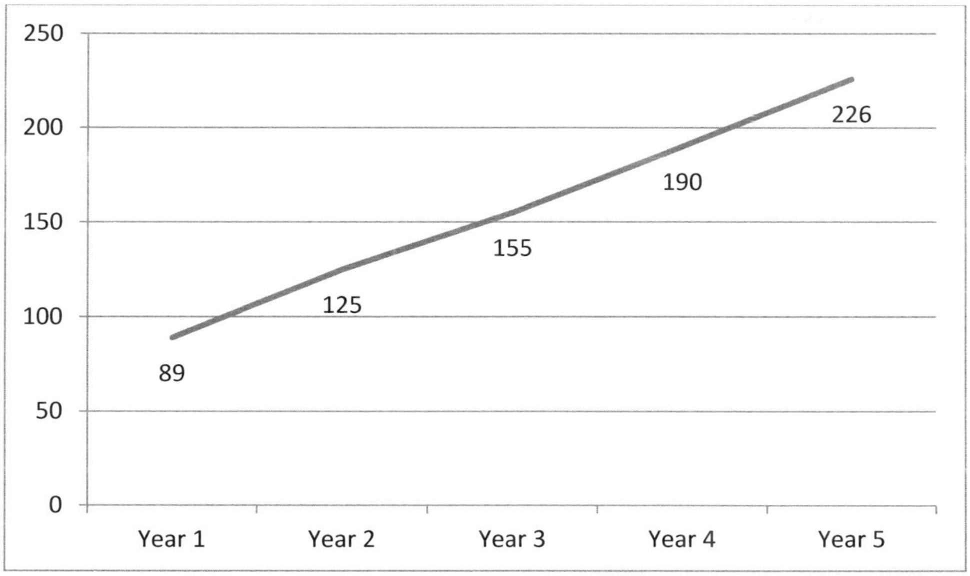


**Which of the following is the best estimate for the number of cars the dealership will sell in Year 9?**

a. 306
b. 366
c. 426
d. 506

**44. The bar graph below represents teacher preferences for different vacation states.**

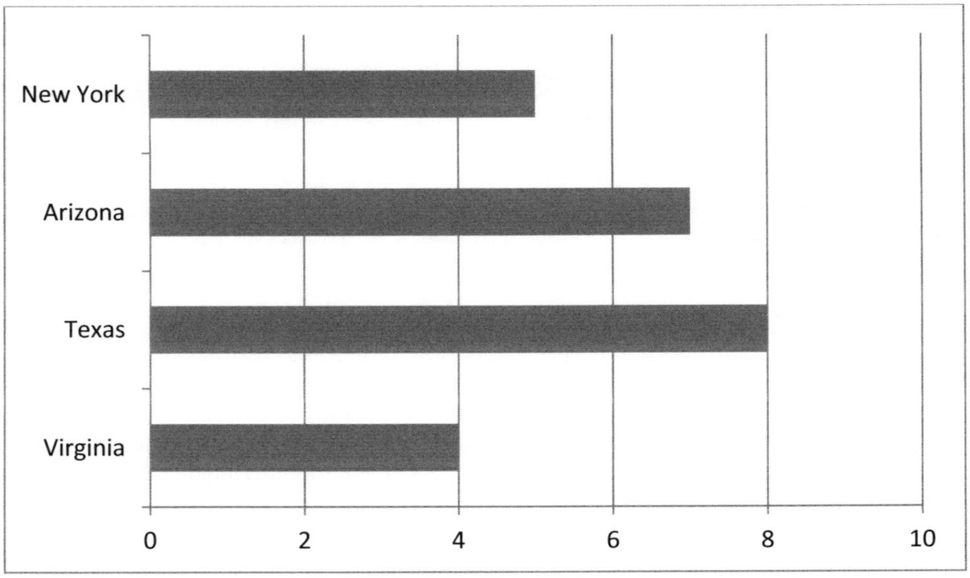


**Which state was preferred by the fewest number of teachers?**

a. Virginia
b. Arizona
c. Texas
d. New York

**45. Alana can choose from 2 shirts, 2 pairs of jeans, 3 pairs of socks, and 2 pairs of shoes. How many possible outfit combinations can she make?**

| | |
|---|---|
| 0 | 0 |
| 1 | 1 |
| 2 | 2 |
| 3 | 3 |
| 4 | 4 |
| 5 | 5 |
| 6 | 6 |
| 7 | 7 |
| 8 | 8 |
| 9 | 9 |

# Answer Key and Explanations for Mathematics Test #2

**1. A:** The numbers can first be compared by examining the value of the number in the hundred thousands place. All have a 1 in this place, so move to the ten thousands place. 118,002 and 119,802 are less than 124,283, 124,321, and 126,094; 118,002 is less than 119,802 because the 8 in the thousands place, in 118,002, is less than the 9 in the thousands place, in 119,802; 24,283 is less than 124,321 because the 2 in the hundreds place, in 124,283, is less than the 3 in the hundreds place, in 124,321; 126,094 has the greatest value.

**2. A:** The number, 802,428,986, is less than 802,430,298 because the 2 in the ten thousands place, in 802,428,986, is less than the 3 in the ten thousands place, in 802,430,298.

**3. A:** The place value is assigned by the position of the digit. The places from left to right are ones, tens, hundreds, thousands, ten-thousands, etc. Since the digit 5 is in the ninth place from the left, it is in the hundred millions place. The value of the digit is 5 X 100,000,000, which is 500,000,000.

**4. B:** The fraction, $\frac{8}{12}$, is equivalent to the fraction, $\frac{2}{3}$. The numerator and denominator of the given fraction are both divided by 4 to obtain the model for $\frac{2}{3}$; the fractions are proportional.

**5. B:** The fraction, $\frac{5}{15}$, is equivalent to the fraction, $\frac{1}{3}$. The numerator and denominator of the given fraction are both divided by 5 to obtain the model for $\frac{1}{3}$; the fractions are proportional.

**6. D:** The first diagram represents $\frac{1}{2}$, while the second diagram represents $\frac{2}{6}$. The model has an addition sign between the two fractions, so the problem is $\frac{1}{2}+\frac{2}{6}$. In order to add fractions, the denominators must be the same. The least common denominator of the two fractions is 6. That means $\frac{2}{6}$ can stay the same; however, $\frac{1}{2}$ will need to be changed to $\frac{3}{6}$. This can be done by multiplying both the numerator and the denominator by a factor of 3. Once the denominators are the same, add the two fractions together. The numerators will be added, but the denominator will not change. Thus, $\frac{3}{6}+\frac{2}{6}=\frac{5}{6}$.

**7. C:** The flat is $\frac{8}{10}$ shaded, which is 0.80; $\frac{4}{5}=0.80$. Also, $\frac{8}{10}$ reduces to $\frac{4}{5}$.

**8. C:** The sum of the dollar amounts is equal to $\$156 + \$173 + \$219$, or $548.

**9. B:** Since Andrea paid $120 per month more last year, the amount she paid per month last year is equal to the difference of $763 and $120, or $643.

**10. C:** The diagram represents the sum of $\frac{3}{10}$ and $\frac{8}{10}$, or $\frac{11}{10}$, which is equivalent to $1\frac{1}{10}$, or 1.10. The decimals, 0.30 + 0.80, can also be added, which equal 1.10.

**11. C:** Forty-eight unit "squares" will fit in the product section of the model. The squares will be placed to the right of the ones "units", shown on the left side of the diagram and underneath the six ones "units" at the top of the model; $6 \times 8 = 48$.

**12. C:** The array includes 3 rows and 7 columns. Thus, the array represents the number sentence, $3 \times 7 = 21$.

**13. B:** Since Eli will equally share his crayons, he will divide 42 crayons into 6 groups; $42 \div 6 = 7$.

**14. C:** Alex will be $3 \times 12$ gallons of milk in 12 weeks, or 36 gallons of milk.

**15. C:** The number of candles sold can be rounded as follows: 20 candles, 40 candles, and 20 candles. Thus, a good estimate of the number of candles sold is $20 + 40 + 20$ candles, or 80 candles.

**16. B:** The distance Isabelle drives can be rounded to 1,500 miles; 1,500 miles divided by 5 days is equal to 300 miles driven per day.

**17. B:** The consultant's earnings can be rounded to \$18,000; \$18,000 divided over 6 months is equal to \$3,000 per month.

**18. C:** The missing number sentence in the fact family is the other division number sentence, which reads: $72 \div 8 = 9$.

**19. C:** The value of each number in the pattern is a multiple of 100. Therefore, the 14$^{th}$ number represents the value of the product of 14 and 100; $14 \times 100 = 1400$.

**20. 132.** The value of each number in the pattern is a multiple of 11. Therefore, the 12$^{th}$ number represents the value of the product of 12 and 11; $12 \times 11 = 132$.

**21. D:** Brad drives 275 miles each day. Thus, the total number of miles driven, over a period of days, can be found by adding 275 miles to the number of total miles driven for each previous day. In other words, after 4 days, he drove 1,100 miles. After 5 days, he drove 1,375 miles. After 6 days, he drove 1,650 miles. After 7 days, he drove 1,925 miles. After 8 days, he drove 2,200 miles.

**22. A:** The values in the second column are indeed 12 more than the values in the first column. Note. 16 is 12 more than 4; 19 is 12 more than 7; 24 is 12 more than 12; 26 is 12 more than 14; and 31 is 12 more than 19.

**23. C:** The total amount of money donated is \$300 more each additional year. Thus, the total amount donated, over a period of years, can be found by adding 300 dollars to the amount donated for each previous year. In other words, after 6 years, the total amount donated was \$1,750. After 7 years, the total amount donated was \$2,050. After 8 years, the total amount donated was \$2,350. After 9 years, the total amount donated was \$2,650. After 10 years, the total amount donated was \$2,950.

**24. C:** The fraction $\frac{12}{4}$ as a division problem is 12 divided by 4. Option A cannot be correct since it is 4 divided by 12. Option B cannot be correct since this model represents the fraction $\frac{4}{12}$ or $\frac{1}{3}$. Option D cannot be correct since it models the multiplication problem 12 times 4.

**25. D:** The first place to the right of the decimal point is the tenths place, the second place is the hundredths place, and the third place is the thousandths place. Since the underlined digit is one place to the right of the decimal point, it is in the tenths place. It is important to distinguish between the tens place and the tenths place. The tens place is two places to the left of the decimal point.

**26. C:** The lines are parallel and do not intersect. However, the most accurate description includes the fact that the lines remain the same distance apart. Note. Lines may not intersect and not be parallel.

**27. D:** Perpendicular lines form four right angles, or 90 degree angles. The lines shown for Choice D form four right angles.

**28. B:** A square pyramid has 5 vertices, with 4 at the base of the pyramid and 1 at the top.

**29. B:** A triangular pyramid has 4 faces, with 1 triangular face at the base and 3 more triangular faces.

**30. B:** A cube has 8 vertices, with 4 vertices at the top of the cube and 4 more vertices at the bottom of the cube.

**31. C:** A trapezoid has 4 sides and only one pair of parallel sides. A square, parallelogram, and rectangle all have two pairs of parallel sides.

**32. D:** The probability that Robert will select a blue card is $\frac{7}{25}$. The total number of possibilities needs to be determined first. $3 + 7 + 9 + 6 = 25$. Since there are only 7 blue cards, the probability that a blue card will be drawn is 7 out of 25.

**33. C:** The number line is divided into tenths. Thus, between the whole numbers, 5 and 6, lie the decimals, 5.1, 5.2,5.3, 5.4, 5.5, 5.6, 5.7, 5.8, and 5 9. Point P represents the decimal, 5.8.

**34. D:** The number line is divided into fourths. Thus, between the whole numbers, 3 and 4, lie the fractions, $3\frac{1}{4}$, $3\frac{2}{4}$, and $3\frac{3}{4}$. Point A represents the fraction, $3\frac{3}{4}$.

**35. A:** The barn measures approximately 1.5 inches, in length.

**36. C:** A normal semi-truck has a mass of approximately 8,164 kilograms. The other choices are much too small.

**37. B:** A pencil weighs approximately one-half of an ounce. The other choices are too heavy, in measurement.

**38. A:** There are 16 ounces in one pound. Thus, her approximate weight, in ounces, is equal to the product of 27 and 16; $27 \times 16 = 432$. She weighs approximately 432 ounces.

**39. 08.** There are 2 cups in 1 pint and 2 pints in 1 quart. There are 4 pints in 2 quarts. Thus, there are $4 \times 2$, or 8 cups, in 2 quarts.

**40. B:** The dimensions of the card round to 4 inches and 6 inches. The area of the card can be determined by finding the product of the dimensions. Thus, the approximate area is equal to $4 \times 6$, or 24 square inches.

**41. D:** From 7:35 to 8:35, one hour has passed. From 8:35 to 9:25, 50 additional minutes have passed. Therefore, the elapsed time is 1 hour, 50 minutes.

**42. B:** The total number of students surveyed is 40, but the only information needed to make a bar graph is the number of students that like each season. Thus, the fall bar should be at 7 on the y-axis

The winter bar should be at 3. The spring bar should be at 12, and the summer bar should be at 18. The bar graph, shown for Choice B, correctly represents these percentages.

**43. B:** The dealership sells approximately 35 more cars each year. So, a good estimate would be 261 cars sold in Year 6, 296 cars sold in Year 7, 331 cars sold in Year 8, and 366 cars sold in Year 9.

**44. A:** There were 4 teachers who preferred Virginia; 4 teachers is less than any other number of teachers displayed on the bar graph.

**45. 24:** The possible outfit combinations are equal to the product of the number of different types of each clothing piece. Thus, the possible outfit combinations are equal to $2 \times 2 \times 3 \times 2$, or 24.

## Online Resources

Due to our efforts to try to keep this book to a manageable length, we've created a link that will give you access to all of your online resources:

mometrix.com/resources719/vsolg4

# It's Your Moment, Let's Celebrate It!

Share your story @mometrixtestpreparation